"Holly Carey's carefully planned and clearly written book comes to life at the intersection of examination of the women in the Gospels and appreciation for the distinctive literary narratives of the Gospels and Acts in order to create this engaging exploration of female discipleship in the Gospels. Contexts are crucial: the context of women's world in the first century; the context of the distinctive narrative moves of Mark, Matthew, Luke-Acts, and John; and the context of Bible readers who are also members of Christian churches today. With scholarly, professorial, and pastoral attention to each of these contexts, Carey shows how these women take action as disciples of Jesus—as Women Who Do."

—Elizabeth Struthers Malbon
Virginia Tech

"If asked to name Jesus's disciples, most of us would focus on the well-known men—Peter, James, John, and the rest. In this important, well-crafted study, Holly Carey fills out that picture by emphasizing Jesus's overlooked female disciples while demonstrating how the women in Jesus's life exemplified best the nature of faithful discipleship. If we want to talk about what it means to follow Jesus, we do well to take her advice: Follow the women!"

—Joel B. Green
Fuller Theological Seminary

"This study of women as disciples in the Gospels is a very welcome addition to recent studies confirming the place of women in the New Testament. Carey argues cogently and with clarity for the activity of women as full disciples in the ministry of Jesus across the Gospels and Acts of the Apostles. This is a well-written and carefully researched study, which portrays the remarkably positive role of female discipleship in the sociopolitical context of the ancient world where women had little power."

— Dorothy A. Lee
University of Divinity, Melbourne

T0370126

Women Who Do

Female Disciples in the Gospels

Holly J. Carey

William B. Eerdmans Publishing Company
Grand Rapids, Michigan

Wm. B. Eerdmans Publishing Co.
4035 Park East Court SE, Grand Rapids, Michigan 49546
www.eerdmans.com

Published 2023

Book design by Lydia Hall

Printed in the United States of America

29 28 27 26 25 24 23   1 2 3 4 5 6 7

ISBN 978-0-8028-7915-8

Library of Congress Cataloging-in-Publication Data

A catalog record for this book is available from the Library of Congress.

Unless otherwise indicated, Scripture quotations are the author's own translation.

Scripture quotations labeled NRSVUE are from the New Revised Standard Version, Updated Edition.

For
Aidan, Cameron, Landon, and Chloe

May you always find inspiration
from the women in your life
along The Way.

Contents

Preface

This book has been brewing for some time now. It began with a paper delivered to the SBL Mark Seminar over five years ago, where I argued that it was the women around Jesus who best displayed the qualities of discipleship, in contrast to the apostles who repeatedly fail. As I worked through the Gospel of Mark, I began to wonder if there was a similar theme in the other gospels, and if so, how they communicated that in their distinctive ways. And so, this book is born out of that process of exploration and discovery. Yes, female discipleship is ever-present in the Gospels, and these women are models of discipleship. They are exemplars not only for their contemporaries (including the Twelve) but also for Christians today. In this book I argue that we should acknowledge a through line that stretches from the positive portrayal of female disciples in the Gospels to the work of female disciples in our own contexts. We should invite these stories into our conversations and allow them to inform our understanding of what women are capable of and what so many already do in the church.

It has been my privilege to have been accompanied by many readers along the way to the book's completion. As I teach my students, we should always be reading Scripture with people who are not exactly like us—nothing serves us better in our close readings of the text than the conversations that blossom out of a diversity of perspectives. This has certainly been my experience with this study. Drafts of these chapters have been graciously read and commented on by old and new friends, Christians and non-Christians, men and women, biblical scholars and people whose expertise lies in other areas, egalitarians and complementarians, readers across multiple generations, students and colleagues. I was even able to coax a couple of family members into reading them (that's real love!). The result, I hope, has been a much more strengthened and insightful reading of the texts.

I am so grateful for the time that each of these friends has spent with various iterations of the final product. Thank you to Chris Keith, Jenn Craft, Wye Huxford, Emily Plank, Derek Sweatman, Heather Gorman, David McCabe, Josh Rice, Sarah Huxford, David Bauer, Heather LoGiacco, Barry Blackburn, and Warren Carey. A special thanks to A-J Levine, who offered hours of her time in dialogue on the penultimate draft. A conversation with A-J is always a lively, entertaining, and fruitful one! She has taken this "baby feminist" under her wing, and I will be forever grateful for her mentorship.

I would also like to express my appreciation to Point University, an environment that encourages research and publication and provides a collegial atmosphere among the faculty that has made me feel so supported during my tenure there. Without our stellar librarians Mike Bain and Adam Solomon, this project would not have been possible. Their timely responses and genuine enthusiasm for the book have been a boon to the otherwise lonely affair of putting thoughts to paper.

There have been several spaces where I have been welcomed to test out some of the material that has made it into this book. In addition to the college-student guineapigs in my Women in the Bible course, I have been warmly received at the 2022 Stone-Campbell Journal Conference as a plenary speaker and at the Dinner and Lecture Series at Atlanta Christian Church. I would also like to thank the SBL Mark Seminar group for its unique comradery and for offering an inviting place for scholars in all phases of their career. And as I was finishing up the draft for submission, it was my privilege to participate in the 2022 Wabash Workshop for Mid-Career Faculty Teaching at Evangelical Theological Schools and Seminaries. The hospitality, respite, and emotional and practical support offered by the Wabash Center for Teaching and Learning in Theology and Religion at our on-campus retreat was extremely timely for me as I was racing toward a deadline. So many of my colleagues at the workshop expressed support and interest for the book and contributed insights that have impacted my reading of these texts in profound ways. I am grateful for these spaces that have allowed me to sharpen my thinking with such good conversation and scholarship.

The team at Eerdmans has been wonderful to work with, making a potentially stressful process significantly less so. Special thanks to Trevor Thompson for championing the idea and helping make the transition from concept to book a reality. I am also thankful to *Catholic Biblical Quarterly*, who graciously allowed portions of my article on female discipleship in Mark to be utilized here.

Finally, I cannot adequately express how much my family's support has meant to me during this time. This support comes from all of my people—my chosen and biological family. Particularly enthusiastic have been my ride-or-dies: Emily, Sarah, Jenn, Heather, and Mandy, who have been cheering the small and big wins for over twenty years, and who are always there to give an attagirl and a Starbucks drink as needed. As a mother of four children, I have little time to spare, and all too often our kids bear the brunt of that. The writing process has required a sacrifice of a good deal of my time and attention from them, particularly in the summer months. While I am deeply in pool-time debt with them, they have been so understanding and are genuinely excited to see the final product. Lastly, more than any other, my husband, Warren, has been my constant rock throughout my career and during these last few years on this project. None of this would be possible without him by my side.

Introduction

Female Discipleship in the Gospels

This is a study of the women who followed Jesus. More specifically, this is a study of *the kind of discipleship* that these women modeled during Jesus's ministry. It turns out that Jesus had quite an entourage that went with him throughout his travels, and yet it is easy to read through the gospel narratives and get the wrong impression about the makeup of that group—that the only people who were consistently with Jesus were the twelve male apostles. But this is an incomplete reading of the concept of discipleship in the Gospels. A closer look reveals that in each of the four gospels women were with Jesus all along. They followed him as he preached and taught and healed and performed miracles throughout Galilee, Judea, and the surrounding gentile regions. They functioned as his benefactresses, funding his ministry and providing for the others who were part of their community. The gospel writers laud many of the women whom Jesus encountered along the way, presenting them as exemplary in their faith or for their insight into who he was or what he could do. He uses women as examples of faith in his teachings and parables. Some women went toe-to-toe with Jesus on the interpretation of the Torah and what their place should be in God's kingdom. And it was women who were there at the end, following the body of Jesus as he was placed in a tomb, then returning to care for it only to find that he had risen. It was these same women whom angels first commissioned with the task of "going and telling" of his resurrection to the others who followed him. Women were everywhere in Jesus's ministry.

Women as Model Disciples

Before going any further, it would be helpful for the reader to know why I am writing this book. I grew up in a context where women were not accepted as leaders or viewed as models for discipleship in the church. Although in my community the restriction was more implicit than explicit, women rarely served in visible ways apart from participating in the worship music on a Sunday morning or providing meals in the kitchen. They did not serve Communion. They did not lead as elders or deacons. And they most certainly did not preach any sermons. Once the children of the church graduated to the middle school classes or were invited to the youth group events, no longer were they taught by women in any official capacity (although women were still allowed to be youth chaperons on trips). Again, most of this was implicit, meaning that at my church the pastors didn't preach *against* female leadership—we just never saw it taking place.

I was a sophomore in college when I realized that all I really wanted to do was teach the Bible. Bible nerd that I am, this realization dawned on me while sitting in a class on the life of Jesus. It rocked my ordered little world, and I could not stop thinking about it. I remember quite vividly sitting across the desk from my professor the very next day and asking him, "Can I do this?" To be clear, this was not a question about my ability to teach. I knew that I could teach if I completed the requisite training and equipped myself well along the way. The question "Can I do this?" would have been better phrased "*May* I do this?" This was about permission. It was a question about whether I, as a woman, was allowed to teach the Bible. Embedded in this question was the recognition that teaching is a form of leadership, and it was sparked by the realization that I had never been exposed to a female leader in a faith context.

To his credit, my professor emphatically and unequivocally answered in the affirmative. And his support launched me into a new world: the world of biblical scholarship. This scholarship exposed me to the insights and leadership of many women. Along the way, I wrestled with the "hard passages" of Scripture that seemed to restrict women in the church and in the home. Texts such as 1 Timothy 2:8–15, 1 Corinthians 11:2–16 and 14:34–36, and Ephesians 5:21–6:9 undoubtedly have something to say about female leadership (more about these later). But as a scholar who increasingly specialized in the Gospels through my academic journey, I began to wonder why *those* texts weren't also included in the discussion. Why weren't we also talking about Elizabeth, Anna, Martha, and Mary? Where do the Samaritan woman at the well and Priscilla and Tabitha and Lydia fit into the conversation?

I am drawn to stories. In my own experience, when my views have changed about an issue, the catalyst hasn't been a principle, an instruction, or a command newly heard or learned. Rather, any change in my perspective has come through the human experience—through real stories of real people. When it came to female leadership in the church, I began to realize that in my own experience there was a path that ran parallel to that of so many women who followed Jesus: just like these female disciples in the gospel stories who get overlooked, the women in my life who followed Jesus were often unseen in their own communities. They were allowed to serve, but only insofar as they were under male authority. They were allowed to lead, but only when their charges were too young to know any better. They were allowed to have all kinds of roles in the church, but only those that did not put them up front or allow them to have a seat at the decision-making table. Just as the influence of these women was taken for granted in my communities of faith, so also were the contributions of women in the gospel stories overlooked as the male disciples took center stage in our conversations about discipleship.

So, why don't we see the women in the Gospels as disciples? One of the causes of our blindness to female discipleship in the Gospels is the way we tend to apply the term "disciple" (*mathētēs*) and the mental image that has developed around the word. Unfortunately, "disciple" has become synonymous with the twelve apostles, such that the default assumption is that it refers to one of the twelve men who make the apostles lists in each narrative.[1] This has no small effect on our understanding of discipleship and on our reading of these stories.[2] Al-

1. Matt 10:2–4; Mark 3:16–19; Luke 6:14–16.

2. See Mercedes Navarro Puerto, "Female Disciples in Mark? The 'Problematizing' of a Concept," in *Gospels: Narrative and History*, ed. Mercedes Navarro Puerto and Marinella Perroni, vol. 2.1 of *The Bible and Women: An Encyclopaedia of Exegesis and Cultural History* (Atlanta: SBL Press, 2015), 147: "These texts, given their concrete narrative form, full of gaps, favor a patriarchal, androcentric reading. The absence of explicit information has served as an excuse to fill holes with gender stereotypes." See also Victoria Phillips, "Full

though all the people who consistently followed Jesus and committed to him during his ministry are included in the group called *mathētēs*, the narrower application of the term often wins the day, affecting the ways we picture the narrative events and the people who are involved in them. *But women were there too,* ministering right alongside men. An example of this (and our tendency to overlook it) is found in Acts 9:1–2, where Luke tells his audience that Saul's goal was to bring men *and women* to prison for being followers of Jesus.[3] Perhaps it would be helpful to keep in mind that, as a rule, if the language used in a passage is not gender-specific or the context of the story does not indicate a particular gender, then masculine plural terms for the groups suggest a mixture of men and women. Very often this is true of the term *mathētēs*.[4] The application of this rule is also consistent with the use of the term in the ancient world, which meant "adherent" and held space as a reference for both men and women.[5]

One of the tasks of this book, then, is to broaden our application of the term, clarify when the texts are referring specifically to the Twelve (this can be determined by context, as even the gospel writers will use "disciple" interchangeably with "apostle" sometimes), and correct our vision of discipleship that too narrowly focuses on these men alone. Attention to the actions of the group or individual also encourages us to expand our definition of what discipleship is beyond the narrowly

Disclosure: Towards a Complete Characterization of the Women Who Followed Jesus in the Gospel according to Mark," in *Transformative Encounters: Jesus and Women Re-viewed*, ed. Ingrid Rosa Kitzberger, Biblical Interpretation Series 43 (Leiden: Brill, 2000), 13–31.

3. Teresa J. Calpino, *Women, Work and Leadership in Acts*, Wissenschaftliche Untersuchungen zum Neuen Testament 361 (Tübingen: Mohr Siebeck, 2014), 150.

4. Suzanne Dixon, "Exemplary Housewife or Luxurious Slut: Cultural Representations of Women in the Roman Economy," in *Women's Influence on Classical Civilization*, ed. Fiona McHardy and Eireann Marshall (London: Routledge, 2004), 58–59; and Calpino, *Women*, 150. To that point, Calpino notes that only four out of twenty-nine times when the term is used in Acts does it apply to a specific individual (who can be identified as male or female): 9:10, 36; 16:1; 21:16. All other cases are masculine plural, Luke's preferred way of referring to disciples in his second volume. We will see how Matthew uses the term differently and contributes to the confusion.

5. In-Cheol Shin, "Matthew's Designation of the Role of Women as Indirectly Adherent Disciples," *Neotestamentica* 41 (2007): 401–2.

defined groups that meet very specific characteristics usually thought to be required of a disciple. While some scholars argue that a *mathētēs* must have been called,[6] or have demonstrated a continuing relationship with Jesus,[7] or have received the label "*mathētēs*" in the gospel,[8] some characters in the narratives who are presented as disciples do not strictly meet those qualifications. Expanding our definition allows us to consider those who might otherwise be excluded—most notably for our purposes, the women who interact with Jesus. Added to this, key discipleship verbs such as *akoloutheō* (to follow), *diakoneō* (to serve), and *synanabainō* (to come up with) are applied to women throughout the gospel narratives.[9] In sum, a disciple of Jesus either is committed to following him physically in his ministry (as part of his entourage) or demonstrates in their interactions with him some of the

6. See M. J. Wilkins, "Disciples and Discipleship," in *Dictionary of Jesus and the Gospels*, ed. Joel B. Green, Jeannine K. Brown, and Nicholas Perrin, 2nd ed. (Downers Grove, IL: IVP Academic, 2013), 205–6, for a list of characteristics of the disciples.

7. Robert C. Tannehill, "The Disciples in Mark: The Function of a Narrative Role," *Journal of Religion* 57, no. 4 (1977): 388, believes this to be the single most important characteristic of discipleship in Mark. His narrower definition might exclude some who could be considered disciples of Jesus, although it is hard to know that those who were healed by Jesus, for example, did not have a continued relationship with him, as the absence of an explicit declaration of this in Mark does not necessarily mean it did not exist.

8. Robert P. Meye, *Jesus and the Twelve: Discipleship and Revelation in Mark's Gospel* (Grand Rapids: Eerdmans, 1968), 170–71, argues that "disciple" is reserved for men in Mark (and also in rabbinic writings), and that "neither following nor ministering is sufficient in itself as a definition of discipleship in Mark." By contrast, John P. Meier, *A Marginal Jew: Rethinking the Historical Jesus*, vol. 3, *Companions and Competitors*, Anchor Bible Reference Library (New York: Doubleday, 2001), 77–79, argues from a historical-critical approach that women who are not called *mathētēs* should still be viewed as disciples. See also Winsome Munro, "Women Disciples in Mark?," *Catholic Biblical Quarterly* 44, no. 2 (1982): 225–41, who argues that we should view the women near the cross (Mark 15:40–41) as disciples, despite Mark's reluctance to present them as such. Although her methodological approach and her conclusions concerning Mark's agenda toward women differ from what follows, we agree that Mark 15:40–41 functions as a key text regarding female discipleship in the gospel.

9. E.g., Mark 1:31; 5:24; 15:41. See Joan L. Mitchell, *Beyond Fear and Silence: A Feminist-Literary Reading of Mark* (New York: Continuum, 2001), 58; Elisabeth Schüssler Fiorenza, *In Memory of Her: A Feminist Theological Reconstruction of Christian Origins* (New York: Crossroad, 1983), 320.

qualities or characteristics expected of a disciple. This is important because it means that the female followers of Jesus have something to teach us about what it means to be a disciple. The portrait of discipleship that excludes these women and focuses only on the twelve apostles paints with strokes that are broad and monochromatic. A portrait that is more true to life will include much more detail and diversity.

Not only that, but the kind of discipleship that the twelve male disciples model is rather faulty. The gospel narratives consistently depict these men as willing to follow, but only with conditions—when they understand Jesus's plan to be consistent with their own hopes and vision of God's kingdom. There are times when Jesus teaches something they do not like or understand, and they seek to correct him or even resist him. This creates a tension throughout the Gospels of unrealized expectations and of success and failure—a tension that increases as the gospel narratives progress. They drop everything to follow him, only to question him, doubt him, and betray, deny, and abandon him in the end. They have moments of real insight, only to be rebuked for their narrow-minded application of that insight. They sacrifice many things, but with the hope of gaining greater glory and power. They have insider access to Jesus's teachings and interpretations, only to fail to have the ears to hear and the eyes to see. The Twelve are a complex combination of faithfulness and unfaithfulness as they vacillate between a calling of self-sacrifice and a concern for self-preservation. By contrast, we do not get that same sort of portrait of the women who follow Jesus. While they do not always get the type of airtime that the men get, when they are mentioned, it is more likely that Jesus will laud them for their faithfulness. Many times, when there is a male in or near their story in the narrative, if the man gets it wrong, the woman gets it right. Women display profound insight and understanding, growth from misunderstanding to belief, and a willingness to follow through in their discipleship in ways that male disciples often do not. These women are indeed assertive women.[10]

Throughout the gospel narratives, we constantly find Jesus coaching the Twelve and the larger group of disciples. Jesus's consistent expectation is that discipleship means action. The act of following

10. William E. Phipps, *Assertive Biblical Women*, Contributions in Women's Studies 128 (Westport, CT: Greenwood, 1992), provides my favorite label for this type of woman, as it rightly emphasizes her actions.

Jesus means *doing* something that shows a commitment to him or to the ideals and values he advocates. He expects his followers to act in ways that demonstrate their faithfulness and embody the kingdom that has come in him.

It turns out that Jesus has quite a lot to say about what it means to follow him. He washed the apostles' feet, demonstrating and demanding that their discipleship requires embracing a life of service for others (John 13:15–17). He calls his followers to be faithful even when it means taking up their cross in sacrifice of their lives (Mark 8:34–38). He urges them to welcome the least among them, just as he does (Mark 10:13–16). He even sends them out on the first-century equivalent of an internship, giving them practice in healing and exorcizing demons as they travel around preaching the good news (Luke 10:1–16). And while the male disciples tend to fall short, the women who are with Jesus often model the kind of discipleship that Jesus instructs. We will see throughout this book that female discipleship is a discipleship of action.

Jesus not only taught about discipleship—he also modeled it for his followers by his own actions. Throughout, the Gospels present Jesus as the primary exemplar for his disciples. Just as he is a servant, they should be as well. They must be willing to take up their cross like he will take up his. A place at the table involves the willingness to drink from the same cup. In telling their stories, the gospel writers emphasize the importance of action in the life of a faithful disciple both by presenting Jesus as the exemplar and by telling his story in a way that underscores his own actions in being faithful to God. Since discipleship is supposed to be about following Jesus, we should expect that true discipleship would indeed involve movement, just as Jesus is constantly on the move. We should expect this concern to be indicated throughout the Gospels, then, in the stories they tell of Jesus's interactions with others, in their responses to him, and in his teachings of the kingdom, which are given priority of place and emphasis.

Jesus also expects that the words they proclaim will match up with their actions. This also follows the example he gives in his own life (and death). In the Gospel of John, for instance, Jesus's words match up with his actions, both literally and figuratively. He declares that he is "the light of the world," and promptly restores sight to a blind man (John 9:5). He is "the bread of life," a claim that follows his miraculous provision of bread and fish for the crowd as they wander in the wilderness following him (John 6:35). He is "the resurrection and the life," a title earned when he brings Lazarus back from the dead (John 11:25). It is noteworthy that the order of words and action changes depending on the circumstance. Sometimes the words prompt the action or prepare the audience for what is to come. Other times the actions precede the words of explanation. The fluidity of order further emphasizes the integral ways the gospel writers weave together words and actions to portray the truth of the identity of Jesus. In the same way, we will see women encounter Jesus, speak truth about him in confession, and follow through with those words in their actions or engage in an activity that leads to understanding and a confession of Jesus's identity. While no one comes to a perfect understanding of Jesus, female disciples show a consistency between their words and actions in ways that mirror Jesus much more often than male disciples do. And in these texts it is difficult—even impossible—to truly understand the weight of the words they utter without seeing them through the lens of their actions.

As a whole, the women who followed Jesus were the ones who most consistently took action—who quite literally followed Jesus in ways that his closest companions failed to do. Since a crucial component of discipleship is to *do something*, then we must conclude that the women in Jesus's life were often the best models. In other words, I will argue that what sets apart good discipleship from failed discipleship is *action*, and that the people who are consistently active in ways that draw Jesus's commendation and model his personal practice are *women*. In terms of proportion and narrative impact, the women who interact with Jesus demonstrate a life of faith and practice that is far more consistent with his own actions than do the Twelve. While there are far fewer episodes that include female disciples than episodes that include male disciples, and while explicit references to women who follow Jesus feature much less prominently in the Gospels than references to men, this disproportionate notice serves to make their appearances catch the eye (or ear) of the audience. The women stand out as outside the norm. Some men do indeed follow Jesus faithfully in the Gospels (Bartimaeus and Jairus, for example, pursue Jesus), but the ratio of action-women to other women as opposed to action-men to other men functions to emphasize that the women who follow Jesus are more active overall in their pursuit of him.[11] Moreover, the actions of the women who follow Jesus are often linked expressly to belief and faith.

11. The Twelve affect this percentage quite negatively, as they are the most prominent men and yet we will see that they are often characterized by their inactivity.

The Importance of Female Discipleship

The study that follows is necessary for painting a more detailed and accurate portrait of discipleship in the Gospels. Any work that neglects the role that women play as committed followers of Jesus misses an essential component of what discipleship means in his ministry. This book aims to fill a crucial gap in scholarship on the women who followed Jesus. It will provide a comprehensive study of female discipleship in the Gospels, arguing that it is their active discipleship that makes them exemplars for Christians. A biproduct of this work is that it offers a more expansive strategy for understanding women's roles in the church that goes beyond the epistolary instructions and injunctions concerning women and allows the portrait of female discipleship in the Gospels to have something to say about these issues as well.

While there have been very helpful studies on select women who appear in the Gospels, most of these have taken the approach of addressing each woman individually, in relative isolation from each other.[12] Such books on New Testament women will devote a chapter to each selected woman, deep-diving into her historical and social context and the texts that include her story. The goal of these works is to give the reader as much information as possible about the individual women we encounter in the New Testament. This is an extremely helpful enterprise, and these books are valuable resources that we can use to learn about these women. However, by the nature of their approach, they lack a sense of cohesiveness. While the women's individual stories are highlighted, a discussion of their fit into the wider narratives and their impact as followers of Jesus is lacking. An approach focusing on individual women does not demonstrate the unique ways that each gospel writer presents female discipleship.

Other studies engage with the broader issue of women in Jesus's ministry. Such works foreground the relationship between Jesus and the women, with particular attention to what the Gospels say about

12. E.g., see Richard Bauckham, *Gospel Women: Studies of the Named Women in the Gospels* (Grand Rapids: Eerdmans, 2002), for an in-depth study of the women in Jesus's genealogy, Elizabeth and Mary, Anna, Joanna, Mary of Clopas, the two Salomes, and the women in the resurrection stories. Frances Taylor Gench, *Back to the Well: Women's Encounters with Jesus in the Gospels* (Louisville: Westminster John Knox, 2004), focuses on six gospel texts that deal with women, providing exegetical studies of these passages through the lens of feminist criticism.

Jesus by examining how he engages with female disciples.[13] While this work provides an important contribution to our understanding of women in Jesus's ministry, its Christocentric focus leaves the women once again on the margins of study. Works such as these are less about female discipleship and more about Jesus's views on women as expressed in his interactions with them. This book instead focuses on *how* the stories tell their stories of discipleship. In the process, while we will witness how Jesus interacted with women and what he thought about them and their actions, his response will help inform our understanding of the overall depiction of female discipleship. This approach seems to me to be most consistent with the emphases of the Gospels themselves.[14]

More recent studies of women have broadened their focus beyond the Gospels to other New Testament texts or to the wider context of Scripture. The works of Jaime Clark-Soles and Dorothy A. Lee, for example, have contributed to the discussion of women by not only examining the biblical texts in which they are found but also calling for these discoveries to influence the treatment of women within the contemporary church. While both studies contain refreshing interpretive insights on the stories of individual women, each scholar does so with a view toward their efficacy for the church.[15]

13. E.g., Ben Witherington III, *Women in the Ministry of Jesus*, Society for New Testament Studies Monograph Series 21 (Cambridge: Cambridge University Press, 1984), who argues that Jesus revolutionized ways of seeing women in his time. See also Luise Schottroff, *Lydia's Impatient Sisters: A Feminist Social History of Early Christianity*, trans. Barbara and Martin Rumscheidt (Louisville: Westminster John Knox, 1995), whose work focuses on the ways that the Jesus movement was a movement of liberation, particularly for those women who found themselves "at the bottom of the barrel" (11).

14. See also Bauckham, *Gospel Women*, xvii: "Though it was not a matter of conscious intention, I realize now that there is hardly anything in this book about 'Jesus' attitude to women,' not because I find that unimportant or uninteresting, but because I have focused rather on the women's side of their relationship to Jesus and the events of his story. I also realize that this is also how the Gospels themselves largely enable us to see things."

15. Dorothy A. Lee, *The Ministry of Women in the New Testament: Reclaiming the Biblical Vision for Church Leadership* (Grand Rapids: Baker Academic, 2021), takes a broader look at the New Testament in order to argue that women should not be limited in their leadership roles in the church. Jaime Clark-Soles, *Women in the Bible*, Interpretation: Resources for the Use of Scripture in the Church (Louisville: Westminster John Knox, 2020), expands her study to in-

Although works that focus on individual women, foreground Christology, and broadly examine biblical women and their roles in the church and world are much needed, they are less interested in addressing what the Gospels say about female discipleship. These works have paved the way for this study to discuss fully the way that the gospel writers emphasize the crucial role of women as actors in God's redemptive plan, often as a direct contrast to men who are (at first) unwilling to do so. The distinct contribution of this work on discipleship is that it recognizes a direct connection between the actions or inactions of the men and women around Jesus and the quality of their discipleship as defined simply by their level of activity with him.

There are several indications in the Gospels that action plays a crucial role in discipleship and that the women who follow Jesus lead the way, but this has not been given due attention. The following chapters will serve as a corrective to this oversight. This more comprehensive treatment of the subject will fill these female lacunae present in discussions of discipleship in the Gospels. I will demonstrate that the women who feature as followers of Jesus in the gospel stories stand out because of their willingness to do what is required and to model the kind of life and faith that Jesus demands of his disciples.

It should not be surprising that this kind of gap in the conversation on discipleship in the Gospels leads to a gap in the understanding of discipleship in the present day. This is especially true in contexts like the one in which I grew up: among churches that debate this issue or leave no room for debate because they actively refuse to ordain women or invite them into leadership roles. When the crucial function of female disciples as exemplars of active discipleship is overlooked, this gap will have a corresponding effect on any contemporary discussion of female discipleship in the church.

We see this effect play out in the texts that are too often offered for consideration alone. These are the "hard passages" of the Epistles noted above. These texts come in the form of instruction to a community of believers. In 1 Timothy, the author addresses a problem with false teachers who have negatively influenced the worship experience of the church at Ephesus. Most affected by this deception

---

clude women throughout the Scriptures, although a large portion of the work is on women in Jesus's ministry. One of her most important contributions is in her inclusion of a variety of approaches to the texts she examines.

are some women in the church, and so they are instructed to learn quietly at church, refraining from teaching or asserting their authority over men. The author ends his instruction by appealing to the deception of Eve to justify this command. In 1 Corinthians 11, women are instructed to cover their heads in worship, a tradition that is to be continued because of the order of headship of God, men, and women. Later, in 1 Corinthians 14, Paul instructs women in the congregation to ask their questions at home, rather than speaking in worship. And in his version of a household code in Ephesians 5, the author elaborates on what it means to submit, instructing wives to submit to their husbands as they do to the Lord.

The instructional nature of these texts is like a gravitational force pulling readers toward them and away from other texts that might equally inform their understanding of women's discipleship. While these texts must be included in any discussion of women's place in the community of faith, they should not be the only ones to influence theology and praxis. A limited study of these "hard passages" results in a one-sided picture of a multivalent issue. It turns out that, ironically, the instructional passages in the Bible are not the only vehicle for instruction. We do a disservice to our understanding of women and their contribution to the Jesus movement—both in his time and now—if we reduce our formative texts to select Pauline instruction.

The gospel narratives have something to say about female discipleship, both as a historical phenomenon and as a model for future practice. My students have sometimes asked, "How can a narrative be instructional?" Narratives can instruct because we learn from stories. We are exposed to the formative nature of narrative almost from the time we leave the womb (and sometimes even before we were born if our parents read to us in utero!). Aesop's fables, nursery rhymes, and fairy tales shape children's views of good and evil, morality, human interaction, and the world in which they live. Moreover, we think of ourselves and our identities in terms of our story. When we are asked to introduce ourselves to a new group, we often start at a beginning point in our lives and tell the story of how we got to where we are now. Somehow, we are innately aware that our stories play an essential role in who we have become as persons making our way in the world.

For our purposes, the clearest and most relevant example of how stories shape community behavior and understanding is the Torah. These texts functioned as the primary shaper of theology and praxis for God's people for thousands of years. They are authoritative texts for millions of people who regard them as having a direct influence on their individual lives as well as the life of God's people as a whole. And while the term means "instruction," of the five books the Torah comprises, almost three-fifths are narrative. Genesis, Exodus, and Numbers are almost wholly narrative, while Deuteronomy has a mixture of laws and stories. Only Leviticus presents as a strictly "law" book. The implication of all of this is that stories are useful for instructing behavior, and that they can be as effective as laws, rules, or commands (or sometimes can have even greater effectiveness). Each of the stories of the patriarchs, for example, serves as both a cautionary tale and an example of following God. Abraham trusts in God and follows him into the unknown toward a land and a people that is promised him. But along the way he tries to orchestrate the fulfillment of God's promises (by adopting Lot and bargaining for his life, sleeping with his slave, Hagar, to conceive a son, and twice offering his own wife to protect himself; Gen 12:10–16; 13:8–9; 16:1–6; 18:22–33; 20:1–2). And yet he also shows his deep trust in God's promises when he is willing to sacrifice the long-awaited son of promise at God's command (Gen 22:1–19). Like their forebear, Isaac, Jacob, and Joseph all have aspects of faithfulness and failure—their stories are told so that we learn from them.

So, when it comes to female discipleship and the ways that women can and do follow Jesus, it is also the case that the narratives of Jesus's life are informative for instructing behavior and practice. Our understanding of what it means to follow Jesus should be shaped by the stories of real people who did that in real time. And those stories include women. Equally important as a study of 1 Timothy 2:8–15 and Ephesians 5–6 is a study of the women who followed Jesus. God speaks to us through narrative. Contemporary Christians learn from those who have gone before us. A restrictive focus on the Twelve, or male disciples, or these instructional passages alone limits the pool of texts that should influence our own practices.[16]

16. Moreover, the gospel writers were not primarily interested in articulating a blueprint for female discipleship. They were writing about Jesus. Whenever we discuss these issues, we need to be careful not to assume that our questions are always identical to the questions that the gospel writers had, nor that our goals were their goals. See Sandra M. Schneiders, "Women in the Fourth Gospel and the Role of Women in the Contemporary Church," in *The Gospel of John as Literature*, ed. Mark Stibbe, New Testament Tools and Studies 17 (Leiden: Brill, 1993), 123–43.

This book will not offer any explicit conclusions regarding women's roles in the church—that is not the objective of this study. My point here is to urge that the body of evidence considered in this discussion of discipleship includes what we see in the Gospels: the evangelists present female disciples as exemplars for faith. This presentation is a necessary factor to include in any modern debate on what it means to be a disciple of Jesus. If we are committed to doing justice to what it means to follow Jesus, we must conduct a thorough and open investigation of the place of women in the community of faith. We will see in the following chapters that the portrayal of female discipleship in the Gospels does not challenge the call for women leaders but strengthens that call. It is strangely inconsistent for some church bodies today to prohibit women from exercising their calling and their gifts while both Jesus and the gospel writers regard women as perfectly capable, exemplary members of the earliest Christian community who are given responsibilities and demonstrate gifts. Thus, while the hot-button issue of the role of women in the church is not the focus of the book, I hope that my work with the gospel texts will contribute new or more expansive ways of thinking about current female discipleship and leadership. Think of this study of female discipleship in the Gospels as another necessary component of the larger discussion of the place of women in the community of faith.

The Focus of This Study

In the following pages, we will encounter quite a few stories about women. While all four of the gospels include unique stories that are found only in their narrative, some of the stories appear in more than one gospel. Still others are found in all four gospels, albeit with each gospel writer's characteristic take on the events that transpire. One of the goals of this study is to take what each gospel says about female discipleship on its own terms. While we will see quite a bit of overlap and shared themes and emphases, each gospel writer has his own objectives in writing and his own sources of information. Consequently, each story of these women has its own voice to be heard. The primary focus of each chapter will be on that gospel's distinct version of the narrative stories of Jesus's encounters with women who follow him consistently or who engage with him in ways that demonstrate faithfulness in action. This focus recognizes that an understanding of female discipleship is primarily shaped by the story within which these characters are found.

The best way to describe my approach is that I will be engaging in a close reading of the text. A close reading takes the variety of narrative features into account in interpretation. But it is not restricted simply to the components of the individual stories.[17] In the process of the study I will also draw attention to the ways that the gospel writers differ, alter, or adapt the stories they do share to suit their own purposes. My examination will also consider the sociocultural realities and challenges of women in the first century and examine the ways that those realities might have affected their actions. Another crucial aspect of my close reading considers how early audiences would have understood and responded to each story—what would be their likely takeaway?[18] Close attention, then, will be paid to the *way* each gospel writer tells his story of Jesus, particularly as it relates to those who follow or seek him out. It is through the different experiences and responses of these characters (both the Twelve and the female disciples who follow Jesus) that each writer communicates most clearly what a faithful disciple should look like.

These close readings will include all sorts of stories of women in the Gospels—those women who are in the narrative as characters who interact with Jesus and also ones that Jesus uses as hypothetical or implied models (such as in parables or in imagery). In some gospels we will see clear threads or themes that help hold these individual stories together and serve the larger emphases and unique features of that gospel. In the Gospel of John, for example, we will see how the singular focus on individual encounters with Jesus that center on the dialogue between the two main characters (presented in distinctive

17. Such as the groundbreaking work of Schüssler Fiorenza, *In Memory of Her*, 97–241, who devotes a section of her book to female discipleship and employs narrative criticism through a feminist lens.

18. Adele Reinhartz, "From Narrative to History: The Resurrection of Mary and Martha," in *"Women Like This": New Perspectives on Jewish Women in the Greco-Roman World*, ed. Amy-Jill Levine (Atlanta: Scholars Press, 1991), 161–84, uses a similar approach in her treatment of Martha and Mary in the Gospel of John, referring to her methodology as the historical-literary approach: "In my use of the historical-literary approach, therefore, I shall attempt to reconstruct for the reader of the twentieth or twenty-first century the cultural and literary milieu that enabled the first-century reader to interpret the Fourth Gospel (7)."

vignettes) helps serve his portrayal of female discipleship. Overall, the approach holds together the unique features of each gospel writer's presentation while highlighting the ways in which those presentations overlap and offer a consistent portrait of faithful discipleship in action.

In the following chapters, our task will be to view the stories of female discipleship through the lens of each narrative—to focus on how the gospel writers depict women, highlighting both explicitly and implicitly their crucial roles as followers of Jesus and fulfillers of God's plan, both in their contrast to men who fail (the Twelve) and in their inclusion with men who successfully follow. While being sensitive to the way each gospel writer uniquely presents their stories of female discipleship, I will also draw parallels between them. I will conclude with a discussion of what these portraits say about the role of women as models of discipleship in Jesus's ministry, and suggest ways in which their stories might have inspired women who were heavily involved in the ministry and mission of the early church.

Before diving into the Gospels, we must first lay some groundwork so that we can start with a baseline understanding of the world in which these women lived. To that end, chapter 1 examines what life was like for a woman who lived in the Greco-Roman and Jewish cultures of the first century. If we are going to talk about what the women who followed Jesus did, we should understand some of what was expected of women in that time, what would be viewed as unusual or norm-breaking, and what kinds of opportunities were available to them. Did the women in our texts act in ways that were consistent with the social norms and expectations of the time, or were they displaying characteristics or behavior that would be viewed as outside those norms and expectations? Answering this question will help us evaluate the actions of female disciples in the Gospels with an appropriate consideration of the social environment in which they lived—a world that was very different from our own. Topics such as marriage, widowhood, modesty, religious life, and work for women of that time can help illuminate our understanding of these texts.

In chapter 2 we will explore what female discipleship looks like in the Gospel of Mark. As the earliest gospel to be written, Mark's depiction of the women who followed Jesus in his ministry or encountered him on his journey was certain to make its mark among the earliest

Christians.[19] Compared to the other canonical gospels, Mark contains the harshest criticism of the Twelve, who serve as a foil for belief and understanding. We will see that many of the women in this gospel display active discipleship in their service (Simon's mother-in-law, the women at the tomb, and the anointing woman), in their pursuit of Jesus and his redemptive power (the hemorrhaging woman, the Syrophoenician woman, and the women at a distance from the cross and at the tomb), and in their willingness to sacrifice their possessions (the widow who gives away her last coins and the woman who anoints Jesus). And often, while these women display the qualities Jesus requires of disciples, the Twelve fail to do the same.

The Gospel of Matthew shares some of the same stories and themes as the Gospel of Mark. In chapter 3 we will observe how, while the term *mathētēs* is almost always reserved for the Twelve, the women who follow Jesus often function in ways that more closely reflect the meaning of the term. Women faithfully follow Jesus in Matthew, even as the Twelve are presented more positively than in Mark. Perhaps most impactful for his portrait of female discipleship is his unique beginning to the gospel. By explicitly mentioning four of the women in Jesus's genealogy (and by implication reminding his audience of their stories), Matthew sets the tone for the rest of his gospel. His audience is reminded from the outset of the ways in which women have faithfully followed God, leading to the birth of the Messiah.

Chapter 4 examines the role of female disciples in the Gospel of Luke. As is the case in the Gospel of Matthew, the beginning matters. Luke begins his narrative account of Jesus's birth with three formidable women: Elizabeth, Mary, and Anna. While not disciples of Jesus in the technical sense, these women, like the genealogical women of the Gospel of Matthew, model through their actions the faithfulness expected of those who follow God, and ultimately his son Jesus. This theme is continued in the story of the woman who anoints Jesus, an action that demonstrates her love for him. We will also explore the implications of the presence of women who fund Jesus's ministry and join the larger group of followers spotlighted in Luke. These women

19. I am following the scholarly consensus that the Gospel of Mark was written before the other canonical gospels and was used as a source for both the Gospel of Matthew and the Gospel of Luke.

were likely part of those sent out to proclaim the good news of the kingdom. Some of them even show up again at the end of the gospel, as they remain near Jesus even in his death and are therefore present to witness to his resurrection. We will also look at the ways that the Lukan Jesus offers female action as a model for exemplary behavior, both in more traditional narratives and in Jesus's use of parables.

As volume two of Luke's larger project, Acts tells the story of the early church moments after Jesus's ascension. In chapter 5 we will explore how female disciples played a crucial role in the formative moments of the church. In his application of Joel 2:28–32, Peter presents prophecy as one of the signs of God's movement among his people and anticipates that both women and men will have prophetic roles to play. At the end of Acts, we see that the daughters of Philip are known for doing just that, forming an *inclusio* of female active participation through their gifts. In this chapter we will also attempt to "see" the "unseen" women who pray, serve, preach, and testify to God's acts, even when their fellow believers ignore or dismiss them. Lastly, we will examine the women who are presented as leaders in the early church. The disciple Tabitha, the gentile convert Lydia, and Paul's coworker in the faith Priscilla are singled out as exemplars of discipleship. And it is no coincidence that it is their actions that are underscored in their stories and create the most impact in their communities.

Unlike the Synoptic Gospels, the Gospel of John rarely spotlights the Twelve, but several women feature prominently. In chapter 6 we will look closely at several of Jesus's encounters with these women, highlighting the ways in which they model the writer's anticipated trajectory of faith: from misunderstanding to belief. While many of the corresponding males in the text fail to make this journey, we will see that women such as the Samaritan woman at the well, Martha, and Mary Magdalene move from speech to action, from confession to witness, from grief to a lived hope. Women in the Fourth Gospel often take the initiative, their actions leading to miraculous signs, the spread of the gospel outside Judea, and an anticipation of the type of service required of those who follow Jesus.

By working through each of these gospels, we will see that the contrast between male and female disciples comes in varying degrees, depending on how favorable each gospel writer is to the Twelve. Not all the men fail, and not all the women succeed. And even failure can serve a useful purpose. The failure of Jesus's closest companions (the

Twelve) would most certainly have served as both a warning and an encouragement for early Christians, reminding them that redemption will be offered when they inevitably fail too.[20] What is consistent in the Gospels, however, is that on the whole the women in these narratives model a discipleship that reflects Jesus's teachings—it is a discipleship of action. As we look at the ways in which the actions of the women embody Jesus's teachings about the kingdom of God, we will see that these female disciples function more like companions of Jesus than those who are called by him, travel more closely by his side, and are privy to the inner workings of his ministry, because they are presented as *women in action.*

Want to talk about what it means to follow Jesus? Let's follow the women.

20. Tannehill, "Disciples in Mark," 393: "The decision of the author to write a Gospel, including the story of the first disciples, rests on the assumption that there are essential similarities between the situation of these disciples and the situation of the early church, so that, in telling a story about the past, the author can also speak to his present."

One

A Woman's World in the First Century

What was it like to be a woman in the first century? What expectations were placed on her? What limitations were imposed? What opportunities did she have? These are important questions for us to address so that we will have a baseline understanding of women's lives under Roman rule during the time of Jesus's ministry and later, when the Gospels were written to their original audiences. This baseline can also help us fill in the gaps so that we can make sense of what is said or to recognize what goes unsaid in these stories. This historical context, in turn, can help us understand more clearly what women *do* in the Gospels and, more specifically, how to evaluate whether their actions as disciples of Jesus would have been viewed as mundane or exceptional in the time they lived.

The lives of any group of people in any point in human history are influenced by various social factors. This makes the study of all groups complex. Regarding women in Jewish and in Greco-Roman culture, biblical scholars are often tempted to paint their lives with a broader brush than is helpful, particularly when it comes to the restrictions placed on them in their respective communities. While we will see that women were not afforded all the same opportunities as men, had generally lower social status than their male counterparts because of their gender, and were often subject to the rule of the men, we will also see how women were able to influence their communities, to wield the social capital that they did have for their own benefit, and to utilize their power on behalf of themselves, their families, and those whom they supported.

The Historian's Challenge

There are several challenges in securing the answers to the questions I've asked in the opening of this chapter. One of the major hurdles in understanding the lives of women in the first century is that we lack firsthand records from the women themselves.[1] Writing for public consumption was almost universally the domain of the elite and powerful, and for much of human history this privilege remained squarely in the hands of men. This distinction had much to do with the access certain groups had to the type of education that promoted writing, such as philosophy and the classics—subjects that were almost always reserved for male members of an elite family.[2] Even if women wrote for their own personal use (such as in diaries), these have been lost to us. (Remember that our sample size of ancient manuscripts is just that—a sample size. *Most* of what was written in the ancient world has been lost to us.)[3] Consequently, women are portrayed through the lenses of those men. What a woman does, how she acts, and what she says are evaluated and filtered through the eyes of these male authors. She has no way to communicate directly, to have her own voice. This lack of voice renders her powerless, because she is not able to frame her story in her own words.[4] At the very least, then, we must question whether women thought of themselves or their lives in the same ways that the men who describe them did.[5]

1. See Ross S. Kraemer, "Women's Authorship of Jewish and Christian Literature in the Greco-Roman Period," in *"Women Like This": New Perspectives on Jewish Women in the Greco-Roman World*, ed. Amy-Jill Levine (Atlanta: SBL Press, 1991), 221–42.

2. Susan E. Hylen, *Women in the New Testament World*, Essentials of Biblical Studies (New York: Oxford University Press, 2019), 14.

3. Hylen, *Women*, 4, 13.

4. In a recent podcast, while discussing the power that is in the hands of those who are able to tell a story, Beth Allison Barr describes it this way: "History is not just about what happened in the past, it's about who tells the story." See "Faith Adjacent: Beth Allison Barr," *The Bible Binge* podcast, June 17, 2022, https://thebiblebinge.com/bethallisonbarr/.

5. Ross S. Kraemer, "Jewish Women and Women's Judaism(s) at the Beginning of Christianity," in *Women and Christian Origins*, ed. Ross S. Kraemer and Mary R. D'Angelo (Oxford: Oxford University Press, 1999), 53: "Certainly, it is not impossible for male authors to transmit reasonably reliable representations of women's lives and experiences. But ancient male authors often display such hostile attitudes toward women, and such strong assumptions about gender difference, that modern readers may feel quite skeptical."

Another challenge for understanding the lives of first-century women is that the men who write about them had their own motivations for doing so—a fact that is all too easy to ignore when reading these texts. Ancient male authors were not writing about women simply to describe them or what their lives were like for posterity; it would be a mistake to read them simply at face value, as if they were just "stating the facts." In fact, men rarely wrote about women *to write about women*. Instead, women were mentioned to serve other purposes, such as to urge household order or to provide a representation of idealized virtues. Rhetoric was an important part of Greco-Roman writing during this time, and female characterizations or stories could often be utilized by male writers to persuade their audience or to win an argument.[6] Determining factors that influenced these depictions of women could be related to the social setting, the genre of the writing, or the larger rhetorical aims of the author.[7] Attention to the social norms and values indicated by the author's treatment of women can give us clues as to the ways men regarded women. As we will see below, this regard could run the gamut from more restrictive views of women to depictions of women who have social and political influence—women who played active and highly visible roles in their communities.[8]

A third challenge is that the first-century woman is not a monolith. A woman born into the elite stratum of Roman society would most certainly have an altogether different life experience than a slave woman, for example. Women who inherited wealth would live a very different life from a poor woman born to a poor family. To refer to "women" in the first century without recognizing these differences is to ignore the historical reality and to lack the nuance needed to understand the lives of real women at this time.[9] We will see how a woman's opportunities were shaped by the place she held in society.

6. Teresa J. Calpino, *Women, Work and Leadership in Acts*, Wissenschaftliche Untersuchungen zum Neuen Testament 361 (Tübingen: Mohr Siebeck, 2014), 99: "In spite of the moralistic rhetoric and legal restrictions on the books, there was a great deal of latitude for women to inherit, own land and property and conduct business. This suggests that the rhetoric and formal laws were more idealistic than unilaterally descriptive of women in society."

7. Hylen, *Women*, 15: "The purpose of most literary sources was not to communicate information about men and women. These texts had rhetorical aims."

8. See Hylen, *Women*, 26–27, whose intention is to focus on the latter.

9. I have found two works to be extremely helpful in my study of women

For our purposes, a fourth challenge is that most of the women we encounter in the Gospels were products of both Jewish *and* Greco-Roman cultures. Jews in the first century were shaped by their own beliefs and the historical events of their people, but they were also living under the rule of the Roman Empire, whose people were shaped by their own history and the influence of the aesthetics, values, philosophies, and art of ancient Greece. This means that views of women in the first century could be influenced by all three cultures, and this reality should have bearing on how we read the Gospels regarding female discipleship.[10] Sometimes the broader views of Greco-Roman ideals influenced the biblical portrayal of women. Sometimes the Scriptures (the Old Testament) were of primary influence. And sometimes local customs would have the most impact.

Thus, painting an accurate portrayal of women in the first century is a task that offers the historian no little challenge. Adding difficulty to our task is the fact that what the writings present as an ideal for a woman does not necessarily depict reality. In theory, a society might believe that a woman should act in certain ways, but did she always live up to those standards? Did she never? Or is it somewhere in the middle? Again, these authors are males with their own agendas, and so even their treatment of these ideals is colored by their own concerns. It may even be that an ideal is no longer valued by most of the members of the society, but the male authors utilize it because it serves their broader agenda. In this case, the depiction of women is often polemical and therefore highly unlikely to depict reality.[11] These

in the first century. Lynn H. Cohick, *Women in the World of the Earliest Christians: Illuminating Ancient Ways of Life* (Grand Rapids: Baker Academic, 2009), focuses on "the average woman" (23) in Greco-Roman culture, highlighting the similarities and differences between Roman women and Jewish women of the time. Hylen, *Women*, spends much of her book discussing the world of elite women in Greco-Roman society. I agree with Jaime Clark-Soles, *Women in the Bible*, Interpretation: Resources for the Use of Scripture in the Church (Louisville: Westminster John Knox, 2020), 6, who cautions against "softening" the gender disparities of women but encourages us to see them in the contexts described in the works of such scholars as Cohick, Hylen, and Carol Meyers, *Rediscovering Eve: Ancient Israelite Women in Context* (Oxford: Oxford University Press, 2013).

10. E.g., Cohick, *Earliest Christians*, 99, who discusses Greco-Roman influence on marriage customs in the first century.

11. See Cohick, *Earliest Christians*, 80, who offers some helpful tips for de-

ideals could also be used as evidence to argue an entirely different matter that was only tangentially related to women. The Roman philosopher Seneca employs this tactic in his work *De beneficiis*, where he laments that the great number of women who are divorcing their husbands is a result of the new policy of publishing divorce lists for public consumption.[12] His concern is not divorce in itself, nor is it about the role women play in initiating divorces. Rather, he is arguing against using the courts to punish clients who failed to pay their debts to their patron—a posture that lacked the gratitude expected from a client. Thus, Seneca is addressing an entirely different matter by using the trope of the divorcing woman to make his point that private matters now handled publicly would lead to an increase in disrespectful clients, just as divorces made public have encouraged too many women to seek them, rather than properly showing gratitude and subservience to their husbands.

It is difficult, then, to determine how these ideals were applied in real circumstances, or how they affected women in the first century.[13] To assume that the ideal was always followed or that the ideal existed in a vacuum apart from the aims of these male authors ignores these complicated factors. Moreover, what might seem to us as a contradiction of ideal and practice might not have seemed that way to an ancient audience who has a different understanding of the world.[14]

Despite all these challenges, I am convinced that a discussion of the world of first-century women in the Roman Empire can be fruitful. This is because the gospel authors were living in this world too, and so their views of women would most certainly have shaped their portrayal of female disciples. Knowing as much as we can know about the values, norms, ideals, and practices of women during this time will help us understand the ways in which the women who follow Jesus in these stories are presented as people who act within the

---

termining whether a polemic on women in literature reflects reality, including paying attention to any interruptions in the flow of argument (when an author goes off on a tangent) and the tone of the author (if he sounds defensive, it might indicate that he is losing a social battle).

12. *De beneficiis* 3.15–16.

13. Teresa J. Calpino, "'The Lord Opened Her Heart': Boundary Crossing in Acts 16,13–15," *Annali di Storia dell'Esegesi* 28 (2011): 84.

14. This is a key feature of Hylen, *Women*. She focuses on a cultural pattern where female domestic virtues become patterns for civic attributes.

norms and expectations of their communities or who push beyond the restrictions or assumptions that might have been placed on them. In the following pages, we will examine the ideals, expectations, and practices of women regarding hierarchy and status in family life (marriage, childbearing, widowhood, and remarriage), womanly virtues (modesty, loyalty, and self-control), the household, eyewitness testimony, patronage, religious participation, and sexual purity.

A mere chapter cannot provide an in-depth study of the intricacies of the lives of women in the first century. However, my hope is that the following summary of these key areas in the lives of first-century women will provide a foundational knowledge that can help illuminate the stories of female discipleship in the Gospels. Therefore, in the following discussion I will focus on the issues that directly connect to the gospel stories we will be investigating.

Worth by Proxy: Marriage, Family, and Widowhood

In the first century, a woman's value was generally linked to another person or group. She did not have significant value inherently. Although women belonged to almost all levels of social strata in the first century, and therefore had different lifestyles based on their social status, they were still regarded as Other.[15] This manifested itself most clearly in a woman's relationships with her husband, her family (especially her father), and those tasked with her care when her husband had died.

Hierarchy

Women were regarded as inferior to men; wives were inferior to their husbands. With rare exception (described below), women were under the rule of a man their entire lives. This system, known as *patria potestas* (paternal power), meant that a woman was under the power of her father, or her husband if she married. By the first century, al-

15. Judith P. Hallett, "Women's Lives in the Ancient Mediterranean," in Kraemer and D'Angelo, *Women and Christian Origins*, 32: "The notion of all women as Other, and the importance given to gender as a key conceptual category of group differentiation among the Romans, are not incompatible with other Roman assumptions, even aristocratic ones, about women's place in society."

most all Roman marriages were *sine manu*, meaning that the *potestas* stayed with the father—it was not transferred over to the husband as long as the father lived.[16] Apart from the advantage of their gender, husbands were also considered superior in status to their wives because they were often five to ten years older than them when they married (and so had the benefit of age in a world where the elderly were respected and revered for their wisdom).[17] Many women were married as soon as they reached puberty so as to preserve their sexual purity for their future husbands.[18]

Generally speaking, a woman would gain admiration or respect if she were married and had children, and the more children, the better. This created a strong incentive to marry—a decision that was made between the parents, who stood to gain financially by a dowry, or in the increased status that their son or daughter would enjoy. Relatedly, the virtues that were lauded as womanly virtues almost always had something to do with those familial relationships.

The structure of the family in this time was hierarchical, with fathers and husbands being at the top. Because males were viewed as superior to females, male family members held the role of decision-makers. Thus, this perspective "played a key role in the social configuration of the ideals of marriage."[19] In other words, assumptions that men were superior to women had a direct effect on the interpersonal dynamics of marriages. Men were expected to lead their homes, while women were expected to obey their husbands. Obedience to her husband was lauded as a quality to which a wife should aspire. Aristotle, quoting Sophocles, described this obedience as an act of courage. While courage was a characteristic valued in both men and women, he argued that it would display itself in gender-specific ways. A husband's courage should present itself in the form of leadership in the home, while a wife's courage would manifest itself in her obedience to her husband's commands. This view is a direct result of the belief that women had less capacity for rational thought than

16. Hylen, *Women*, 66.

17. Hylen, *Women*, 73.

18. Kraemer, "Jewish Women," 58, describes the experiences of Berenice (first century) and Babatha (second century) as examples of Jewish women who were married young and to older men.

19. Cohick, *Earliest Christians*, 67.

men and would therefore need to follow the lead of their husbands in decision-making.[20]

Even though husbands wielded the decision-making power in the household, they were not completely free to act as they liked. There was a societal expectation that marriages remain harmonious. This may reflect the increased economic and social impact that women had on the household—they had the capability to impact this harmony, for good or for ill.[21]

Actual practices and relationships in marriages were not just influenced by the broader Roman conception of marriage or the laws that were put in place to encourage it. They were also impacted by local customs and assumptions. Marriage ideals in Jewish writings, for example, tended to focus on the stability of the household, adapting Aristotelian views of household submission for wives. Philo, a Hellenistic Jewish philosopher in the first century BCE, argued that women must remain in and care for the house while the men are away in the marketplace and courts, and when the men are at home, women must promote obedience to their superior.[22] Josephus proposed a similar household construct.[23] From the Babatha archive of the second century CE, we learn that a woman named Babatha entered a polygamous relationship after her first husband had died. Even though Roman law forbade polygamy, she followed local Jewish customs that allowed it.[24]

20. Aristotle, *Politica* 1.13 (1260a22–3), and Sophocles, *Ajax* 293. See Prudence Allen, *The Concept of Woman: The Aristotelian Revolution, 750 B.C.–A.D. 1250*, 2nd ed. (Grand Rapids: Eerdmans, 1997), 110–14. For a study of Aristotle's view of women in the political arena, see Richard Mulgan, "Aristotle and the Political Role of Women," *History of Political Thought* 15, no. 2 (1994): 179–202.

21. Hylen, *Women*, 74.

22. Philo, *De specialibus legibus* 3.169–71; *Hypothetica* 7.3, 5.

23. Josephus, *Contra Apionem* 2.199. For a comparative analysis of these, see David L. Balch, *Let Wives Be Submissive: The Domestic Code in 1 Peter*, Society of Biblical Literature Monograph Series 26 (Atlanta: Scholars Press, 1981), 51–59.

24. Yadayim 10, 14–19, 26. However, Jacobine G. Oudshoorn, *The Relationship between Roman and Local Law in the Babatha and Salome Komaise Archives: General Analysis and Three Case Studies on Law of Succession, Guardianship and Marriage* (Leiden: Brill, 2007), 393, argues that it is possible that Babatha had married Judah after he was divorced.

A Civic Matter

We have already recognized the challenges for the historian that come with the recognition that the instructions and ideals of the time were overwhelmingly given by men and seen through the male view of the world. These ideals were so pervasive that they were often used as a *topos* in writings on another topic (indicating that these ideals were a basic assumption that all could agree on).[25] They could also be utilized as propaganda to serve the most powerful males in society, whereby domestic virtues were lauded as ideal civic attributes. One example of this utilization can be found in the *Lex Iulia et Papia Poppaea*, a collection of marriage laws Augustus enacted.[26] These laws incentivized marriage and remarriage after the death of a spouse, made adultery a crime (moving it from a family matter to a matter of the state), and created rewards for successful childbearing. Regarding children, Augustus's creation of the right of *ius liberorum* offered a reward to family members for having multiple offspring. The ordinances operated on the view that having children was a matter of honor. A father could be given preference for political office if he had three children. Likewise, a woman with three children could be granted the right to act in her own interests without a guardian. Even a freedwoman (formerly a slave) could represent herself if she had four children who survived the high child mortality rate. "Such legal changes made marriage and childbearing matters of civic responsibility, and they rewarded both male and female citizens who contributed in this way to the public good."[27] It was believed that marriage and the creation of a family were not just personal affairs but contributed to the stability of the community.[28]

Augustus also crafted his own image to model domestic virtues. The Roman historian Suetonius put a spotlight on the emperor's family life as a way of extolling his personal virtue as the emperor.[29] As the *paterfamilias* (father of the family) of the empire, Augustus was the final word on all things, the fatherly figure who was in the best po-

25. Cohick, *Earliest Christians*, 70.

26. James A. Field Jr., "The Purpose of the *Lex Iulia et Papia Poppaea*," *Classical Journal* 40, no. 7 (1945): 398–416.

27. Hylen, *Women*, 38.

28. Hylen, *Women*, 72.

29. Suetonius, *Divus Augustus* 61–73.

sition to make decisions for the family because he was the head of the Roman Household. It was important, then, to show that his personal family life modeled the same virtues and priorities of the imperial "family," which was the state. Later, as the concept of the *paterfamilias* became increasingly tied to property ownership (and therefore power), it could even be applied to childless men or women of a certain social standing.[30]

While maintaining restrictions on women in the household and in family life (e.g., expecting unreserved obedience to their fathers and husbands), the domestic language in civic discourse does insert women into the center of political life, and this is an important reality.[31] The effect of this presence is that women were not completely ignored in public discourse on virtue. Rather, the virtues that they were to uphold were seen as models for all citizens. As women were to obey their husbands, so people in the empire were to obey the emperor.

Status

A woman's status had the potential to trump the restrictions that her gender typically placed on her in society. This trumping happened on an individual basis because status involved several factors: family of origin, wealth, citizenship, gender, and one's standing as an enslaved, freed, or freeborn person.[32] Within each of the categories was its own hierarchy. As men were perceived as superior to women, free people were superior to slaves, the highborn were superior to those from a lower class. Such hierarchies further complicated the status of a woman, who could have a strike against her for her gender but could have gained status in another social category. If an elite woman married with property, for example, she could often exercise power over it.[33] Moreover, by the first century, the rules regarding guardianship over a woman's property were loosened. Formerly, a Roman

30. Kate Cooper, "Closely Watched Households: Visibility, Exposure and Private Power in the Roman *Domus*," *Past and Present* 197 (2007): 4.

31. Hylen, *Women*, 39.

32. Hylen, *Women*, 95.

33. According to Richard P. Saller, *Patriarchy, Property and Death in the Roman Family*, Cambridge Studies in Population, Economy and Society in Past Time (Cambridge: Cambridge University Press, 1994), 204–24, women owned roughly one-third of the property during the Imperial period, which indicates

woman needed the signature of a male guardian to legalize some transactions, such as dealing with slaves or selling property. Female masters, for instance, could not legally free their slaves, while male masters had the power to do so.[34] This law reflected the belief that a woman could not be trusted or was not capable of making decisions that would be in the best interests of the family and so needed to be monitored by a male who could be trusted.[35] The loosening of such a law meant that she could have direct control over decision-making. Yet even though there were opportunities for women to become independent from men in Roman society, they were never granted official status that made them equal to men. On the whole, regardless of their particular circumstances, women were viewed as inferior to men. Husbands generally had greater access to the potential to gain honor or authority than their wives did, although if a woman inherited a significant amount of property or had a powerful father, an exception could be made.[36]

This tension is demonstrated in the story of Lucretia, a Roman noblewoman who lived at the beginning of the Roman republic.[37] In a tale demonstrating the virtues of rejecting a king to establish democratic rule, the Roman historian Livy portrays modesty as the primary motivator for a people to throw off the tyranny of a monarch. Lucretia represents the ideal wife, who displays industry and modesty by working wool late into the night. The king's son, Sextus Tarquinius, lusts after her and extorts her to sleep with him by threatening to kill her and make it look like she had committed adultery. After giving in to his demands, she calls on her male relatives to avenge her and then takes her own life. Tarquinius is driven into exile, and her relatives found the Roman republic. Here we see a wealthy woman of high status (with family connections that will birth an empire) who has limited choices at her disposal because of her gender. She feels compelled to sleep with Tarquinius but afterward takes matters into her own hands by taking her own life in a dramatic act of honor. In

that there would be some cultural familiarity with women exercising authority and status in this way.

34. Hylen, *Women*, 79.

35. Hylen, *Women*, 67.

36. Cooper, "Closely Watched," 7.

37. Traditionally dated to 509 BCE. Livy, *Ab urbe condita* 1.57–59, and Valerius Maximus 6.1.1.

the process, she spurs her family on to throw off the tyrannical rule of kings. While her gender cannot save her, her status provides a way for her death to impact an entire nation.

Another example of the tension between gender and status for women is in the intertestamental text of Susanna.[38] Susanna is the daughter of a pious and respected Jewish family in Babylon. Two of the elders in the community spy on Susanna while she is bathing and approach her, demanding that she have sex with them. If she refuses, they will accuse her of adultery. In a poetic and introspective moment, Susanna describes her quandary and weighs her options: "I am completely trapped. For if I do this, it will mean death for me; if I do not, I cannot escape your hands. I choose not to do it; I will fall into your hands rather than sin in the sight of the Lord" (Sus 22–23). Unlike Lucretia, Susanna refuses to succumb to the men's desires and instead faces the reality that she will be accused and executed unjustly. Ultimately, it is Daniel's Solomon-like wisdom that uncovers the lies of the elders, and Susanna is saved. In this story, Susanna chooses death rather than deception—even her status cannot save her from the false testimony of the men in power over her. Apart from her brief monologue of deliberation, she is allowed no voice to defend herself. Her defense rests on Daniel's wisdom and advocacy.

Widowhood and Remarriage

What was a woman's life like if her husband died? Widowhood was a pervasive issue in the first century. Because men often married much younger women, the likelihood that wives would outlive their husbands (if they survived childbirth) increased. The numbers are staggering. Richard Saller cites data from Egypt from this period that indicates more than half of women were likely to be widows by their late thirties.[39]

A widow's situation would depend greatly on her social and economic status while her husband was living. She might have property at her disposal and experience some level of freedom after her husband's death, had she those advantages during her marriage. Yet if

38. The date of the text is debated.
39. Saller, *Patriarchy*, 68.

she had children or other family members, she would be expected to consider their interests, and so there was societal pressure to use her resources in ways that may or may not benefit her personally.[40] Other women would be worse off financially when their husbands died. If a widow was poor when she married, she would remain poor when her husband passed away. If her husband had been a laborer, she had no way to maintain that income when he died, as women were restricted in the types of work they could do outside the home. Added to this precarity is the fact that it was fairly common for people to target these poor widows, as they were among the most vulnerable members of society.[41]

The *Lex Iulia et Papia Poppaea* laws decreed by Augustus strongly encouraged widows to remarry. The laws gave widows and widowers two to three years to maintain the legal benefits of marriage before removing those if they failed to remarry. This decree was, however, an incentive only—it was not illegal to remain unmarried; it would just be to a woman's disadvantage, particularly if she was short on resources or lower in status.[42]

Societal views on widows varied and at times even appear contradictory. Widows who chose not to remarry could be criticized for being immodest (sexually promiscuous) or lazy.[43] Yet while Augustus's decrees for young widows incentivized them to remarry, a woman who elected to remain single could also be seen as virtuous. Some texts lauded the *univira*—the term given to a woman who married only once and remained unmarried after the death of her husband as a way to honor his memory.[44] Relatedly, the Jewish ascetic group in Egypt called the Therapeutics—known to us through Philo—admitted women into their community and lauded those who chose to remain

40. Hylen, *Women*, 83.

41. Hylen, *Women*, 83–84.

42. Hylen, *Women*, 81.

43. E.g., Cicero, *Pro Caelio* 38, who plays on the trope of a frivolous and sexually promiscuous widow who lives without self-control. Hylen, *Women*, 82, notes that while he is not referring to a historical person, his comments do display a cultural anxiety about widows and the potential difficulties they might face if they chose not to remarry.

44. Marjorie Lightman and William Zeisel, "Univira: An Example of Continuity and Change in Roman Society," *Church History* 46, no. 1 (1977): 19–32.

virgins into old age.[45] Miriam, the sister of Moses, is not linked to any husband in the Pentateuch.[46] Judith, the Jewish heroine after whom the text is named, is revered for her choice in remaining a widow, lending her the credibility and trust of the elders to go about her plan to defeat Holofernes without disclosing the details.[47] Moreover, evidence from early Christian communities indicates that there were some who believed that singleness would be advantageous for the mission of the church—a view that increasingly became popular and influenced later Roman legislation on the subject.[48]

A Woman's Place: Virtues, Expectations, Opportunities, and Practice

Women in the first century were expected to demonstrate and embody the virtues that were understood to be womanly at the time. Ancient authors wrote about the ideal characteristics that a woman should display in her relationships and in her community. These virtues influenced the wider cultural acceptance of women in certain spheres of life. Whether or not real women consistently displayed these virtues, their function as ideals would certainly impact a woman's life. Either she would live up to these expectations or she would not. In the following discussion we will look at some of the virtues that ancient authors lauded as womanly, and we will discover how those expectations actually played out.

45. Philo, *De vita contemplativa* 8.68.

46. Although later Jewish tradition links her to a husband. See Josephus, *Antiquitates judaicae* 3.54 (Hur, Exod 17:10–12), and Rabbah 48:4 (Caleb).

47. Jdt 8:28–36. To combat the assumption that her widowhood might incline her to use sexually suspect means to defeat Holofernes, the text repeatedly testifies to her sexual purity and her commitment to widowhood as a *univira* (Jdt 8:5–8, 29; 12:16–13:10, 15–16; 16:21–25), although it does not use the term *univira*.

48. Bonnie Thurston, "Who Was Anna? Luke 2:36–38," *Perspectives in Religious Studies* 28 (2001): 50. See Paul's advocation for singleness in 1 Cor 7:8–9, 39–40; Tertullian, *De exhortatione castitatis* 13; and Adolf Berger, "Secundae nuptiae," in *Encyclopedic Dictionary of Roman Law* (Philadelphia: American Philosophical Society, 1953), 693, on later Roman legislation affected by this view, which from the fourth century on financially restricted men and women who were married a second time and favored the children born of first marriages.

Virtues: Modesty and Loyalty

We have already seen that a first-century woman was praised for being an obedient wife, and that bearing children would be regarded as a fulfillment of her duties as a good member of her community and of the empire. Another expectation of women was that they conduct themselves modestly. This was important because a woman's conduct was a direct reflection on her husband. Modesty could be manifested in a wife's sexual self-control by remaining committed to her husband and refraining from sexual relationships with others. While it was not considered morally egregious for Roman men to have sex outside marriage, their wives were not afforded this same freedom. In terms of dress, the virtue of modesty was less about avoiding revealing attire (as it is in contemporary contexts) and more about wearing simple clothing. Ultimately, modesty was about showing self-control rather than being self-indulgent.

Not only could such modesty be manifested in a woman's choice of clothing, but it could also be reflected in her careful speech—even in being silent in the presence of her social superiors.[49] When all other things were equal (including status), women were inferior to men. So they were expected to show modesty by being silent among them.[50] This was true even of the few women who were educated and intellectually capable of going toe to toe with men in public speech. Juvenal, a second-century Roman poet and satirist, represents a quite hostile view of women who engage in public speech. He harshly criticizes a woman who dares to speak on Homer and Virgil at a dinner party:

> Still more exasperating is the woman who begs as soon as she sits down to dinner, to discourse on poets and poetry, comparing Virgil with Homer: professors, critics, lawyers, auctioneers—even another woman—can't get a word in. She rattles on at such a rate that you'd think all the pots and pans in the kitchen were crashing to the floor or that every bell in town was clanging. . . . Wives shouldn't try to be public speakers; they shouldn't use rhetori-

49. Hylen, *Women*, 45–46. This was also true for men as well as women, who could show deference to their social superiors in age or status by being silent and listening, rather than insisting on being heard.

50. Hylen, *Women*, 46.

cal devices; they shouldn't read all the classics—there ought to be some things women don't understand.[51]

Here Juvenal is criticizing a woman for trying to be a philosopher, when he regards such things as an exclusively male domain. She should refrain from this type of behavior and maintain the status quo of modesty in silence, even though she be educated and capable.[52] This is one example where the rhetorical impact of male writings had real-world consequences for women. By portraying modesty as silence and controlled speech, Juvenal painted this virtue not as a response of passivity but as an active choice worthy of being praised—a laudable act rather than a prohibition.

Still, there were exceptions to the rule. The main factor in whether a woman's speech was considered modest was her social status in relation to her audience's. Silence before her social superiors was a hallmark of self-control, while frankness of speech could be praised if she were in the presence of peers. The ability to calculate when to speak and when not to speak was an important skill to develop for women, and depended more on who was in the room than the space that was being occupied.[53] It also had something to do with what was being said. For example, a woman who freely spoke among her husband's business partners would be judged for her lack of modesty, while she might use the same space to discuss family matters with relatives or to order her slaves in their daily tasks. Likewise, if she made a speech that extolled traditional virtues valued by the community, she might be praised for her words, especially if they had to do with virtues that were deemed particularly relevant for women. Thus, in this context a woman had many factors to consider before she opened her mouth to speak.

In practice, modesty was a complicated matter because as a virtue it could sometimes create tension with other cultural values. For instance, because wealth influenced social status—another important factor in a woman's quality of life—wearing simple attire created a

51. Juvenal, *Satirae* 6.434–456. See Sarah B. Pomeroy, *Goddesses, Whores, Wives, and Slaves: Women in Classical Antiquity*, 2nd ed. (New York: Schocken, 1995), for a useful survey of the life of a woman in classical antiquity.

52. Cohick, *Earliest Christians*, 244.

53. Hylen, *Women*, 150–51. This was true of men as well.

problem. While a woman might desire to avoid gaudy or eye-catching clothing in principle, it was also advantageous for her and her family to move up the social ladder. An outward demonstration of wealth would enhance this likelihood, making it tempting to show off her wealth in the kind of clothes she wore.[54] In another example of the complicated nature of modesty, even though in theory husbands were free from the expectations of sexual modesty that were placed on their wives, ancient authors recognized the tension that this could create within the marriage. A husband's infidelity could threaten the harmony of the household, which was also greatly valued. Thus, philosophers such as Plutarch encouraged men to have self-control so that the marriage would remain harmonious.[55] Sexual modesty, then, was believed to impact the stability of the household and the state, a matter that we've already seen was of great concern in the first century.[56]

Another virtue expected of women was loyalty to her husband. This included the requirement of sexual fidelity, but also of shared interests with her husband. If a woman came to the marriage with money and property, she was expected to offer them for her husband's use. This was a manifestation of the wife's general subordination as the inferior partner in the marriage: the husband had the status and perceived ability to manage her affairs better than she could ever do. If the marriage was *sine manu*, it would be up to her, however, to relinquish that control. This expression of the virtue of loyalty would ultimately serve his interests.[57] Another example of a wife's loyalty could be expressed after her husband's death, if she chose to become a *univira*—a woman who remained unmarried after widowhood. The *univira* came to represent the ultimate act of loyalty to her husband and to his children.

A Well-Ordered Home

We have already discussed how women were seen as integral to the running of the household. Both Roman and Jewish writings of the first century reflect the belief that the focus of a wife should be her home,

54. Hylen, *Women*, 43–44.
55. Plutarch, *Conjugalia praecepta* 44.
56. Hylen, *Women*, 47.
57. Hylen, *Women*, 55.

with varying degrees of allowance for other areas of influence. Prior to the last decade, scholars preferred to describe this as a matter of a "public" versus a "private" domain—that women were restricted to the private home, while men would be expected to contribute to the public life of the community. More recent discussions, however, have called the usefulness of that distinction into question. In some ways it is true that women were restricted in public life—at least in terms of the ideals set forth by male authors of the time. But it is not true that women had no influence on what went on in the community outside the home. A strict dichotomy between public and private spheres does not reflect the real-life practice of women at the time.

Philo represents a more restrictive view of women at the time: "The women are best suited to the indoor life which never strays from the house. . . . A woman, then, should not be a busybody, meddling with matters outside her household concerns, but should seek a life of seclusion. She should not show herself off like a vagrant in the streets before the eyes of other men, except when she has to go to the temple."[58] For those who held to this view, wives should focus on the area of most concern and impact on them—the home. We have already seen how Philo and Josephus assimilated Aristotelian views of the household hierarchy, and this Aristotelian influence is evident in the way that Philo describes an ideal wife as one who is secluded from other men besides the one who rules over her—her husband. When we read texts such as Philo's, we might get the impression that women were never allowed out of the home, had no social life whatsoever, or had no opportunities to influence the wider community beyond their own families. When viewed in this way, the "public" versus "private" descriptor seems apt. However, modern definitions of these words differ from ancient ones.

In first-century Roman life, what was considered public was a much narrower set of activities, usually referring to political functions or to the judicial realm. Not only were these off limits to women, but they fell squarely into the purview of elite men (and so it was restricted not wholly by gender but also by status).[59] Likewise, what was considered private would include all kinds of activities that might originate or impact the home but would be carried out in the

58. Philo, *De specialibus legibus* 3.169–170.
59. Hylen, *Women*, 33.

community. Commerce and the production of goods, for instance, served the household. Moreover, the household was often the center of this work, and so wives would be actively involved in these activities.[60] Acts of patronage could also originate or be conducted in the home, with women at the center of the decision-making and their oversight. Even the architectural design of houses blurred the lines between public and private, since elite families had multiple rooms from which they could do housework and host visitors (thus inviting the community into the home). Even poorer households would share courtyards with their neighbors.[61] It was also seen as honorable if a man's private possessions were utilized in such a way as to benefit his city or the empire.[62] If we continue to talk about the "public" and "private" distinction, we must keep in mind that the former term was much narrower and the latter much more expansive than we often envision them.[63] Ultimately, this means that the sphere of influence for a woman in charge of her household was often quite a bit wider than we assume.[64]

As a microcosm of the state, the household was seen as a key indicator of the greatness of the Roman Empire. If a wife failed to manage the household in the ways that were expected of her, this could be interpreted as a subversive act with far-reaching effects. A well-ordered household meant a well-ordered state.[65] This put a great deal of so-

60. See Cooper, "Closely Watched," 21–22.

61. Hylen, *Women*, 34. See also Cooper, "Closely Watched," 14–17, on the relationship between the house structure and its visibility and the honor ascribed to the family.

62. Cooper, "Closely Watched," 5.

63. See Carolyn Osiek and Margaret Y. MacDonald, *A Woman's Place: House Churches in Earliest Christianity* (Minneapolis: Fortress, 2006), who resist the framing of public versus private as a polarity by examining the ways that women were involved in house churches in early Christianity.

64. While Hylen, *Women*, 34–35, suggests that we abandon the terms altogether, I do think they have some value, as they reflect accurately the reality that women were not completely unrestricted in the first century—they were able to influence their communities only through the avenues allowed them at the time. Maintaining a nuanced definition of "public" and "private" also allows us to hold together the tension between the ideals set forth by authors such as Aristotle and Philo and the recognition that wives generally had much greater influence in real life.

65. The concern for a well-ordered home was also reflected in Jewish writings such as Sir 26:16.

cial pressure on husbands to maintain control over their wives and households, and on wives to be obedient and in concert with their husbands in every way.[66]

Women as Witnesses

It has been a common view among biblical scholars that women were not considered reliable witnesses in a Jewish court of law during this time. This conclusion derives from a combination of factors, including the lack of explicit mention of women functioning as witnesses in the Scriptures (an argument from silence), that some rabbinic texts restrict women from witness testimony, and that Josephus concludes that women were too "light" and "presumptuous" and so were prohibited by Mosaic law from serving as legal witnesses.[67] Adding to this is the fact that Origen later must defend the reality of Jesus's resurrection because of Celsus's dismissal of the accounts as the testimony of a "hysterical female."[68] Women were regarded as inferior to men in the Greco-Roman world, and while they were encouraged to have self-control in the company of males by limiting their speech, a generalization such as the claim that women could not serve as witnesses lacks nuance. There is evidence that suggests that women in the first century could serve as eyewitnesses under certain circumstances.

According to the Mishnah, a rabbinic collection of oral traditions that date from the third century CE but likely reflect earlier Jewish practices and beliefs, while women could not testify under normal circumstances, and were not compelled to do so if the concern involved bringing a case against another, there were exceptions to the rule. They could do so if the case involved the virginity of a woman (because they would be in a unique position to confirm this).[69] If she were the only one to witness a man's death, a woman could testify that he did indeed die, freeing his wife so that she could remarry.[70] A woman could take

66. Cohick, *Earliest Christians*, 68–69.

67. Josephus, *Antiquitates judaicae* 4.219.

68. Origen, *Contra Celsum* 2.55.

69. See also 4Q271 3:13–14.

70. See Judith Romney Wegner, *Chattel or Person? The Status of Women in the Mishnah* (New York: Oxford University Press, 1988), 120–26, 188–89, and Moshe Meiselman, *Jewish Women in Jewish Law*, Library of Jewish Law and Ethics 6 (New York: Ktav/Yeshiva University, 1978), 73–80.

an oath to swear that she had not cheated someone in a business transaction. And whatever the circumstance, if the case was very urgent, a woman's account of the matter would be accepted.[71] Further, women were believed to be legally competent to take vows and oaths of a religious nature, they could make religious confessions, and they were widely recognized as prophets. Generally speaking, female testimony was often allowed if the matter was viewed as a womanly issue or an issue that involved them directly. [72] The underlying assumption is that these women, when allowed to testify, were functioning as equals to men under these specific conditions, and so the same criteria applied to male testimony was applied to female testimony.[73]

The Essenes listed additional scenarios for female testimony. Women in the community were encouraged to testify against their husband's sexual indiscretions. Relatedly, if a woman was accused of adultery herself, she was allowed to give her own defense.[74] Both of these scenarios underscore how important sexual purity was to the group. It also indicates that they were willing to take the word of a woman over the word of a man.[75]

Religious Life in the Community

In the first century, women were actively engaged in the religious life of their communities. In Greek and Roman worship, women could serve as priestesses and could pray and prophesy in religious services. Likewise, in Jewish writings women such as Deborah, Hannah, and Aseneth are revered for their prayers and prophecy, their content often included in the texts at length.[76] According to Philo, female members of a group he calls the Therapeutics (the women were called

71. *Rosh Hashanah* 1:8.

72. Robert G. Maccini, "A Reassessment of the Woman at the Well in John 4 in Light of the Samaritan Context," *Journal for the Study of the New Testament* 53 (1994): 36.

73. Wegner, *Chattel or Person?*, 120–21.

74. 4Q270 4 and 4Q266 12. This is an adaptation of Num 5:11–31. Philo, *De specialibus legibus* 3.52–63, also contains this provision. Cf. Cecilia Wassen, *Women in the Damascus Document*, Academia Biblica 21 (Atlanta: Society of Biblical Literature, 2005), for a full-length study of women among the Essenes.

75. Cohick, *Earliest Christians*, 204–5.

76. Judg 5; 1 Sam 2:1–10; Jos. Asen. 12–13, 21.10–21. See also Pseudo-Philo's *Liber antiquitatum biblicarum* (LAB), which includes expanded prayers of fa-

Therapeutrides) were engaged in the interpretation of the law in their community and even wrote hymns that reflected their theological understanding.[77] There is even some evidence that women held the title "leader of the synagogue" and were regarded as such.[78] And as we will see from our study of discipleship in the Gospels, there is ample evidence that women were actively involved in the religious life of the earliest Christians.

One of the most important aspects of religious life for women in the first century was the societal expectations of purity. We have already seen that this concern resulted in the early marriage of young women at the time, to guarantee their virginity for their husbands. The Jewish writer Jesus ben Sira is an example of someone obsessed with this concern for a daughter's sexual purity.[79] His concern is with the impact that the shame of a daughter's indiscretions would have on her father, as it would result in public dishonor. Ben Sira's writing taps into the common belief at the time that women were unable to regulate or control their own urges and therefore unable to practice virtues without the oversight of their father or husband.[80]

---

mous women in the Scriptures such as Jael (31.5–6), Deborah (32.1–17), and Jephthah's daughter (40.5–7).

77. Philo, *De vita contemplativa.* For a detailed study of the Therapeutrides, see Ross S. Kraemer, "Monastic Jewish Women in Greco-Roman Egypt: Philo Judaeus on the Therapeutrides," *Signs* 14 (1989): 342–70.

78. Bernadette J. Brooten, *Women Leaders in the Ancient Synagogue*, Brown Judaic Studies 36 (Atlanta: Scholars Press, 1982), 30–33, argues that the title *archisynagōgissa* (the feminine form *archisynagōgos*) was not just an honorific title or a reference to her relationship to her husband, the synagogue leader (like "pastor's wife"), but that the term indicates the leadership role she would have held in her own right.

79. Claudia V. Camp, "Understanding a Patriarchy: Women in Second Century Jerusalem through the Eyes of Ben Sira," in Levine, *"Women Like This,"* 20–22, speculates that Ben Sira's obsession with sexual purity reflects his general lack of trust in all people and his anxiety concerning what he cannot control. Sexual activity is one thing he can control, and so this becomes an important focus of his advice to men.

80. Cohick, *Earliest Christians*, 49. For example, in describing the bravery of the mother of the seven sons who are martyred for their faith, the writer of 4 Maccabees seems unable to conceive of this bravery as an inherently female virtue, but rather lauds the woman for displaying manly characteristics of courage and reason. Cohick works through other contemporary literature to show that Ben Sira's harsh commentary does not match other portraits of Jewish women from that period (e.g., Tobit, LAB, Joseph and Aseneth): "We should probably not assume that Ben Sira speaks for all families when he decries the

A person's purity was believed to have an impact that went well beyond the individual. While those in Greco-Roman societies expected women to be sexually pure regarding their marriages, there was no restriction placed on their religious participation or community engagement during menstruation. This contrasts with Jewish purity laws, which have been understood as an injunction against community interaction with menstruating women or women with discharges.[81] However, like some of the other womanly ideals we have examined thus far, it is likely that a strict prohibition or separation was a far cry from reality. While Jewish women may not have been able to participate in worship in the temple during times of uncleanness, examples from the Therapeutrides and women in the Essene community, female involvement in the leadership of synagogues, and women in Jewish resistance movements such as Masada and the Bar Kokhba uprising suggest that women could continue in daily and religious activities alongside men.[82] These laws, then, did not preclude women from being actively engaged in their communities or in joining the men in religious movements.[83]

Avenues of Influence: Work and Patronage

Despite the limitations we have surveyed for women in the first century, there were areas where women could have great influence. The level of influence, the means used to do so, and the recipients of this influence would depend on several of the cultural factors we have already observed, such as status and wealth, since these were the kinds of cultural realities that could trump the limitations of their gender.[84] The major avenues of influence for women in this time were through their work and in the practice of patronage.

---

birth and care of a daughter—with one exception. Ben Sira probably reflects the widespread conviction that a daughter's sexual purity is of paramount importance" (54).

81. Lev 12:1–7; 15:19–30; 18:19; 20:18; Num 5:1–4.

82. Cohick, *Earliest Christians*, 222–23, reiterates the important observation that these purity restrictions on cleanness never implied sinfulness, and that it "did not cast a moral shadow" over the woman.

83. See Amy-Jill Levine, "Second Temple Judaism, Jesus, and Women: Yeast of Eden," *Biblical Interpretation* 2 (1994): 15–20, who argues against generalizing purity laws as overly restrictive in first-century Judaism.

84. Cohick, *Earliest Christians*, 22–23.

Although some literary sources condemn or criticize women who engage in business transactions, the existence of this criticism indicates that it was a common enough practice to pose a threat to the idealized view of women advocated by these authors.[85] Evidence from inscriptions shows that women owned ships as merchants and engaged in the wine trade. The remnants of Pompeii prove that women owned businesses in that community and worked alongside their husbands in family businesses. Rome and Pompeii contain iconography and inscriptions that show that women were working in the community, most commonly as artisans and with cloth.[86] The extent to which elite Roman women had public personas as businesswomen or dealt with business matters primarily behind the cover of a male guardian or tutor is debated, but it is clear that the women were behind these endeavors.[87] This is another example that underscores the tension between the portrayal of the ideal woman espoused by ancient authors and the reality of actual women living under real circumstances.

One of the characteristics of being an "ideal" woman was to be an industrious woman. Women were expected to contribute in many ways to the running and maintenance of the household, including the production of goods and the making of clothing. Again, we see here that the relationships between the private economic state of the household and the public business interests of the family were held together by the wife and were mutually impactful for the family because of her actions.[88] The types of work that a woman engaged in would also be influenced by her social status and access to money. A poor woman would find herself doing more hands-on manual labor, while an elite woman would likely have the responsibility of managing slaves who would do that same work. Regardless of status, however, "woolworking" became code language for a woman's skill in her work and her productivity for the family's benefit.[89] The expectation of a

85. E.g., Cicero, *Pro Caelio* 2, 31, 33, who accuses a man and a woman (Caelius and Clodia) of engaging in illicit sexual relations because money has exchanged hands between them.

86. Sandra R. Joshel, *Work, Identity, and Legal Status at Rome: A Study of the Occupational Inscriptions* (Norman: Oklahoma University Press, 1992), 141.

87. Calpino, "'Opened Her Heart,'" 84–85.

88. Hylen, *Women*, 51.

89. Hylen, *Women*, 51–52. Recall the image of Lucretia modestly working wool in her home.

woman's industry fed the perspective that women should oversee the running of the household, and this widespread view indicates that they were given some authority in this space.[90]

Another way that women could exercise influence in their communities was to act as benefactresses. The patron-client relationship was a foundational one in Greco-Roman culture, as it had significant economic benefit in a system that did not afford equal opportunities for its residents.[91] Elite women could use resources at their disposal to benefit their community through this established system of patronage. These women would give gifts and fund financial and social needs in their cities, and they were often acknowledged publicly for doing so, bringing honor to them and to their families for their good works. At times the extent of their role as benefactresses would lead to a more official role as representatives of the city than is often realized. When this happened, the lines between private and public authority and power were blurred, as these women were using their private means for the public good.[92]

An example of a first-century patroness was a businesswoman in Pompeii named Eumachia. She worked alongside her husband in the family business, but what is interesting is that her name is listed as the benefactress on a large building dedicated to the city, not his. She was clearly known as a patroness in her own right—there was even a statue dedicated to her in the city.[93] Moreover, patronage was not an exclusive domain of elite men and women. Anyone could be a patron, raising their status in the community, even if they were of limited means.[94] Patronage is yet another example of how status—fueled by action—could be a means by which women could overcome some of the cultural limitations placed on their gender.[95]

90. Hylen, *Women*, 120–22. The woman of Prov 31 is also lauded for her industry in the home.

91. Cohick, *Earliest Christians*, 288: "Benefaction greased the wheels of the economy, so that any woman in business was also a part of the patronage system."

92. Cooper, "Closely Watched," 6.

93. See Calpino, *Women*, 125–26.

94. Hylen, *Women*, 107.

95. Zeba Crook, "Honor, Shame, and Social Status Revisited," *Journal of Biblical Literature* 128 (2009): 591–611.

Conclusion

Our brief survey of the social and political factors that most influenced first-century women has revealed a complex portrait. While many of the ideals expounded by the male authors of the time likely reflected general societal expectations for women's behavior, there is also evidence that women were not always bound to those ideals in their real lives. While the ideal might be for women to remain at home to tend to the family affairs in the household, we have seen that women actively engaged in the business affairs of the family, often alongside their husbands, and were even publicly recognized for the benefaction they bestowed on their communities. Moreover, it was not uncommon for there to be tension between two sets of ideals, resulting in some choices for women that could each lead to praise or honor. A widow could be rewarded by the state for remarrying after her husband's death, her new marriage viewed as an important contribution to the *familia* of the empire. On the other hand, she could choose to remain loyal to her dead husband by remaining a *univira*—unmarried until her own death. What we can say with certainty is that the cultural assumptions, values, and norms provided a setting where there were many advantages for men because of their gender and, conversely, many disadvantages for women because of their gender.

How can all of this information help us? When we study a topic such as female discipleship in the Gospels, it is useful to have a sense of what opportunities women had at the time to understand and evaluate the actions of the women who followed Jesus. It is also important not to paint with broad strokes that ultimately fail to be helpful in our task. As we have seen, first-century women had greater opportunities than is often assumed to act inside or outside the ideals articulated by contemporary male authors.[96] But I would also caution us from swinging the pendulum too far back in the opposite direction. Women's lives were not unrestricted, and it is important to recognize how much status played a role in their opportunities. If a woman belonged to an elite class with power and wealth, she would have more avenues for action and influence outside her household. But a woman with lower social standing and more limited resources would experience much less choice and much more difficulty in acting outside those ideals and norms.[97]

96. Hylen, *Women*, 85.

97. While I think the perspective of Hylen, *Women*, rightly calls for a rec-

While restrictions were placed on women in the first century, women were not without influence in their own communities. For our purposes, this is one of the most fruitful outcomes from the more recent studies of first-century women. In the following chapters, I will highlight the ways in which the women who followed Jesus or acted in ways consistent with faithful discipleship contributed to their communities. We will see that it is precisely in these actions that female discipleship becomes the model for all disciples.[98] In the process we will find that some of the womanly ideals of the time were not adhered to by these women, providing another example of the difference between these ideals and the reality of their lives as reflected in the Gospels. Finally, we will see that female disciples were in a unique position to follow Jesus precisely because of the limitations of their opportunities in the first century. Women were accustomed to being regarded as less than men in their culture. Jesus's description of discipleship as being "last" instead of "first" would most certainly have resonated with these women. Being a disciple of Jesus did not require a dramatic change in their social status—in fact, it was a way to actively embrace what was formerly imposed on them. It meant a reevaluation of their current situation in light of the cross.

---

ognition of the opportunities afforded women at the time, she focuses much of her discussion on elite women. Women of lower classes would likely experience the same hardships that scholars often ascribe to all women. It is useful to have a more nuanced discussion and to recognize the extent to which status aided women's freedoms at the time, while also recognizing that there were more women of lower class and status in the ancient world than women of the elite classes, and so the difficulties and lack of choices described by most scholars would accurately describe most women at the time.

98. As we have seen, it is not uncommon for women to be thought of as models of behavior and practice at the time (e.g., domestic life as a model for civic attributes).

Two

Female Discipleship in the Gospel of Mark

Discipleship is an important theme in the Gospel of Mark—this is not a groundbreaking claim to make.[1] Mark communicates this theme in a number of ways. Jesus calls disciples and others to follow him, literally (1:16–20; 10:17–22). Thus, discipleship means following Jesus in terms of proximity. Moreover, the "new exodus" language in the gospel—first introduced in its opening conflated citation—provides a framework for understanding discipleship in terms of Israel's story (1:2–3). Mark utilizes this exodus theme by presenting his citation in the context of Isaiah's words of promise about restoration for God's people back to the land. Like his former promises to Israel in Exodus, God promises that he will bring his people out of bondage, this time from Babylon exile (Isa 40:3). By including a citation from Isaiah that is itself an allusion to the exodus event, Mark fashions a triple-layer cake of interpretation: just as God's people were in slavery in Egypt, and in exile in Babylon, so also are they in bondage at the time that Jesus begins his ministry. John the Baptist is the voice God has now sent to prepare the way for his deliverance through Jesus Christ, the Son of God (Mark 1:1). The exodus event at its core was about following God out of Egypt.[2] The wilderness wanderings that began shortly thereaf-

1. This chapter is an adaptation of my previous publication, Holly J. Carey, "Women in Action: Models for Discipleship in Mark's Gospel," *Catholic Biblical Quarterly* 82, no. 3 (2019): 429–48.

2. See Rikki E. Watts, *Isaiah's New Exodus in Mark*, rev. ed. (Grand Rapids: Baker, 2001), and Joel Marcus, *The Way of the Lord: Christological Exegesis of the Old Testament in the Gospel of Mark* (Edinburgh: T&T Clark, 1992): 12–47, on the influence of the "new exodus" theme on the Gospel of Mark.

ter found Israel's movement stagnant and purposeless, where God's people were most often doing wrong or doing nothing at all. The entry into the land by the new generation represents a new chapter of following God and promises blessings along the way (Deut 30:15–20). These blessings were eventually squandered by Israel, as both Israel and Judah experienced destruction and displacement from the land by their enemies. By invoking remembrances of this "story behind the story" at the beginning of his gospel (and placing reminders throughout), the gospel writer is surely underscoring the continued movement of God's people with him, this time alongside his Son, Jesus.[3] This notice is undergirded by the fact that the Markan Jesus is the ultimate example of right relationship with God.[4] Thus, following Jesus means following his example.

What it means to follow Jesus is at the heart of this gospel, but scholarly discussions tend to center on Jesus's teachings about discipleship to the Twelve and their repeated missteps. When the focus is on this group alone, discipleship as a theme in the Gospel of Mark has the running threads of failure, misunderstanding, and disappointment throughout.[5] What if the focus is turned elsewhere or is broadened to include another category of Jesus followers in the gospel? What if we

3. This movement imagery is also bolstered by Mark's use of *hodos*, particularly in the middle section of the gospel (see 8:27; 9:33, 34; 10:17, 32, 46, 52). Adela Yarbro Collins, *Mark*, Hermeneia (Minneapolis: Fortress, 2007), 398, notes that the mention of Jesus's going on ahead of them in 10:32 "suggests that the literal journey to Judea symbolizes discipleship." See also Joan L. Mitchell, *Beyond Fear and Silence: A Feminist-Literary Reading of Mark* (New York: Continuum, 2001), 60.

4. Emphasized in many places in the gospel but perhaps most clearly in his role as "son of God" in Mark 1:11; 9:7; 15:39.

5. Explanations for the failure of the Twelve, in particular, are as diverse as they are numerous. See, e.g., Theodore J. Weeden, *Mark: Traditions in Conflict* (Minneapolis: Fortress, 1971), and Werner H. Kelber, *The Kingdom of Mark: A New Place and a New Time* (Philadelphia: Fortress, 1974). Although they offer different theories on the matter, both believe the purpose of the Twelve's negative portrayal in the gospel is polemical (against those who put their hope in a *theos anēr* [Weeden], and those in the Jerusalem church who misunderstood Jesus's eschatological teachings [Kelber]). See also C. Clifton Black, *The Disciples according to Mark: Markan Redaction in Current Debate*, Journal for the Study of the New Testament Supplement Series 27 (Sheffield: Sheffield Academic, 1989), for a study of the various redaction-critical approaches to the disciples in Mark.

consider the women whom Jesus encounters and who are committed to his ministry in our discussions of discipleship? How might this change in focus alter the way we view the landscape of discipleship in the gospel? In this chapter we will examine the ways in which Mark underscores the active role of female disciples in his gospel, and how this dynamic provides a corrective to the disproportionately bleak portrait of a discipleship that only narrowly considers the Twelve.

When the failures and successes of the Twelve are compared with the actions of the women who serve, pursue, and sacrifice, the gospel creates a two-sided impression. Mark tells readers both what to avoid and what to embrace in their own discipleship. In our survey of the texts involving female discipleship, we will see that Mark urges the Christians in his community to avoid the failures of the Twelve while embracing the faithful action of the women who engage with Jesus. Following Jesus, it seems, means being as active as he is.[6]

Mark champions the kind of discipleship modeled by these women in several ways. First, he emphasizes the action of the women in their seeking out Jesus and their response to him. Second, he depicts the insufficient discipleship of the Twelve by repeatedly underscoring what they do not do (their inactivity) or what they do that is misguided or characterized by misunderstanding. These women provide a model for discipleship (what *to* do), and the Twelve often provide a foil for discipleship (what *not* to do, or what *not* to be caught *not* doing).

Of the four canonical gospels, Mark is widely seen to contain the harshest treatment of the Twelve. In this gospel the Twelve have few redemptive qualities during Jesus's ministry and few successes—which are often immediately tempered by some sort of failure or misunderstanding. This results in several moments of frustration on the part of Jesus toward these men. Notably absent is Jesus's frustration directed toward

6. Suzanne Watts Henderson, *Christology and Discipleship in the Gospel of Mark*, Society for New Testament Studies Monograph Series 135 (Cambridge: Cambridge University Press, 2006), has a very helpful study on the incomprehension of the Twelve in the Gospel of Mark, and in it she emphasizes the role of the Twelve as being primarily about the men's presence with Jesus and *practice*. For her, "practice" is about continuing "Jesus' practice of wielding the power associated with God's apocalyptic reign" (4). Although there are some significant differences between her work and this study in terms of focus and scope, her underscoring of the importance of action for the Twelve is congruent with the present argument.

female disciples. While no one is perfect apart from Jesus, the women who follow him get it "right" more often than their male peers.

Discipleship as Action

A fair bit of attention in Markan scholarship has been paid to the role of women in the gospel. This important work involves various kinds of approaches. Some have surveyed the role of females in Mark and compared and contrasted this with the role of the Twelve and other men who follow Jesus. In these studies some have regarded female discipleship in the gospel as the model of true discipleship.[7] Others have found the women in Mark to fall just as short of true discipleship as the men who follow him, together creating a complex composite portrait of discipleship.[8] Another sort of study, undertaken by feminist scholars, seeks to reclaim these texts on female disciples for the purpose of letting the women have their own voice in the story.[9] Lastly, some work has been done on the individual women in Mark or biblical texts that deal specifically with female followers of Jesus.[10] All of these studies have been very useful in their contribution to the discussion of discipleship in the gospel, and some have been seminal in their own areas.

It is significant that Mark presents an active Jesus both in the way he writes and through the theme of discipleship in his narrative. The Markan style of fast-paced, choppy storytelling (with abrupt, short sentences and little regard for sophisticated grammar), the portrayal of an on-the-go Jesus that takes up almost three-fourths of the narrative (Mark 1–12), and the way Mark significantly limits the inclusion of the

7. E.g., see Mary Ann Beavis, "Women as Models of Faith in Mark," *Biblical Theology Bulletin* 18 (1988): 3–9.

8. The most compelling argument thus far has been made by Elizabeth Struthers Malbon, "Fallible Followers: Women and Men in the Gospel of Mark," *Semeia* 28 (1983): 29–48.

9. See Elisabeth Schüssler Fiorenza, *In Memory of Her: A Feminist Theological Reconstruction of Christian Origins* (New York: Crossroad, 1983), 316–23; the collection of essays that focus specifically on Mark in Amy-Jill Levine, ed., *A Feminist Companion to Mark* (Sheffield: Sheffield Academic, 2001); and Warren Carter, *Mark*, ed. Sarah J. Tanzer, Wisdom Commentary 42 (Collegeville, MN: Liturgical Press, 2019).

10. There are too many to list here. Those that are directly relevant to this study are discussed below.

content of Jesus's teachings—all unique features of the Gospel of Mark as compared to the other canonical gospels—might not be just a stylistic feature, quirky habit, or indication of incompetency on the part of the author. Instead, perhaps it is precisely through these features that Mark is indicating what should be a crucial priority for his audience of Jesus followers—movement in service of the gospel. And for an early audience that is primarily hearing rather than reading the story, the effect of this kind of presentation of Jesus—an emphasis that begins quite dramatically in the very first chapter—would be profound.[11]

For this gospel, action is crucial. Movement is crucial. Ultimately, what the author includes and what he excludes is done in the service of getting Jesus to the cross and beyond. Thus, Mark is prioritizing the action of Jesus's followers theologically. Jesus is a man of constant action and movement (he does not waste time), and the Twelve move very slowly, if at all, and tend to stall any progress that seems to be made as the narrative progresses. We can see this in the way that the dialogue that is initiated by the Twelve and their questions of misunderstanding often bring the action to an abrupt halt. It is no surprise, then, when Jesus is often frustrated by their misunderstanding.[12]

By contrast, every time a female disciple's story is told, it calls to mind the announcement of the kingdom of God in Mark 1:14–15, which is characterized by repentance and belief in the gospel—both of which are actions required in response to the inauguration of God's kingdom in the person of Jesus.[13] Thus, in the Gospel of Mark the author guides his audience to recognize when actions are taking place as indications of faithful discipleship, because he links action with the entrance of the kingdom in Jesus's ministry. True discipleship is a discipleship that moves toward Jesus, toward Jerusalem, and toward the kingdom.[14] In contrast, it is often the case that if the Twelve move

11. Joanna Dewey, "Mark as Interwoven Tapestry: Forecasts and Echoes for a Listening Audience," *Catholic Biblical Quarterly* 53, no. 2 (1991): 221–36, argues for "reading" Mark with a view toward audience (hearing). She emphasizes ways in which Mark weaves together material to create connections, rather than breaking them apart to study them individually without attention to co-text.

12. Mark 6–8, for example. Worse, his enemies move in total opposition to Jesus throughout the narrative.

13. Although Mark surprisingly has little to say about repentance in his narrative, the importance of faith is underscored throughout (2:5; 4:40; 5:34, 36; 9:23, 24, 42; 10:52; 11:22–24, 31).

14. Dewey, "Interwoven Tapestry," 234, notes the impact of the "oral chaining method" on a narrative, where the author builds narrative connections that

at all, they are moving *away* from the kingdom of God—rebuking, fleeing, denying, and even betraying Jesus.

Women in Mark: Token Followers or True Disciples?

Mark presents women in the gospel in several ways. Some are named, while others are known only by their action, circumstances, or relationship to more prominent characters in the narrative. Some interact directly with Jesus, while others serve only to provide object lessons for Jesus's teachings to the Twelve. Some are included to explain how certain circumstances have arisen and are therefore not the focus themselves. For our purposes, the following discussion is limited to either those women who interact with Jesus directly or those whom Mark presents as models of discipleship.[15]

Each section begins with some brief observations of their stories and then highlights the ways that their actions demonstrate what it means to follow Jesus faithfully. Rather than working through the stories in narrative order, I have divided the discussion into three "action" categories—women who serve, women who pursue, and women who sacrifice—in order to highlight the specific nature of their discipleship.[16]

Women Who Serve

The very first active woman Mark introduces in his gospel is Simon's (Peter's) mother-in-law (1:29–31). Immediately after Jesus's first successful public exorcism, he enters the house of Simon and Andrew and is told that she is bedridden with a fever. Once notified, Jesus goes

---

call back to prior mention in the story. One can also see this type of retroactive effect in Mark 15:40–41.

15. Excluded from the discussion will be those who are presented as antithetical to Jesus's ministry. The intention here is not to imply that all women in the Gospel of Mark are faithful followers and all men are not. Herodias and her daughter (Mark 6:14–29) are clearly not disciples of Jesus. Mary, Jesus's own mother, does not appear to buy into what Jesus is doing (Mark 3:19b–35). Although certainly presented negatively, none of these women make a statement about discipleship, because they are not presented as disciples. Whereas Jesus's mother is depicted as a disciple in other gospels, in Mark 3 she follows Jesus only in an effort to interrupt or even end his ministry because of the rumors circulating about him (3:21, 31).

16. Although these categories are not mutually exclusive, each woman/group of women is placed in the category that is most emphasized in the narrative itself.

to her, takes her by the hand, and lifts her up. When he does so, her fever leaves. Without even starting a new sentence, Mark tells us that she began to serve Jesus and the disciples who were with him.[17] In this action she demonstrates the hospitality expected of the time and shows that her management of her household has not skipped a beat. This action emphasizes the immediacy of the healing and the way that service to Jesus can be exercised through tasks that might otherwise be considered expected and even mundane. Two additional matters are of particular note. First, the episode is told in typical Markan fashion. By excluding dialogue, Mark prioritizes the action of Jesus and the action of Simon's mother-in-law. Second, it is ironic that Jesus has just called Simon, Andrew, James, and John to be "fishers of men," emphasizing what they will learn to *do* when they are with Jesus (1:17). Yet they quite literally do nothing besides enter their own house and witness two people—Jesus and the mother-in-law—engage in service. Jesus has just served the young man who was demon-possessed

17. Marla J. Schierling, "Women as Leaders in the Marcan Communities," *Listening* 15 (1980): 252, sees Mark 10:45 as the programmatic statement for discipleship and leadership in underscoring the importance of service. She argues that there are three central concepts to service—suffering, following, and denying oneself—and argues that women in Mark engage in all three. Winsome Munro, "Women Disciples in Mark?," *Catholic Biblical Quarterly* 44, no. 2 (1982): 232, argues that serving should not be understood as a menial task, and sees a connection between the calling of the first four disciples (1:16–20) and of Levi (2:13–14), the role of the angels (1:13), and Jesus's own sacrifice (10:45). Susan Miller, *Women in Mark's Gospel*, Journal for the Study of the New Testament Supplement Series 259 (Edinburgh: T&T Clark, 2004), 22, notes that Simon's mother-in-law is unique in that she is the only character in the gospel to respond to a healing with service. On the other hand, Deborah Krause, "Simon Peter's Mother-in-Law—Disciple or Domestic Servant? Feminist Biblical Hermeneutics and the Interpretation of Mark 1.29–31," in Levine, *Feminist Companion to Mark*, 37–53, argues that there is tension between Jesus's compassionate healing of the woman and her response of the kind of service that would be expected in her role as mother-in-law. Accordingly, Krause calls into question whether she should be considered a disciple at all. While Krause's call for nuance and recognition of the tension in the story is valuable, I do not think that Mark's audience would miss the connection between Simon's mother-in-law and the women at the end of the gospel, who are both described as serving Jesus (*diakoneō*, 15:40–41). Although there would be a cultural expectation for her to serve in her home given her familial role, this does not take away from the reality of her appropriate action toward Jesus—she is serving not just anyone; she is serving the Christ.

(1:23–27), and now he has served Simon's mother-in-law by healing her. She has served Jesus. And one-third of the future "Twelve" have looked on all the while.

Perhaps it is not accidental that the gospel begins its depiction of female followers as people who are actively serving, because it ends in exactly the same way.[18] The women who go to the tomb after the Sabbath to anoint the body of Jesus are also serving him (16:1). Mark tells us that these women—Mary Magdalene, Mary the mother of James, and Salome—are the same ones who witnessed the crucifixion of Jesus (15:40–41).[19] At this point, Mark announces that these women followed Jesus during his ministry and provided for him while he was in Galilee. The introduction of this information—that these women have been in the background of the story all along—serves to underscore their presence here, in this moment. The twelve disciples who have been featured in the gospel are nowhere to be found. But the women who have been there in the background continue to stay. This, then, is not the first time that these women have sought to serve Jesus. They intend to serve him in death just as they served him in life, and they do this by bringing spices to his tomb in order to anoint his dead body.[20] With this intention they join the woman who had anointed Jesus before his arrest—an anointing that anticipated his burial (14:3–9). According to Jesus, this first anointing is an action that will be proclaimed alongside the gospel. Jesus elevates her act of anointing as an integral part of his story, and it is retained as part of her own story too, keeping the audience's attention on her as well as her action's effect on his own ("what she has done will be told in remembrance of her" [NRSVUE], *kai ho epoiēsen hautē lalēthēsetai eis mnēmosynon*; 14:9). Once again, women show a desire to care for Jesus's body as a way of

18. In fact, apart from the description of Jesus's own role as servant in Mark 10:45, *diakoneō* is only applied to women in the gospel (excluding the angels of 1:13).

19. This assumes that "Mary the mother of James the younger and of Joses" (15:40) is the same Mary mentioned in Mark 15:47 ("Mary the mother of Joses") and 16:1 ("Mary the mother of James"). Unless there is evidence to the contrary, it would be natural for an audience hearing the gospel read to assume that these are the same person.

20. The emphasis on their following Jesus's body and witnessing his burial in Mark 15:47 fits well within the second category, women who pursue, and thus will be discussed there.

showing him honor—an honor that would normally be withheld for someone who has died in such a shameful way.

Noticeably absent from the cross and the tomb are the Twelve. In the Gospel of Mark, the last to leave Jesus—Peter—completes a rejection of his own discipleship during the trials, failing to serve his master when recognized by a servant girl by denying he ever knew him (14:66–72). The play on the concept of service here is another instance of Markan irony. While the words are different (the term used to describe the girl is *paidiskē* rather than *diakoneō*), the audience would not likely miss the irony that a person whose identity is defined by her job of serving her master would be the most vocal in identifying Peter's master. And yet, when his connection to Jesus is made public, Peter denies him—the master whom he has served for years. It is a servant girl who exposes him for who he is, and when she does so, his last words in the gospel are a denial of the truth of which the audience is well aware: while Peter has followed Jesus from the beginning, in the end he leaves him to fend for himself at the hands of his enemies. When Peter's own life hangs in the balance, it turns out that he is not willing to pay the cost of discipleship.

Women Who Pursue

The majority of women who follow Jesus in the Gospel of Mark are characterized by their pursuit of Jesus. Mark presents two women who are determined to be beneficiaries of Jesus's power, and a group of women who follow Jesus even after his closest companions fail to do so.

Mark 5 contains a rapid-fire succession of three healing stories: the exorcism of the Gerasene demoniac (5:1–20), the healing of the hemorrhaging woman (5:25–34), and the healing of Jairus's daughter (5:21–24, 35–43). All of these have the running thread of pursuit. After his healing, the former demoniac begs Jesus to allow him to follow him into the boat and across the sea, just as the townspeople beg Jesus to leave altogether. Jesus denies him, giving him the task of witnessing to his home and friends. Immediately after landing, Jesus is inundated with the masses clamoring for his attention. Among them is a synagogue leader, who begs for Jesus to act in healing his daughter who is gravely ill. Her situation is so dire that Mark uses *sōzō* (to save) to describe the required action it would take to make this child well again.[21] The use of the term implies a more comprehensive healing of some kind, rather than simply a medical act. This salvation is emphasized even more in the following story—a story that interrupts the account of Jairus and his sick daughter. As he is on the way to see the little girl, Jesus is involved in an inadvertent healing of another female. A woman who has been bleeding for twelve years, desperate for intervention and destitute both financially (she "spent all she had" on doctors[22]) and relationally (she was ceremonially unclean in her condition and therefore on some level isolated from her community; see Lev 15:19–30), takes matters into her own hands, sneaks through the crowd, and touches Jesus's cloak from behind in order to be healed (also *sōzō*; Mark 5:28, 34). Positioned as the centerpiece of the intercalation of the healing of Jairus's daughter and her own story of healing, the hemorrhaging woman's salvation from physical and social death becomes the primary focus of the narrative.[23] She is presented as one who risks everything for the chance to touch the cloak of Jesus, banking on the stories she has heard about his great power to heal (5:27).

What is she risking? She is risking further ostracization from her community by publicly exposing herself and her condition in the midst of the crowd. While it has been argued that the woman would not technically have been considered contagiously unclean unless she sat down and contaminated a place where others might sit,[24] that does not preclude the crowd from frowning on her willingness to expose them.[25] The most natural reading of the text here suggests that the

21. Mark had other options at his disposal, such as *therapeuō* (1:34; 3:2, 10; 6:5, 13).

22. Mark 5:26: *dapanēsasa ta par' autēs panta.*

23. In terms of the resolution of the stories, hers is also the center of the three stories of healing, as Jairus's daughter does not experience healing until after she does, although the daughter's circumstances are introduced in Mark 5:21–24a before the woman's plight. In the device of intercalation, it is the middle part that functions as the "meat" of the text.

24. Lynn H. Cohick, *Women in the World of the Earliest Christians: Illuminating Ancient Ways of Life* (Grand Rapids: Baker Academic, 2009), 208, argues that the woman would not necessarily have been regarded as an outcast because she would not transmit her uncleanness except in places she sat down, and that this explains why "no one seems worried that she is jostling in their midst."

25. We would do well to listen to our Jewish brothers and sisters who urge us to adopt a more nuanced view of Levitical purity legislation regarding

woman has more to lose than what she has already lost. It is easy to imagine that the last thing she would want to endure, on top of everything that she has already endured, is a public humiliation in front of a crowd who also seeks something from Jesus. This may best explain her rather stealthy approach to Jesus (in contrast to Jairus's public request) and her fear of being called out in front of the crowd. But other factors might also make her fearful. In his version of the story, Mark emphasizes the relationship between her touch of his cloak and the power that goes out of Jesus as she is healed.[26] Her experience of feeling and receiving the effects of that kind of power could have made her fearful that Jesus would object to what she has done. It is also likely that her lack of status compared to Jairus (for whom Jesus is traveling) would have made her acutely aware of her presumption in interrupting Jesus's mission—she is moving in on Jesus's time to heal Jairus's daughter (and it turns out that her concerns were valid, as Jesus arrives "too late" to heal and must restore the dead girl back to life). The woman has been bleeding for as long as the little girl has been alive. She is destitute and desperate—her chronic illness makes her less important than the child who is on the brink of death.

Mark makes quite an issue of the woman's condition, giving details he would not normally supply, like the length of time she has been bleeding and the fact that she has exhausted her resources. It seems unlikely that her uncleanness has nothing to do with her choices in the way she engages with Jesus here, but those emphases are not in isolation from the surrounding narrative. The intercalation of the stories of Jairus's daughter and the hemorrhaging woman mimic the interruption of Jesus's momentum in healing the little girl. The woman

---

women. See, e.g., Amy-Jill Levine, "Second Temple Judaism, Jesus, and Women: Yeast of Eden," *Biblical Interpretation* 2 (1994): 15–20, who argues that "society did not shut down during their menstrual cycles." Rather, they continued to be engaged in the public sphere (16). She cautions against an overconcern with purity that views Pharisaic practices as the standard for all Jews at the time and that assumes that Pharisees had a negative view of women.

26. Candida R. Moss, "The Man with the Flow of Power: Porous Bodies in Mark 5:25–34," *Journal of Biblical Literature* 129 (2010): 507–19, argues, on the basis of Greco-Roman views of the body, that Mark presents both Jesus and the woman as "leaky." Jesus is porous enough for her to draw power from him, and she who was once leaky is dried up as a result of his healing power. See also Candida R. Moss and Joel S. Baden, *Reconceiving Infertility: Biblical Perspectives on Procreation and Childlessness* (Princeton: Princeton University Press, 2015), 201–8.

would be considered a lost cause and a bother; the daughter of a synagogue leader has her whole life ahead of her. Moreover, Jairus seems to have easy access to Jesus, despite the large crowd that surrounds him. Mark gives no indication that Jairus's approach to Jesus required any effort—he simply goes to him.[27] The contrast of each character's path to Jesus is striking: Jairus has a clear and easy approach to Jesus, while the woman must jostle the crowd and approach in stealth mode to "steal" some time and power from Jesus.

As the power leaves Jesus and he asks the crowd who has touched his clothes, his disciples condescendingly question his ability to sense this, failing to acknowledge his power just as the woman testifies to it in her willingness to approach Jesus and in the reality of her own miraculous healing. By their response of incredulity, the male disciples align themselves with Jesus's enemies, since up to this point in the gospel it has been the scribes and Pharisees who have increasingly challenged Jesus's ability, his authority, and the source from which he is able to do such things.[28] While they doubt—and ultimately side with Jesus's enemies—she believes.

Meanwhile, Jairus's daughter has died. Jesus speaks words of comfort and hope to the synagogue leader and announces to the crowd that has gathered to mourn her that "the child is not dead but sleeping" (5:39).[29] He proceeds to enter the room and commands her to "get up," which she does immediately (5:41–42). Although the primary active figures in the story are Jairus (in pursuing Jesus and begging him to heal her) and Jesus, the daughter does indeed comply with Jesus's command to rise.[30] The disciples who are present in the room, however, are merely spectators of this flutter of activity.

Another woman who pursues Jesus is the Syrophoenician woman in Mark 7:24–30. Mark tells us that Jesus is hiding out in a house

27. Echoes of the effort of the hemorrhaging woman to access Jesus are also found in the story of the Syrophoenician woman, who must resort to hunting Jesus down during his vacation in order to intercede for her daughter (Mark 7:24).

28. Cf. Mark 2:6–7, 16, 24; 3:1–6, 22–30.

29. *To paidion ouk apethanen alla katheudei.*

30. See Janine Luttick, "Little Girl, Get Up and Stand on Your Own Two Feet!," in *Reading the Gospel of Mark in the 21st Century: Method and Meaning*, ed. Geert van Oyen, Bibliotheca Ephemeridum Theologicarum Lovaniensium 301 (Leuven: Peeters, 2019), 631–42, who argues that Jesus functions as the authority figure of the household in this story.

in Tyre, continuing a not uncommon practice of retreat from the overwhelming crowds (e.g., 1:35; 3:9–10; 14:32). Somehow a gentile woman from the region hears of his whereabouts and comes to the house to petition him concerning her daughter.[31] Mark emphasizes her gentileness by specifying her origin as Syrophoenician, and also in the riddle Jesus gives her. Although Mark underscores the fact that she is a gentile, her femaleness is not irrelevant. In the surrounding narrative of Mark 5:21–24 and 35–43, a father comes to petition on behalf of his daughter, and his daughter is also healed. The similarities of posture (bowing down/falling at his feet), request (healing/exorcism), and result (health) would surely not be lost on an audience who has heard these stories read so closely together. But this time it is a mother who acts as an advocate for her daughter. Moreover, it is not a synagogue leader who has easy access to Jesus, but a gentile woman who must go to great lengths by chasing him down when he seeks to get away, just to get an audience with him. As in the case with the hemorrhaging woman, the author is again emphasizing the determination of the women who pursue Jesus, even when there are overwhelming obstacles ahead.

Although her petition appears to be rejected, the Syrophoenician woman refuses to take no for an answer.[32] Instead, she responds to Jesus's riddle in kind, and it is her clever retort that inspires Jesus to comply with her request. Thus, the woman doggedly pursues Jesus twice in one episode: by tracking him down at his hiding place and by going toe to toe with him in a rhetorical sparring match until she gets what she wants. Much like the Therapeutrides described by Philo, she is portrayed as perfectly capable of engaging with him in matters of the law and its relationship to her as a gentile. This is especially evident in the fact that Jesus has just been arguing with some Pharisees and teachers of the law, but the result of their exchange is entirely different.

31. Mark applies the term "immediately" (*euthys*) to her hearing of Jesus. Her actions follow thereafter in rapid succession.

32. See Holly Carey, "Jesus and the Syrophoenician Woman: A Case Study in Inclusiveness," *Leaven* 19, no. 1 (2011): 28–32, for the argument that Jesus never intended to permanently reject the woman's request but rather uses her as an opportunity to play devil's advocate by demonstrating the misguided view of purity represented by his opposition (and described in the previous pericope, Mark 7:1–23) and then aligning himself with her more inclusive view of Jewish/gentile relations.

They are given no chance to counter Jesus's interpretations—he simply wins the argument and Mark moves on to explain the imagery he uses to his followers (7:5–17). Furthermore, in the episode of Jesus's sparring session with the Syrophoenician woman, the Twelve are nowhere to be found. Mark makes no mention of them—whether they are in the house with Jesus, or whether they are even in Tyre at all. The most recent mention of them comes in the previous pericope, where Jesus becomes exasperated with their lack of understanding at his teaching on purity (7:7–23). Thus, the Twelve fail to understand Jesus, while, immediately following, a gentile woman displays the mental (and spiritual?[33]) acumen equivalent to Jesus himself.

Finally, the last women to pursue Jesus in the gospel are those found at a distance from the crucifixion scene (Mark 15:40–41). Much of the passion-resurrection narrative up to this point has emphasized the utter abandonment of Jesus by the Twelve. Mark begins by giving his audience an indication that Judas Iscariot has plotted with Jesus's enemies to betray him (14:10–11). Jesus confirms this in his prediction at the Passover meal shared with the Twelve (14:18–21). Jesus again predicts his suffering and the "scattering" of the Twelve by citing a messianic prophecy from Zechariah 13:7 (14:27). When Peter rejects Jesus's prophecy and proclaims his commitment to him, Jesus specifies exactly how he will abandon him (14:29–31). In Gethsemane, Peter, James, and John—with bellies full—cannot keep from falling asleep even though Jesus expressly asks for their companionship and prayer as he agonizes over his future (14:32–42). When the soldiers come, Judas betrays Jesus with a kiss (14:44–45), the others run away in terror (14:50), and one even leaves his clothes in his hasty exit (14:51–52)! Finally, with all the audience's hopes placed on the one who has been the most vocal in his commitment to Jesus, it is Peter who succumbs to the temptation of self-preservation, denying Jesus three times just as Jesus said he would (14:66–72). In Mark, Jesus dies on the cross surrounded by his enemies, not his friends.

There is one meager bright spot in this sad turn of events. Some of the women who have followed Jesus during his ministry and have

33. Although Jesus commends her words specifically (*dia touton ton logon*), it is likely that, given the parallels with the hemorrhaging woman's circumstances, pursuit of Jesus, and equal determination, the audience would infer that the Syrophoenician woman's words display her faith as well.

been providing for him remain to watch Jesus's crucifixion from a distance (15:40–41). Although they are not by his side as he dies, Mark's mention of these women certainly comes as a contrast to the Twelve, who are nowhere to be found. Of those who had followed Jesus in his ministry, it is these women who are the most committed to him, even in death.[34] These same women make their way to the tomb to care for Jesus's body after the Sabbath (16:1–2). Thus, by narrowing the distance between him (as they think he is in the tomb) and themselves, they are in the unique position to hear the announcement of good news, "He has risen!"

Women are the first to be tasked with witnessing to the resurrection. And it is important to recognize that Jesus did not have to go to them. Nor did a representative or other disciple have to seek them out to arrange a meeting with Jesus, as will be the case with the Twelve (16:7). The women come to the tomb of their own volition. These women are still following him, even though they do not yet realize just how far they still must go. They come to the tomb at first light (16:2), with no thought of the logistics of what they are trying to do (they think about the challenge of rolling away the stone only after they have started their journey; 16:3).[35] This displays a profound sense of urgency and longing on the part of the women to care for Jesus's

34. Contra Munro, "Women Disciples," it is not likely that Mark is reluctantly mentioning these women now because his hand is forced by the (passion narrative) tradition. Rather, perhaps Mark withholds his mention of these women's discipleship during Jesus's ministry precisely because he is contrasting their presence with the absence of the Twelve at the climax of the narrative. In other words, their commitment to Jesus is made all the more moving when contrasted with the abandonment of all the male disciples who are more prominent in the gospel up to this point.

35. The glimpse that Mark gives us into the concerns of the women about how to remove the stone is interesting because they express them only after they are already on the way to serve. This aspect of the account underscores the supernatural removal of the stone before they arrive (as does Mark's emphasis on the size of the stone; 16:4). Larry W. Hurtado, "The Women, the Tomb, and the Climax of Mark," in *A Wandering Galilean: Essays in Honour of Seán Freyne*, ed. Zuleika Rodgers, Margaret Daly-Denton, and Anne Fitzpatrick-McKinley, Supplements to the Journal for the Study of Judaism (Leiden: Brill, 2009), 433–34, is correct in observing that their notice of the stone's removal is the first "action" they take when they arrive. Contra Andreas Lindemann, "Die Osterbotsghaft des Markus. Zur Theologischen Interpretation von Mark 16.1–8," *New Testament Studies* 26, no. 3 (1980): 304–6, who argues that fear/astonishment is their first response to the empty tomb.

body. Narratively, these women have taken the first step toward Jesus, which is more than any of the other disciples have done.[36] With the Twelve running away from Jesus to preserve their own lives, women who have supported Jesus's ministry are there to care for his body at the end. Moreover, their role as observers is underscored (15:40–41, 47; 16:4–6).[37] Their presence gives them the unique opportunity to go and tell others that the tomb is empty. Because they are the primary eyewitnesses to Jesus's resurrection, the cultural implication is that his resurrection has a direct bearing on them and their lives *as women*. Their primary role no longer involves the rituals of mourning and care for the body of Jesus, as would be expected of women at the time. They now serve as first witnesses to the resurrection. And their presence legitimizes the veracity of what they witness.

Did they continue to take more steps? Much has been written on the enigmatic ending of the Gospel of Mark in 16:8, where the women flee the tomb in terror and "[say] nothing to anyone" (*kai oudeni ouden eipan*).[38] Space simply will not allow a thorough discussion of

36. It is not clear that Joseph of Arimathea is portrayed as a disciple in the Gospel of Mark. Yes, the author describes him as one who "was waiting for the kingdom of God" (*ēn prosdechomenos tēn basileian tou theou*, 15:43), and he does respect Jesus enough to bury him properly. But there is no other indication that he followed Jesus in any meaningful way. He seems to be a character on the cusp of discipleship. These can show respect to Jesus and recognize truths about him that others do not (see the centurion of 15:39), without Mark going so far as to present them as true and committed followers of Jesus.

37. Hurtado, "Climax of Mark," 431–32.

38. Some interpret this as evidence that the women were failures as the Twelve were: Andrew T. Lincoln, "The Promise and the Failure: Mark 16:7, 8," *Journal of Biblical Literature* 108, no. 2 (1989): 289; Bas M. F. Van Iersel, "Failed Followers in Mark: Mark 13:12 as a Key for the Identification of Intended Readers," *Catholic Biblical Quarterly* 58, no. 2 (1996): 258; Weeden, *Mark*, goes so far as to suggest that the Twelve never received the good news and that this fits the Markan polemic against this group. Others argue that the women said nothing to anyone *else*—i.e., that the women actually did tell the Twelve in Galilee: Hurtado, "Climax of Mark," 427–50. Many scholars see in the ending a challenge and charge for the audience to fill in the gap and participate in the sharing of the good news, even in the midst of their own fears: Morna D. Hooker, *Endings: Invitations to Discipleship* (Peabody, MA: Hendrickson, 2003), 25; Schüssler Fiorenza, *In Memory of Her*, 322–23, also believes that the women did ultimately tell the Twelve; Paul Danove, "The Characterization and Narrative Function of the Women at the Tomb (Mark 15,40–41.47; 16,1–8)," *Biblica* 77, no. 3 (1996): 395–97, argues that the women's failure to tell creates space for the implied reader to finish their task and proclaim the good news. Still others believe

this debate here. For the purposes of this study, the most important question is not whether they went and told the Twelve as they were instructed to do, but rather what it means if they did not go and tell. Does this undo all that has been argued up to this point—that the women who follow Jesus are more faithful disciples because they are women of action? Taking into account the ways the narrative has shaped the views of the gospel's audience on faithful women who petition and follow Jesus throughout his ministry—and especially their presence near the cross when all others have abandoned him—the answer must be no. Even if the best reading of 16:8 is that the women did not obey the instructions of the young man at the tomb, this does not negate all that they have done up to this point.[39] The women are *there*; the Twelve are not. The task of telling the "good news" is given to the ones who are present—who have followed Jesus even in death.[40] And as many have noted, the open-endedness of the last verse leaves the audience with the question "What will *you* do?"

Women Who Sacrifice

The willingness to make sacrifices for the sake of the gospel is a necessary characteristic of discipleship—ranging from giving up one's

---

Mark's purpose is to depict the women as having an appropriate response to the epiphany they've experienced: e.g., Yarbro Collins, *Mark*, 800; Mitchell, *Beyond Fear*; Marie Sabin, "Women Transformed: The Ending of Mark Is the Beginning of Wisdom," *CrossCurrents* 48, no. 2 (1998): 161; David Catchpole, "The Fearful Silence of the Women at the Tomb: A Study in Markan Theology," *Journal of Theology for Southern Africa* 18 (1977): 3–10; Rudolf Pesch, *Das Markusevangelium II*, Herders theologischer Kommentar zum Neuen Testament (Freiburg: Herder, 1977), 535. See also Victoria Phillips, "The Failure of the Women Who Followed Jesus in the Gospel of Mark," in Levine, *Feminist Companion to Mark*, 222–35, who argues that the women have an appropriate response to the news because they have been excluded from information that would help them make sense of it—information that was given to the Twelve but withheld from them.

39. *Pace* Gerald O'Collins, "The Fearful Silence of the Three Women (Mark 16:8c)," *Gregorianum* 69, no. 3 (1988): 489–503. Although his main argument is that the women have an appropriate response to the divine revelation they are experiencing, he cautions against equating the failures of the male disciples with that of the women.

40. And, strictly speaking, in terms of "following" Jesus, these women are instructed to tell Peter and the other disciples to follow—they are not told to do it themselves.

possessions to giving up one's own life. Throughout the gospel, Jesus makes it clear that discipleship is less about what someone can gain from knowing him and more about what they will have to give up or give away. The Gospel of Mark depicts some characters who are successes in this regard as well as others who are failures. As might be expected, there are more failures than successes in the narrative as a whole, but there are some bright spots. Two of the most important examples of sacrificial discipleship are women: the widow who gives away her last coins (12:41–44) and the woman who anoints Jesus in Bethany (14:3–9).

In Mark 11–12, Jesus has been spending a significant amount of time in the temple, teaching his disciples and arguing with his enemies on matters of the law and the Scriptures. Although Mark rarely gives us large blocks of didactic material, these chapters are an exception. Jesus's last public teaching is his condemnation of the superficial piety of the scribes, who want honor among the people, but who take advantage of the least in the culture—widows—rather than ensuring their provision and protection (12:38–40). In essence, Jesus is accusing them of violating the commands of God in Exodus 22:22. Immediately following, Jesus sits in view of the treasury, watching people present their offerings. As he sees the rich put in large sums of money, he calls his disciples' attention to the offering of a poor widow. Although she has only put in two small coins, the gift goes beyond their monetary value. Jesus prioritizes her giving because it is done sacrificially; she has given all she had to live on (*holon ton bion autēs*, 12:44). Mark's commentary here emphasizes the precarious nature of her position. As a poor widow, she would have no economic means of providing for herself and no property to bring her passive income. Also absent is any mention of sons or other male family members who could ensure her welfare or economic stability. Thus, her offering is an embodiment of her trust in God, who has provided both an institution (the temple) and instructions (the Torah) that should provide the security she lacks.[41] But this trust is under threat by those religious leaders who

41. See Amy-Jill Levine, "'This Poor Widow . . .' (Mark 12:43): From Donation to Diatribe," in *A Most Reliable Witness: Essays in Honor of Ross Shepard Kraemer*, ed. Susan Ashbrook Harvey et al., Brown Judaic Studies 358 (Providence, RI: Brown University, 2015), 183–94, who cautions against reading her example as a story that extolls poverty: "The very temple to which she gives her last two coins will be the institution that will provide for her" (186).

will abuse the system for their own social benefit. The sacrifice of her coins, then, is a sacrifice of herself—she is placing her life in God's hands. This is a discipleship of the whole person—a person who gives all that is in her power to give, as God commands.[42]

The context of Jesus's saying here is important. He is deliberately contrasting the false piety and honor-mongering of the scribes, who have made a practice of opposing his ministry, with the authentic piety of the widow.

Later, as Jesus dines with his disciples in the house of Simon, "the one suffering leprosy," a woman enters the house and anoints Jesus's head with expensive ointment. Her action prompts immediate and unequivocal condemnation from "some" in the house. As evidenced by their response, not only does this woman make a monetary sacrifice to honor Jesus, but she also risks sacrificing her reputation as she is publicly shamed for what she has done. Yet instead of rejecting her or shaming her, Jesus defends her, lauding her kindness in doing "what she could,"[43] and claiming that her action is so meaningful as to merit its remembrance as an integral part of the gospel story (14:9). In terms of narrative impact, the fact that the anointing at Bethany is surrounded by the plotting of Jesus's death by his enemies (14:1–2) and one of his own (14:10–11) underscores even further the inevitability of his own sacrifice and the profound significance of the woman's sacrificial gift.[44] Who is like Jesus, following him in his path toward the cross? It is this anonymous woman and not the Twelve.

42. Yarbro Collins, *Mark*, 590, argues that the use of *bios* here suggests that the widow is doing discipleship because she is giving of her whole life. She sees this as an allusion to Deut 6:5, where there is precedent in the Dead Sea Scrolls to interpret the terms "power" or "strength" (*ischys*) as "wealth" or "property" (CD 9:10b–12; 1QS 1:11–15; 3:2–3)—so in giving of her wealth she is giving all of her "strength" and therefore following the great commandment.

43. Mark 14:8: *eschen epoiēsen*. This description of her action has echoes of Jesus's description of the widow's sacrifice (Mark 12:44). Both have done all that they can do in their service to God.

44. Stephen C. Barton, "Mark as Narrative: The Story of the Anointing Woman (Mk 14:3–9)," *Expository Times* 102 (1991), argues that the framing of the story with these two episodes highlights the contrast between these groups and the woman: "Those of whom the reader should expect most—the religious leaders of the people and one of the specially chosen intimates of Jesus—turn out to be the perpetrators of the greatest ill. Instead, it is a nameless woman who does what is right" (231).

Ultimately, what makes both of these women among the clearest representatives of sacrifice in the gospel is Jesus's own elevation of their role as exemplars.[45] Although Joseph of Arimathea gives up his tomb for Jesus's body (15:46), and the hemorrhaging woman risks something to pursue Jesus in the crowd, neither of them is explicitly presented as a model for action. Neither have their actions been immortalized by Jesus. By contrast, Jesus elevates the widow and the woman at Bethany as models of faithful sacrifice.[46] In both cases Jesus underscores their giving to those who would otherwise have missed its importance (the Twelve in 12:43)[47] or rejected it outright (the unnamed criticizers in 14:4–6).[48]

On the other hand, some followers of Jesus in the gospel display a disinterested attitude toward sacrificial discipleship. Still others reject the notion altogether. The four men to be called by Jesus early in the gospel might seem at first to be well on their way to successful discipleship. Simon Peter, Andrew, James, and John immediately respond to Jesus's invitation (1:16–20). Their lack of hesitancy is remarkable for a number of reasons (most notably that this appears to be the first time they have ever encountered Jesus, and that they appear

45. *Pace*, Dewey, "Interwoven Tapestry," 233. Beavis, "Women as Models," 3, argues that the *chreiai* (pithy sayings that focus on a character in the narrative) about these two women (as well as the hemorrhaging woman of 5:24–34 and the Syrophoenician woman of 7:25–30) show "women understanding Jesus better than men." Note that the type of *chreia* attributed to these women highlights the action they take rather than what they say.

46. Beavis, "Women as Models," 6, observes that the widow is the only Markan character other than Jesus and John the Baptist to give "all her life" in service to God.

47. Yarbro Collins, *Mark*, 589, sees in Jesus's summoning of his disciples a call back to the summoning of the disciples in Mark 8:34 (to teach them about suffering discipleship) and 10:42 (to teach them about a discipleship of service): "The similarity suggests that the action of the widow is relevant to the question of discipleship." Elizabeth S. Malbon, "The Poor Widow in Mark and Her Poor Rich Readers," *Catholic Biblical Quarterly* 53, no. 4 (1991): 596, sees the widow's gift of her "whole life" as a contrast to Peter's complaint when Jesus declares his willingness to give his life (10:45). Thus, the widow demonstrates what it means to be a true disciple, while one of the Twelve resists the required sacrificial component. In addition, Peter's declaration in 14:31, and then his failure to follow through with that promise, also contributes to this contrast.

48. It is unclear whether the Twelve were present at the anointing in Mark, although later gospel tradition locates them there and blames them as the primary criticizers of her actions (Matt 26:8–9; John 12:4–5).

willing to abandon their family's livelihood). It creates an expectation among the narrative's audience that their enthusiasm and active pursuit of Jesus will continue and increase during his ministry.[49] In great storytelling fashion, however, Mark has set his audience up! Instead of logging success after success from their time with Jesus, Mark shows that they repeatedly misunderstand, rebuke, and reject Jesus's teachings of the kingdom. At the height of Jesus's teachings on the required sacrifices of discipleship and the anticipation of his own suffering and death, they are found arguing among themselves about who will be given the most prestige in the new kingdom (10:35–45). And in the end they are not willing to follow Jesus out of the garden and toward the cross. What starts as a promising beginning ends with utter disappointment.

We have already observed how the scribal attitude of false piety is a cover for their exploitation of widows, and that this provides the primary contrast for the widow's authentic sacrifice in Mark 12:41–44. Perhaps there is also a subtler contrast with the Twelve in Mark 13:1, in the disciples' exclamation concerning the opulence of the temple. Here Jesus has just lauded the sacrificial generosity of a woman whose experience was likely to be that of the other widows—to have her house "devoured" by the religious leadership.[50] On top of this, Jesus must call their attention to her sacrifice, as they fail to notice it on their own.[51] The next words out of the mouths of the disciples are to express awe at the grandeur of the temple. The juxtaposition of these

49. In fact, it has been argued that the first six chapters of Mark create an expectation of success in discipleship, as the Twelve are depicted as being close to Jesus and sharing in his mission: Günther Schmahl, *Die Zwölf im Markusevangelium* (Trier: Paulinus-Verlag, 1974). Robert C. Tannehill, "The Disciples in Mark: The Function of a Narrative Role," *Journal of Religion* 57, no. 4 (1977): 397, however, is correct to critique Schmahl for his one-sided emphasis on the positive aspect of the Twelve's behavior in the gospel.

Although the four men leave the family business, it is clear that they did not sever all ties from their family. It is likely that Jesus's base of operations in Capernaum was Peter's house (1:29; 2:1). Perhaps, then, Peter's claim that they had "left everything" to follow Jesus (10:28) is a bit of Petrine hyperbole, and soon after Mark indicates that at least some of them thought this was an investment in their future, rather than being purely sacrificial (10:35–37, 41).

50. See 12:40: *hoi katesthiontes tas oikias tōn chērōn*.

51. Malbon, "Poor Widow," 595, sees in this passage a deliberate connection between the neglect of the widows by the religious authorities and the neglect

interactions is key. Jesus has just warned against the superficiality of outward appearance in matters of holiness, and yet the Twelve are still awed by the facade of the temple. He is interested in the sacrifice of "lives" for the gospel; they are concerned with outward expressions and material possessions.[52] It is only fitting, then, that Jesus's prophecy of the destruction of that very structure is a focus of his Olivet discourse. Once again, the leaders of God's people have demonstrated a penchant for misplaced priorities and corruption of God's house (11:17).[53]

Other would-be followers and disciples also reject their chance to embody the sacrificial nature of discipleship. The rich man in Mark 10:17–27, who has so much going for him in terms of status (as his disciples note with confusion) and who desires to "inherit eternal life," is not willing to give up his possessions and risk it all to follow Jesus. And alarmingly, one of Jesus's own Twelve rejects his vision of the kingdom and plots to betray him (14:10–11). That this incident comes directly on the heels of the anointing at Bethany suggests the possibility that Judas's actions were motivated by his dissatisfaction with Jesus's support of the woman's decision to "waste" the ointment on him rather than sell it for a large sum of money.[54] Rather than selfless action, Judas chooses to look out for his own interests.[55]

Do Something! The Role of Active Faith

The first words Jesus says in the Gospel of Mark are described as "the good news of God" (*to euangelion tou theou*, 1:14). With his arrival comes the kingdom of God—a fulfillment of what God has prom-

of this widow by Jesus's own disciples. If this is so, it is a damning rebuke of Jesus's followers.

52. See also Mark 10:35–45.

53. See also Louis Simon, "Le sou de la veuve: Marc 12/41–44," *Etudes théologiques et religieuses* 44 (1969): 115–26, who argues that the episode of the poor widow is significant in its juxtaposition with the fig tree/temple episodes.

54. Although Mark does not tell his audience this explicitly (as in John 12:4–5), it seems reasonable to think that an audience would infer this from the juxtaposition of these two pericopes and from the fact that the chief priests offer him money for the job (Mark 14:10–11).

55. Malbon, "Poor Widow," 599, notes the irony of the contrast between the portrayal of the woman who gives up money to honor Jesus by entering a house and Judas who leaves a house to give up Jesus for money.

ised (1:15). But Jesus is not content to simply make that proclamation. As with John's own ministry of preparation, the people of God are supposed to respond to the good news. In other words, there is an expectation that the hearers of Jesus's teaching will *do something*. Being part of the kingdom as disciples of Jesus, then, requires action.[56] In response to the good news of the kingdom's arrival, God's people should repent and believe.

Although the theme of repentance does not feature prominently in the Gospel of Mark,[57] the role of faith in response to Jesus surely does. And, whether implicitly or explicitly, the actions of the women that we have surveyed relate to Jesus's vision of the kingdom of God in Mark because they demonstrate a level of faith and commitment to Jesus that surpasses even that of the Twelve. The much-longed-for healing of her body is due to the faith of the woman who has been hemorrhaging for twelve years (5:34). Jesus credits the Syrophoenician woman's words for the powerful long-distance exorcism of her daughter, but it is her pursuit of him that puts her in a position to dialogue in the first place (7:25, 29).[58] Whereas the rich man fails to enter the kingdom because it requires him to have faith enough to relinquish his hold on his wealth, the widow steps out on faith that God will provide for her even as she drops her last two coins in the treasury (10:21–23; 12:42–44).[59] By contrast, the Twelve display very

56. Leif E. Vaage, "An Other Home: Discipleship in Mark as Domestic Asceticism," *Catholic Biblical Quarterly* 71, no. 4 (2009): 742, rightly sees significance in the placement of Jesus's teachings on finding, receiving, and entering the kingdom in the middle of the gospel, where there is also the highest concentration of Jesus's teachings on discipleship.

57. Mark is clearly drawing an explicit connection between John's ministry of repentance and Jesus's own ministry, particularly in terms of its role in preparing God's people for his return (1:4). Yet repentance is mentioned only one other time in the remainder of the gospel (6:12), characterizing the trial-run ministry of the Twelve. Interestingly, this work of the Twelve also calls to mind John's ministry—so much so that people believe him to have been raised from the dead (6:14).

58. The juxtaposition of the episode with Jesus's teachings on true purity also suggests that it is more than a clever retort that inspires Jesus to act. See Carey, "Syrophoenician Woman." David Rhoads, "Jesus and the Syrophoenician Woman in Mark: A Narrative-Critical Study," *Journal of the American Academy of Religion* 62, no. 2 (1994): 345–46, also sees in her actions the faith that is called for in Jesus's programmatic statement on the kingdom in Mark 1:14–15.

59. Barton, "Mark as Narrative," 232, sees in the narrative framing of Mark 13

little faith in Jesus, especially with regard to his supernatural abilities (4:38; 6:37, 52; 8:4), and doubt their own abilities even after they have had successes in the ministry—a result of their faithlessness (6:12; 9:18–19).

Discipleship that reflects the kingdom of God also requires a consistency of talk and action that the Twelve simply lack. This dynamic in the narrative creates a consistent thread of disappointment on the part of the hearer. The first men who are called follow Jesus "immediately," and the audience starts out feeling optimistic about this group (1:20). But as the narrative progresses, these men leave behind them a string of empty promises. Meanwhile, there are anonymous women who do not speak at all, yet whose actions demonstrate faithful discipleship worthy of emulation and remembrance—such as we have seen in the anointing woman at Bethany and the women near the cross and at the tomb.[60]

Lastly, the passion-resurrection predictions and the teachings of Jesus that correct the Twelve's misunderstandings concerning discipleship immediately thereafter (8:31–38; 9:31–37; 10:33–45) teach that discipleship in the kingdom of God requires the willingness to suffer. Following Jesus means being willing to take up your cross, to risk everything, to "endure many things" at the hands of those who oppose God. This combination (*polla* + *paschō*) is found only three times in the Gospel of Mark—twice to refer to Jesus (8:31; 9:12) and once to describe the experience of the hemorrhaging woman before Jesus heals her (5:26). The woman's suffering is ended with the coming of the kingdom as expressed through Jesus's power, but the suffering at the hands of persecution will be a hallmark of discipleship, as it is the path that Jesus himself must travel.[61] By linking the story of the

---

with two sets of stories that contrast "exemplary women and villainous men" (scribes vs. the widow in 12:38–40 and 12:41–44; the chief priests and scribes vs. the anointing woman in 14:1–2 and 14:3–9) an indication that these women are examples of those who are willing to give up everything for the kingdom. Thus, we see in these stories a real connection to Jesus's kingdom message in his apocalyptic discourse.

60. Dewey, "Interwoven Tapestry," 233.

61. See Joanna Dewey, "'Let Them Renounce Themselves and Take Up Their Cross': A Feminist Reading of Mark 8.34 in Mark's Social and Narrative World," in Levine, *Feminist Companion to Mark*, 23–36, for a very thoughtful essay on the meaning of suffering in the first century, Mark's view of the place of suffering

hemorrhaging woman with Jesus, Mark connects their experiences. Moreover, in the case of many of the women we have surveyed, their actions demonstrate a willingness to risk social persecution and perhaps physical persecution as they seek to be in close proximity to Jesus, even as he heads toward the cross and death.

Conclusion

It is not incidental that while so many women are presented as faithful followers of Jesus in the Gospel of Mark, the twelve who should fill this role fail to do so on numerous occasions. Memorable stories of females who serve, pursue Jesus, and make sacrifices punctuate the narrative all the way to the empty tomb: "Mark mentions woman at the beginning and at the end of the gospel. Woman is always near yet not always at the center of activity. She is there in the crowds, as disciple, as healed and healer, and as grave preparer."[62]

Female discipleship in Mark models what it means to be a follower of Jesus, the one who has brought the kingdom of God near. Social status does not function as the primary determiner of a person's role in the kingdom. It is rather her willingness to do as Jesus does—to actively respond to the good news. This kind of discipleship is risky, as many of these women demonstrate in their interactions with Jesus and in their worship of God. Some have to resort to extreme measures. Some risk further ostracizing and physical danger. Some give all that they have. Each woman represents the cost of following Jesus.

---

in the kingdom, and a critique of a decontextualized glorification of victimage that has been applied to women by a misreading of these texts.

62. Schierling, "Women as Leaders," 252.

Three

Female Discipleship in the Gospel of Matthew

Among biblical scholars, there is quite a lot of discussion about how Matthew uses the term "disciple" (*mathētēs*), who qualifies as a disciple, and what discipleship entails. For the most part, the gospel writer reserves the term for the twelve male companions of Jesus.[1] Because he applies it so exclusively, we should ask, "Are there other disciples of Jesus in the gospel beyond the Twelve?" The answer to this question will have great bearing on our understanding of female discipleship in Matthew.

Apart from the Twelve, only one other person who follows Jesus is given the label "disciple." Joseph of Arimathea, a rich man, has his first (and last) appearance in the narrative during Jesus's burial scene. Here Matthew retroactively notes that he has been a disciple of Jesus, which explains why he would offer his own tomb for Jesus's body (27:57).[2] By contrast, Matthew calls no woman a "disciple." However, Joseph of Arimathea's exception to this practice of reserving *mathētēs* for only the Twelve is significant, as it indicates that while Matthew's preferred application of the term is to the Twelve, he recognizes that others can also be regarded as Jesus's disciples. This exception indicates that there were likely others who followed and served Jesus—people who were not expressly called "disciples." These people were also committed to Jesus, and their stories can provide insight into

1. Matt 10:2–4. This is also the only place where he uses the term *apostolōn* for the Twelve.

2. The verb form, *emathēteuthē*, indicates that Joseph had been a disciple during Jesus's ministry, and emphasizes the action of *being a disciple*.

what it means to be a disciple, according to Matthew.[3] This broadened perspective is key. Some scholars limit their discussion of discipleship to the actions and stories of those who are only explicitly called "disciples" in the gospel.[4] However, others have rightly argued that we should think of Matthean discipleship as being less about membership in a formal character group, "the disciples," and more about having the proper response to belief in Jesus.[5]

This more expansive consideration of discipleship is further substantiated by the ways that Matthew uses two verbs, "to follow" (*akoloutheō*) and "to serve" (*diakoneō*).[6] I think it is right to see *akoloutheō* used both literally and metaphorically—sometimes emphasizing the actual movement of Jesus's followers alongside him in his travels, and sometimes connoting their deepening commitment to follow his teachings in word and deed.[7]

Context and character development help determine whether the actions of a person or a group constitute the type of following that is required for discipleship.[8] Notably, Matthew uses *diakoneō* only

3. See In-Cheol Shin, "Matthew's Designation of the Role of Women as Indirectly Adherent Disciples," *Neotestamentica* 41 (2007): 400, who argues that the use of *mathētēs* in Matt 26:17–19 refers generally to a larger group of disciples, since the Twelve are distinguished from them in 26:20. It is also notable that Matthew does not refer to the Twelve (*dōdeka*) until 10:1.

4. Georg Strecker, *Der Weg der Gerechtigkeit: Untersuchung zur Theologie des Matthäus* (Göttingen: Vandenhoeck & Ruprecht, 1962), 191, argues that *mathētēs* is a term that is identical to the Twelve. Patrick J. Hartin, "Disciples as Authorities within Matthew's Christian-Jewish Community," *Neotestamentica* 32 (1998): 392–93, challenges this, arguing that it refers more generally to the master-pupil relationship.

5. Janice Capel Anderson, "Matthew: Gender and Reading," *Semeia* 28 (1983): 16.

6. Jack Dean Kingsbury, "The Verb AKOLOUTHEIN ('To Follow') as an Index of Matthew's View of His Community," *Journal of Biblical Literature* 97 (1978): 56, thinks it significant that Matthew uses *akoloutheō* more frequently than the other Synoptics.

7. Kingsbury, "Index," 58–61, makes a sharp distinction between the two, but I wonder if it is more helpful to think of this as a *spectrum* of discipleship. For example, Kingsbury argues that the crowds only follow Jesus literally and that this is not to be regarded as discipleship. However, I think the narrative leaves open the possibility that there is hope of them being *on their way* to genuine discipleship.

8. Craig S. Keener, "Matthew's Missiology: Making Disciples of the Nations (Matthew 28:19–20)," *Asian Journal of Pentecostal Studies* 12 (2009): 15–18, ar-

five times. Of the five, two of them refer to the actions of women who serve Jesus (8:15; 27:55), much like the angels who do so at the beginning of Jesus's ministry (4:11). Elsewhere, Jesus describes his own death as an act of service (20:28), expects the same service of his disciples (25:44), and calls those who follow to take up their cross, even if it leads to a division within their own families (10:34–39). This last requirement, which describes the potential cost of discipleship, pertains to both men and women who want to follow Jesus.[9] Moreover, when his mother and brothers request an audience with him, he redefines what his family is by including those who are with him, pointing to his disciples (*mathētēs*) and exclaiming, "Here are my mother and my brothers! For whoever does the will of my Father in heaven is my brother and sister and mother" (12:49–50 NRSVUE). By applying the term to a group that can be called both brothers and mothers/sisters, the text suggests a broader group of disciples than the Twelve—a group that includes women.[10] Throughout the narrative, then, several of the women who follow Jesus demonstrate the type of action that is expected of his disciples and will define his own work.[11]

Are there female disciples in the Gospel of Matthew? The answer in part depends on whether we restrict the pool of candidates to those who are explicitly labeled "disciples." If so, then the women who follow Jesus are excluded from any discussion of the subject. But when we reject that narrow definition, it becomes clear that there are stories of women in the gospel that contribute in significant ways to Matthew's overall portrayal of discipleship.[12] Even when those women come up

---

gues that Matthean discipleship requires one to value Jesus above job security, residential security, financial security, and social obligations, and to take up one's cross to follow Jesus. Shin, "Matthew's Designation," 404, and Robert H. Gundry, *Matthew: A Commentary on His Literary and Theological Art* (Grand Rapids: Eerdmans, 1982), 406, both regard the blind men in Matt 20:34 as examples of disciples.

9. Cf. Jane Kopas, "Jesus and Women in Matthew," *Theology Today* 47 (1990): 16–17.

10. See also Mark 3:31–35.

11. Anderson, "Gender and Reading," 19, argues that the use of *diakoneō* indicates that the servant role that was willingly taken up by the women was one that the Twelve should have pursued.

12. Some try to bridge this gap by regarding women as "auxiliary" disciples (e.g., Anderson, "Gender and Reading," 20–21) or "indirectly adherent disciples"

against difficulties and challenges that are an effect of the restrictions they would normally encounter (owing to their social status as women), the narrative presents these women in ways that subvert cultural assumptions and cast female disciples as faithful followers of Jesus, often in contexts where the Twelve are less than faithful.[13] Thus, Matthew displays a bit of irony when he regularly uses *mathētēs* as a shorthand term for the Twelve (excluding other followers) and yet often presents other followers as more faithful in their response to Jesus.[14] Those who are not called "disciples" end up doing a better job of disciple-ing![15]

(e.g., Shin, "Matthew's Designation," 399) because they are outside the Twelve by nature of their gender and social status.

13. Kopas, "Jesus and Women in Matthew," 13, notes that on first examination women do not appear to be all that significant in the Gospel of Matthew (they are in the background or are important only in their association with men), "yet a closer examination of the roles they do play reveals a somewhat more complex picture. It is one in which Matthew struggles to incorporate women moving from the periphery to greater public involvement and from being victims and survivors to being disciples and leaders." See Dorothy Jean Weaver, "'Wherever This Good News Is Proclaimed': Women and God in the Gospel of Matthew," *Interpretation* 64 (2010): 391–93, who gives a helpful summary of the ways in which Matthew depicts women in the sociocultural restrictions of their time only to subvert them with his "upper-level portrait": "To bring God into the story of women is ultimately, for Matthew, to overturn conventional social and religious perspectives and to grant women extraordinary and unanticipated significance for the life and the faith of the people of God" (391). On balance, women were not completely excluded from religious life in the first century, with evidence that women attended the public synagogue worship services—a more gender-inclusive practice than in most Greco-Roman worship services. See Anders Runesson, "Saving the Lost Sheep of the House of Israel: Purity, Forgiveness, and Synagogues in the Gospel of Matthew," *Melilah* 11 (2014): 8–24.

14. Carlos Olivares, "The Term *oligopistos* (Little Faith) in Matthew's Gospel: Narrative and Thematic Connections," *Colloquium* 47 (2015): 287–88, highlights the "minor characters" who operate in contrast to the Twelve because of their faith, some of whom will be discussed below.

15. Elaine M. Wainwright, *Towards a Feminist Reading of the Gospel according to Matthew*, Beihefte zur Zeitschrift für die neutestamentliche Wissenschaft 60 (Berlin: de Gruyter, 1991), 335, believes that the Matthean community received the tradition that the disciples were distinctively male, and so by placing that tradition alongside women's stories of faithfulness, he indicates that term should be more inclusive, representing all who were adherents to Jesus. This accounts for the ambiguity between Matthew's exclusive application of *mathētēs* to men and his inclusion of stories of female discipleship.

In this chapter I will explore the ways in which Matthew depicts female discipleship in stories that overlap with their companion stories in Mark.[16] Changes in emphasis may indicate what Matthew is trying to accomplish regarding his views on the requirements of discipleship and how women fare when it comes to following Jesus. We will look at the ways, for example, that his more positive portrayal of the Twelve impacts his presentation of female discipleship.[17] Are the characters placed in new settings that could influence the way we understand the role of these women in Jesus's ministry? I will also include a discussion of a uniquely Matthean passage on women in Jesus's genealogy (1:1–17) and how it sets the tone for everything that follows. How does the opening of this gospel impact our understanding of what it means to be faithful and to have a part in God's plan through Jesus? As with the chapter on Mark, I will highlight the thematic threads woven through these stories of women as a way of understanding what actions Matthew thinks are crucial and necessary to be a disciple of Jesus.

The Women Who Precede Jesus (Matthew 1:1–17)

One of the unique features of the Gospel of Matthew is his inclusion of women in the opening genealogy.[18] While Luke also has a genealogy, he includes no mention of Tamar, Rahab, Ruth, or "the wife of Uriah" (i.e., Bathsheba) as Matthew does. However, the women in Matthew's genealogy do function somewhat like Mary and Elizabeth

16. I am less interested in how Matthew *redacts* his material than in how he *reads and interprets* Mark.

17. See Richard N. Longenecker, "Taking Up the Cross Daily: Discipleship in Luke-Acts," in *Patterns of Discipleship in the New Testament*, ed. Richard N. Longenecker (Grand Rapids: Eerdmans, 1996), 54–55, who provides a summary of the ways in which Matthew adapts Mark's more negative view of the Twelve into a more positive portrayal. Yolanda Dreyer, "Gender Critique on the Narrator's Androcentric Point of View of Women in Matthew's Gospel," *Hervormde teologiese studies* 67 (2011): 2, is right to observe that, while Matthew's portrayal of the Twelve is generally more positive than Mark's, they still struggle to "get it right."

18. The inclusion of women in genealogies was unusual. Some notable biblical exceptions include Gen 11:29; 22:20–24; 25:1; 35:22–26; 36:10, 22; 1 Chr 2:4, 18–21, 24, 34, 46–49; 7:24. See John C. Hutchison, "Women, Gentiles, and the Messianic Mission in Matthew's Genealogy," *Bibliotheca Sacra* 158 (2001): 163.

(and, to a lesser extent, Anna) in the opening chapters of the Gospel of Luke: although neither text is about discipleship per se, they both help shape their audience's understanding of who Jesus is and highlight the important roles women play in his story. The audience's exposure to these women in the opening of these gospels also increases their capacity to recognize the active part women have played and will play in God's plan of salvation through Jesus.[19] The women included in the genealogy of Matthew have profound impact on Israelite history. Moreover, their stories are implicitly connected with Mary's own role in the conception and birth of the Messiah.

Matthew's genealogy is highly stylized. This indicates that he is trying to communicate something about Jesus by the people he chooses to include and the way that he organizes his material. The list is composed of three sections of fourteen generations, each ending with figures whose stories come at pivotal points in Israel's history: David, at the golden age of Israel's united kingdom (1:6), Jechoniah, at the time of the Babylonian exile (1:11), and Jesus (1:16). As would have been expected at the time, the genealogy is patrilineal, focusing on the male line. For the most part, it also follows a formula that underscores the men in the ancestry of Jesus (male begetting male; *egennēsen*). But disrupting that standard formulaic structure are four women from Israel's history (Tamar, 1:3; Rahab, 1:5; Ruth, 1:5; and the wife of Uriah, 1:6). Each is introduced with the Greek formula "out of" (*ek tēs*) + woman, emphasizing the woman as the source of the child.[20]

At the end of the genealogy when Mary is introduced, even the interruption is interrupted. While still maintaining the "out of" pattern, Matthew emphasizes her importance over against Joseph by making his role as her husband his primary identifier (*ton andra Marias*, 1:16),

19. Anderson, "Gender and Reading," 8: "The superscription and genealogy set the stage for reading the rest of the gospel."

20. The verb applied to the men, *egennēsen*, highlights their role as fathers, while the *ek tēs* draws attention to the moment that the child came *out of* the womb—i.e., their birth. Contra Stuart L. Love, "The Household: A Major Social Component for Gender Analysis in the Gospel of Matthew," *Biblical Theology Bulletin* 23 (1993): 25, I do not think this indicates that the women's inclusion is "secondary" because it is "instrumental." *Pace* Hutchison, "Matthew's Genealogy," 163, who argues that Matthew departs from the common structure in 1:3, 5, and 6 to emphasize the matriarchal information in a parenthetical way to highlight its addition.

and then replacing the active form of *gennaō* (*egennēsen* has been used up to this point in the list) with the passive form (*egennēthē*).[21] This change in structure anticipates the exceptional nature of Jesus's birth, indicated by the fact that Joseph will not be the biological father of the child.[22] In a culturally shocking move, the father has been pushed to the margins and the mother is centered.[23] Moreover, there is a parallel drawn between Jesus being born "out of" (*ek*) Mary—which follows the pattern of the other four women—and being born "out of" the Holy Spirit (*ek pneumatos hagiou*, 1:18, 20).[24] All of the women in the genealogy and the Holy Spirit, then, are intimately tied to the children they produce.[25] Their introduction to the story of Jesus undermines the assumption that the sheer number of men listed in the genealogy indicates that they are of primary importance. Rather, the *ek* functions as an interrupter that calls attention to women and their roles in Jesus's family history, and by the end they find themselves in good company with the Holy Spirit in contributing to God's plan for humanity.[26]

Why these women and not others? What is the connection between Tamar, Rahab, Ruth, Bathsheba, and Mary that would prompt Matthew to include these women in Jesus's genealogy? This question has inspired much discussion among scholars and has led to several suggestions. Some argue that the four women are gentiles, and so Matthew is emphasizing the gentile influence in Jesus's ancestry

21. See also Wim J. C. Weren, "The Five Women in Matthew's Genealogy," *Catholic Biblical Quarterly* 59 (1997): 292.

22. Weaver, "'Good News,'" 394–95, describes this as Matthew "breaking the lineage" between Joseph and Jesus.

23. Amy-Jill Levine, "Women's Humor and Other Creative Juices," in *Are We Amused? Humour about Women in the Biblical World*, ed. Athalya Brenner (London: Continuum, 2003): 120–26, also highlights how Joseph was a reluctant father (wanting to divorce Mary), just as the other partners of Tamar, Rahab, Ruth, and Bathsheba were on some level "undesiring sires" (121). She argues that this contributes to the comedic aspect of the genealogy and the circumstances around Jesus's birth.

24. Weren, "Five Women," 292–93, sees a parallel here with the Bathsheba story, as the father is not her husband but David.

25. Weren, "Five Women," 293, argues that this connection indicates that the motherhood of the other women in the genealogy should also be viewed as special.

26. Weren, "Five Women," 295–96, also sees in this an indication that the women "do not act of their own accord, but are activated by the spirit of God."

as a way to understand the role of the Messiah as one that reaches beyond Judaism: Jesus is the Messiah to the gentiles too.[27] Others have argued that these women are included in the genealogy because they all had scandalous pasts or were known primarily as sinners.[28] Inclusion in Jesus's ancestry, then, would anticipate his inclusion of and concern for sinners in his ministry. A third suggestion has been that each woman does something extraordinary or has something extraordinary happen in her life—something that changes the course of history in a meaningful way and has great impact on the trajectory of God's people in the Scriptures.[29] This third approach tends to focus

27. E.g., Richard Bauckham, *Gospel Women: Studies of the Named Women in the Gospels* (Grand Rapids: Eerdmans, 2002), 17–46; Andrew D. Heffern, "The Four Women in St. Matthew's Genealogy of Christ," *Journal of Biblical Literature* 31 (1912): 69–81; Samuel B. Hakh, "Women in the Genealogy of Matthew," *Exchange* 43 (2014): 109–18, argues that Matthew is showing that Jesus has a "genealogical relationship" with gentiles. Hutchison, "Matthew's Genealogy," believes that these were included to prove that gentiles could have extraordinary faith in contrast to Jews who lacked faith; Keener, "Matthew's Missiology," sees this as an anticipation of the Great Commission in Matt 28:19–20. Edwin D. Freed, "The Women in Matthew's Genealogy," *Journal for the Study of the New Testament* 29 (1987): 3–19, objects to this view, arguing that some of the women were regarded as Jewish converts by the time of Jesus.

28. E.g., Anthony Tyrrell Hanson, "Rahab the Harlot in Early Christian Tradition," *Journal for the Study of the New Testament* 1 (1978): 53–60. But John Paul Heil, "The Narrative Roles of the Women in Matthew's Genealogy," *Biblica* 72 (1991): 540, is right to point out that when sin is explicitly mentioned in Tamar's story, for example, it is Judah who is presented as the sinner. See Gen 38:26; T. Jud. 14.5; Jub. 41.23. The same could be said for Rahab (the men of Jericho are the aggressors, Josh 2:3–7), Ruth (she is rejected by her closest male family member, Ruth 4:1–6), and Bathsheba (the focus of the narrative is on *David's* selfish actions, 2 Sam 11–12).

29. E.g., Michel Remaud, "Les femmes dans la généalogie de Jésus selon Mattieu," *Nouvelle revue théologique* 143 (2021): 3–14; Raymond E. Brown, *The Birth of the Messiah: A Commentary on the Infancy Narratives in the Gospels of Matthew and Luke*, Anchor Bible Reference Library (New Haven: Yale University Press, 1999), 74, combines this with the "sinner" theme by arguing that the women have an unusual relationship with the men in their lives, which often involves sexual scandal, and that each woman took some action to see God's plan through. Against the "sinner" reading, F. Scott Spencer, "Those Riotous—yet Righteous—Foremothers of Jesus: Exploring Matthew's Comic Genealogy," in Brenner, *Are We Amused?*, 7–30, argues that each woman was a "righteous trickster," and that each of their stories has a comedic aspect where the men in the story are outsmarted and proven less faithful than the women.

on the personality, gumption, or ingenuity of the women, who are often successful despite the odds against them.

It would take too much space for our purposes to systematically go through each proposed theory, weigh the pros and cons, and choose one. I am not convinced, however, that this is necessary. None of these is a mutually exclusive option. All of them highlight in some form or fashion that these women were outsiders—socially at a disadvantage whether they were regarded as gentiles, poor, powerless, or stigmatized for their actions. It seems to me that the most important thing to recognize is that Matthew is including women who had numerous obstacles and yet were used by God in unexpected ways.[30] Perhaps the common denominator is that they were *women* and therefore experienced all the difficulties that being a woman could bring. Yet they were still faithful.[31] In fact, it is the actions of each woman that are the focal point of their respective stories regarding their children. Tamar takes initiative to procure a child, even if it means deceiving her father-in-law.[32] Rahab risks her life and the lives of her family members to harbor the enemy and to aid the Israelites in their takedown of Jericho.[33] Ruth risks her safety and security to follow her mother-in-law to a foreign land and does what it takes to care for and provide for her.[34] And Bathsheba, while likely without agency in her affair with King David, later successfully advocates for her son Solomon's claim to the throne.[35] Each of these women's actions change the trajectory of the story.

Mary, too, will encounter obstacles that are placed in her path by virtue of her cultural context. In fact, while Joseph is important insofar as he provides Jesus the Davidic lineage required of the Messiah, his actions are not the focus of the birth account. Instead, the purpose of Joseph's characterization in the story is to highlight the real danger that Mary faces in being divorced from her betrothal because she has shown up pregnant before her marriage (1:19) and to emphasize that

30. See Kopas, "Matthew," 14: "In a move that parallels their role in the history of Israel, Matthew's Gospel shows the way that 'outside' insiders begin to make a contribution to the future of the church."

31. Kopas, "Matthew," 14–15.

32. Gen 38:1–30.

33. Josh 2:1–21; 6:17, 22–25.

34. Ruth 1–4. See also Weren, "Five Women," 99–301.

35. 1 Kgs 1:11–31.

the baby is not his son but God's.[36] Like the threat of Herod in the following chapter, Jesus's life is on the line by virtue of his being "out of" Mary and the Holy Spirit, and it requires a visit from an angel to convince Joseph to follow through with the marriage and stand alongside Jesus's mother when she gives birth to her son (1:20–21). While Joseph provides the security and protection that is required by the social environment in which they live, it is the work of the Holy Spirit and of Mary to bring about the Messiah. Thus, Joseph is introduced in the genealogy as "the husband of Mary," a change in construction (see 1:6) that centers her as the primary actor in Jesus's birth.[37]

It is not coincidental that all four of the women named in Matthew's list of Jesus's ancestors have stories that emphasize their active roles in bringing about God's purposes, often in contrast to the men who are present in their stories and with whom they interact. In a subversion of the genre, Matthew pushes back against any cultural assumption that one's patrilineage is the primary player in God's plan. Instead, those on the margins—gentiles, women, the powerless, those with lesser social capital—are not only found within the household of Jesus but are active participants in what God is doing through the Messiah. God is at work in them against all odds—a theme we will see throughout the Gospel of Matthew.

Women with Healing Faith (Matthew 9:20–22; 15:21–28)

Both Matthew and Mark tell versions of the stories of two women who approach Jesus with the hopes of healing. In the first story, a woman who has been hemorrhaging for twelve years approaches Jesus while he is on his way to heal a community leader's daughter from illness.[38] Matthew gives us a glimpse into her thought process: if she

36. Freed, "Women," argues that Matthew includes the other women in his genealogy to defend Mary's pregnancy by pointing to women whose questionable behavior had been justified in eyes of the Jews because of the extraordinary things they had done that directly benefited the Jewish people. I find this unconvincing, however, because Matt 1:18–25 already serves this purpose. Any conjecture about Mary's sexual activities have been put to rest by the repeated testimony of her virginity (narrator: 1:18; angel: 1:20; narrator/Isaiah: 1:22–23; narrator: 1:25).

37. Kopas, "Matthew," 15.

38. While Mark describes him as a synagogue leader (*archisynagōgō*, 5:22),

could just touch the fringes of Jesus's cloak, she will be saved (i.e., healed from her infirmity, 9:21). Her intent is to avoid calling attention to herself, but Jesus turns and sees her, commends her for her faith, and credits that faith with her instant healing (9:22). In the second story, a woman approaches Jesus for healing, but not for herself. Her daughter is demon-possessed, and the Canaanite woman cries out to Jesus for help on her behalf. Her approach is very different from the hemorrhaging woman, as the Canaanite woman's shouts for help draw public attention and the ire of the disciples (15:22–23). Despite being ignored and refused in three ways, the woman persists, accepting the premise of Jesus's riddle-like retort, responding in kind, and ultimately displaying such faith that Jesus instantly heals her daughter from afar (15:28). These incidents take place in the middle of Jesus's ministry, and each version of the story emphasizes different aspects of the requests and of the women who make them. In addition to their general plotlines, both versions uphold the women as exemplars in some way. In the following discussion we'll explore how Matthew's stories of the hemorrhaging woman and the Canaanite woman shed light on female discipleship in the gospel.

First, we need to recognize the common threads of each woman's story. Both are outsiders, not only because of their being female, but also because of some aspect of their identity or social circumstances. The hemorrhaging woman has an ailment that almost certainly would have caused some strain in her relationships in the community. Matthew's version is sparser in the details of her motivations and does not describe her emotions in her encounter with Jesus. Yet her incognito approach toward Jesus and her strategy to just touch the fringe of his cloak indicate a reluctance to cause a scene or draw attention to herself (*hēpsato tou kraspedou tou himatiou autou*, 9:21).[39] The Ca-

Matthew leaves his position vague (*archon*, "a ruler," 9:18), indicating only that he has some influence in his community.

39. Mark's version underscores her reluctance more clearly by describing her fear of answering Jesus's public demand to know who touched him (5:33). Contra Dreyer, "Gender Critique," 3, who argues that because Matthew does not mention the age of the girl as twelve, he is therefore not calling attention to her age as the time when girls begin to menstruate, which she regards as the primary evidence that the woman is experiencing menstrual bleeding in Mark and is therefore unclean. Thus, she argues that there is no association in Matthew's version with vaginal bleeding. I find this argument tenuous, as it

naanite woman is a gentile, and her daughter—for whom she makes her appeal—is demon-possessed, which would carry with it significant social stigma (15:22). Both women, then, have multiple strikes against them, yet they are so desperate for help in their respective situations that they are willing to risk exposure and ridicule for the possibility that Jesus will heal.[40] As a result of their actions, Jesus commends both women for their faith (9:22; 15:28). The contrast between their precarious status as marginalized women and the gumption they display serves to bring attention to their accomplishments.[41] This is further accentuated by the placement of the hemorrhaging woman's story in the center of the healing of the leader's daughter (9:18–19, 23–26). While he is in a position of power and high social status, she enjoys none of those privileges.[42] And yet, while Jesus consents to go to the man's daughter, the leader is not commended for his faith as the hemorrhaging woman is commended for hers. Even more contrast is made between the women's faith and the lack of understanding on the part of the disciples. In the chapter preceding the narrative of the hemorrhaging woman, Jesus admonishes the disciples for being afraid during the storm, as their fear displays their "little faith" (*oligopistoi*, 8:26). Even though they follow Jesus (*ēkolouthēsan*, 8:23), they fail to have confidence in God and in Jesus's provision when they need it most.[43] Moreover, the male disciples immediately follow this scene

---

assumes that Matthew's audience would not speculate that a *woman* who has been bleeding for twelve years has been doing so in a particularly womanly way. Nevertheless, Amy-Jill Levine, "Discharging Responsibility: Matthean Jesus, Biblical Law, and Hemorrhaging Woman," in *A Feminist Companion to Matthew*, ed. Amy-Jill Levine and Marianne Blickenstaff (Sheffield: Sheffield Academic, 2001), 70–87, cautions against assuming that the woman was unclean and drawing on stereotypes of Judaism that see Jesus as one who frees Jews from overly restrictive purity laws. As she rightly notes, Matthew emphasizes that Jesus came to preserve the law, not to override it (5:18).

40. Anderson, "Gender and Reading," 11, describes this as their "double marginality."

41. Anderson, "Gender and Reading," 16.

42. *Pace* Anderson, "Gender and Reading," 12, this may be why he feels comfortable to approach Jesus publicly, while she prefers a more covert approach.

43. See Olivares, "Thematic Connections," 281, who notes that *oligopistos* is also found in places where the disciples' performance is interrogated, exposing their failure to remember what God does and has done to provide (Matt 6:30; 16:8). This criticism, in turn, teaches what faithful discipleship should be.

by demonstrating that they have learned nothing from Jesus's first miraculous feeding of the crowds, as they wonder aloud where they will get enough bread to feed the crowd of four thousand (15:32–33).[44]

One of Matthew's unique contributions to these stories is to highlight with greater clarity the faith of the women Jesus encounters. In both versions of the story of the hemorrhaging woman, Jesus lauds the woman's faith (Mark 5:34; Matt 9:22), but because there are less additional details in Matthew's version, the audience's focus is drawn more closely to Jesus's exclamation: "Take heart, daughter. Your faith has saved you."[45] The third part of the intercalated passage (where Jesus raises the leader's daughter) is also briefer than Mark's version, excluding many of the details of what happens in the room. But Matthew includes the negative reaction of the professional mourners, who ridicule Jesus for his claim that the girl is only sleeping (9:24). While the woman has faith and is saved (*hē pistis sou sesōken se*, 9:22), those who doubt Jesus are cast out (*exeblēthē*, 9:25).[46] The narrative impact of the hemorrhaging woman's initiative is also on display in its subtle contrast to the following story of the healing of the blind men (9:27–31). While they cry out to Jesus for mercy and follow him, it is Jesus who prompts them to declare their faith (9:28). It is only then that they really act on it, going and spreading the news about him throughout the district (9:31). By contrast, the woman needs no prompting. Her action in pursuing Jesus and her belief that a simple touch of the fringe of his cloak will heal her are enough—he does not require any more proof of her faith.[47]

Matthew also puts a spotlight on the Canaanite woman's faith. While the Markan Jesus lauds the woman for her words (*ton logon*, Mark 7:29), Matthew makes explicit the implications of her actions:

44. Anderson, "Gender and Reading," 15, observes the irony of their misunderstanding in relation to the woman's request: she just wants crumbs, while they are not able to comprehend the surplus.

45. Jesus calls her "daughter" (*thygatēr*, 9:22). The implication is that he has as much concern for her as the leader has for his own daughter.

46. See also Anderson, "Gender and Reading," 12.

47. Anderson, "Gender and Reading," 13, argues that it is significant that the woman's faith declaration is unambiguous, while that of the blind men is ambiguous: "According to your faith let it be done to you" (*kata tēn pistin hymōn genēthētō hymin*, 9:29). But if so, that ambiguity is very brief, as Matthew immediately recounts their healing in the following verse.

it is her persistence, manifested in both the things she says and her dogged perseverance to stay and advocate for herself and her daughter, that demonstrates her faith (Matt 15:28).[48] Not only that, but her faith is not just adequate; it is "great" (*megalē sou hē pistis*). This faith is conveyed by the level of desperation in her actions (she cries out: *ekrazen*, 15:22, 23; she falls down before him: *prosekynei autō*, 15:25).[49] Although her posture might suggest worship, it also accomplishes the very practical goal of forcing him to engage with her—she has physically backed him into a corner as she will metaphorically do in a moment.[50] And not only is she female, which is difficult enough, but she is also a Canaanite woman.[51] Matthew's unique characterization

48. Melanie S. Baffes, "Jesus and the Canaanite Woman: A Story of Reversal," *Journal of Theta Alpha Kappa* 35 (2011): 13, regards this as a challenge-riposte, but Matthew's switch from "words" to "faith" in action suggests that the focus of the narrative goes beyond the words she says to win the argument with Jesus.

49. Kara J. Lyons-Pardue, "A Syrophoenician Becomes a Canaanite: Jesus Exegetes the Canaanite Woman in Matthew," *Journal of Theological Interpretation* 13 (2019): 240, argues that Matthew's tone is more desperate here than Mark's, where the woman "asks" (*hērōta*, 7:26). Jaime Clark-Soles, *Women in the Bible*, Interpretation: Resources for the Use of Scripture in the Church (Louisville: Westminster John Knox, 2020), 18, humorously refers to her as "a loud mother 'other.'"

50. Amy-Jill Levine, "Matthew's Advice to a Divided Readership," in *The Gospel of Matthew in Current Study: Studies in Memory of William G. Thompson, S.J.*, ed. David E. Aune (Grand Rapids: Eerdmans, 2001): 36–37, notes that this is the same type of action that Tamar takes with Judah and Ruth takes with Boaz (Gen 38:14; Ruth 2:10; 3:6–14): "She stops his movement. He can either walk around her, as she literally holds her ground, or he can respond."

51. Given that Jesus appears to be back in Jewish territory (9:1) and that no mention is made of the hemorrhaging woman's ethnicity, it is safe to assume that she was Jewish.

See Alan H. Cadwallander, *Beyond the Word of a Woman: Recovering the Bodies of the Syrophoenician Woman*, ATF 1 (Adelaide: ATF Press, 2008), 3–42, who argues that the image of "dog" wasn't just a generic insult among Jews toward gentiles but was a common gendered slight from men toward women. Alternatively, F. Gerald Downing, "The Woman from Syrophoenicia and Her Doggedness: Mark 7.24–41 (Matthew 15.21–28)," in *Women in the Biblical Tradition*, ed. George J. Brooke (Lewiston, NY: Mellen, 1992), 129–49, argues that the image of a dog was seen as positive by Cynics, and so what Jesus is really doing is recognizing her as a Cynic disciple. The narrative flow of the story from initial rejection to public recognition, however, makes Downing's interpretation less plausible.

of her as a Canaanite emphasizes this, as it most certainly would have called to mind the ancient animosity between Israel and the Canaanites throughout the Scriptures.[52] Perhaps this helps explain why she is thrice rejected before her persistence wins the day: Jesus initially ignores her (15:23), the disciples request that he send her away (15:23), and Jesus responds by stating that his ministry is not for those outside the "house of Israel" (*oikou Israēl*, 15:24, 26). The instinct of Matthew's audience might have been to expect Jesus to reject her request, especially since he has previously sent the Twelve to Jewish towns only (10:5–6). On the other hand, we have already seen the gospel highlight the importance of outsider women in Jesus's genealogy, and Jesus has been willing to heal gentiles up to this point (8:28–34; 14:34–36). Not only that, but he has recently ignored the disciples' request to send a hungry crowd away and has answered their needs with a miraculous provision of food—a request that uses identical language as their request to send away the Canaanite woman (*apolyson tous ochlous*, 14:15; *apolyson autēn*, 15:23).[53] Most importantly, in the immediately preceding passage, Jesus engages with the Pharisees and scribes in a dispute over purity, effectively prioritizing what is in the heart rather than outward expressions of ritual holiness (15:1–20).[54]

52. Lyons-Pardue, "Exegetes," 239; Jim Perkinson, "A Canaanitic Word in the Logos of Christ; or the Difference the Syro-Phoenician Woman Makes to Jesus," *Semeia* 75 (1996): 64, 79. Love L. Sechrest, "Enemies, Romans, Pigs, and Dogs: Loving the Other in the Gospel of Matthew," *Ex Auditu* 31 (2015): 96; Gail R. O'Day, "Surprised by Faith: Jesus and the Canaanite Woman," in Levine and Blickenstaff, *Feminist Companion to Matthew*, 116, interprets the woman's actions as akin to a lament psalm. Others see parallels between the woman and Rahab: Daniel N. Gullotta, "Among Dogs and Disciples: An Examination of the Story of the Canaanite Woman (Matthew 15:21–28) and the Question of the Gentile Mission within the Matthean Community," *Neotestamentica* 48 (2014): 329–31; Heil, "Narrative Roles," 544. Ironically, Jesus's initial response places him squarely in the group of the male partners who resist or serve as a foil to the women in the genealogy of Jesus. See Levine, "Matthew's Advice," 36.

53. J. Martin C. Scott, "Matthew 15.21–28: A Test-Case for Jesus' Manners," *Journal for the Study of the New Testament* 62 (1996): 37: "Given that Matthew's Jesus has not done as they requested on that occasion, the reader is prepared for the fact that the story will not end here, but that Jesus will respond in some way to the woman's request." Scott also sees in the excess basketfuls of "crumbs" an indication that there is more than enough to go around for gentiles too (40).

54. O'Day, "Surprised by Faith," 115, sees the change in geography as another way that Matthew emphasizes the further intensification of his rebuke of the

All these factors impact the audience's understanding and expectations of Jesus on the basis of who he is and what he has already done and taught. These passages, then, suggest that Jesus's response to the woman may have more to it than meets the eye, since a permanent rejection of her request on account of her ethnicity or gender would run counter to what Jesus has already done and taught.

In Matthew the initial opposition to her request functions narratively to provide the platform needed for her to demonstrate her great faith.[55] In other words, by initially rejecting the woman's need, Jesus provides an opportunity to demonstrate what it means to persistently believe that Jesus can heal and do the miraculous works of God.[56] This does not take away from the brutality of Jesus's initial refusal here, but rather enhances it. Matthew's audience has come to expect a Jesus who is liberal in his compassion and generous in his healing. What would be more sympathetic than a mother who comes to plead on behalf of the welfare of her child? Yet, in the face of a potentially devastating disappointment, she is able to demonstrate her belief that Jesus is truly "Lord, Son of David" (*kyrie huios Dauid*, 15:22).[57] Moreover, her great faith is emphasized by the progression of her actions in the story. She begins by shouting (implying distance, 15:22), follows Jesus and the disciples (15:23), comes to him and kneels before him to demand his attention (15:25), and engages in witty dialogue with him (15:26–27).[58] She is both the catalyst for healing and the embodiment of faithful

religious authorities concerning purity. He is moving from a "clean" place to an "unclean" one.

55. It is also possible, *pace* Lyons-Pardue, "Exegetes," 241, that his response about the house of Israel is directed more at the disciples than it is at her. Scott, "Test-Case," 27, argues that Matthew "intensifies" Jesus's "sullenness" by his initial lack of response to the woman, but fails to recognize how Jesus's delayed response moves her to increase her persistence.

56. Baffes, "Reversal," 18, argues that Jesus is portrayed as a learner (from her) rather than the teacher, so that his actions provide a model of transformation for his disciples. Lyons-Pardue, "Exegetes," 249, argues that Matthew is underscoring Jesus's ability to interpret the Scriptures.

57. Scott, "Test-Case," 36–37, is correct in observing that this thoroughly Jewish title is unexpectedly placed on the lips of a gentile. Clark-Soles, *Women in the Bible*, 19, argues that the title recalls Matthew's genealogy, which features Rahab, who is also a Canaanite woman.

58. Matthew increases the harshness of Jesus's initial rejection by leaving out the element of priority that is in Mark (the "children" should be fed first in Mark 7:27).

discipleship. The structure of the narrative, along with her persistence until she gets what she wants, centers her and her actions. [59]

Matthew's version of the story also contains the unique aspect of tension between the woman and the disciples. In the Gospel of Mark, we have already seen that the Twelve were nowhere to be found in this episode. But in Matthew the disciples are portrayed as irritated by the woman's actions. This irritated response contrasts more with her desperate plea for help than it does with Jesus's own initial response, which is silence. They protest her shouting, and their request that Jesus send her away indicates that their primary concern is for their own sanity. Unlike elsewhere when they seem to envision their role as protectors of Jesus (19:13–15), here they just want her to stop shouting at them![60] It is an entirely selfish reaction, and they plead with Jesus to do something about it by sending her away. Ironically, the woman has been willing to go away from her daughter and risk rejection in hopes that her loved one will benefit from Jesus's healing. The disciples act selfishly, while she acts selflessly on behalf of the daughter she loves. She is a woman of great faith, while they will shortly demonstrate that they are men of "little faith" (*oligopistoi*, 16:8).[61]

The Woman Who Anoints Jesus (Matthew 26:6–13)

Like the other canonical gospels, Matthew tells the story of a woman who approaches Jesus while he is dining and anoints him. Of the al-

59. O'Day, "Surprised by Faith," 118: "Matthew 15.21–28 is from beginning to end the story of the Canaanite woman. She initiates the movement of the story with her first petition, refuses to be silenced or ignored, and in the end goes away victorious, having been answered and heard by Jesus. She is insistent, demanding, and unafraid to state her claims. She is the lifeblood of this story. Any attempt to classify this text by placing Jesus at its center will ultimately be inadequate."

60. While it is possible that the Twelve are encouraging Jesus to grant her request so that she will go away (e.g., BDAG, "*apoluō*," 118), the emphasis is on their desire for her to be gone. They do not display compassion or concern for her.

61. Amy-Jill Levine, "Gospel of Matthew," in *Women's Bible Commentary*, ed. Carol A. Newsome, Sharon H. Ringe, and Jacqueline E. Lapsley, 3rd ed. (Louisville: Westminster John Knox, 2012), 474, argues that because the woman is presented as a Canaanite woman who recognizes that salvation will come through Israel's representative (Jesus), she "proves more faithful than insiders" and functions in the story as another Rahab or Ruth who does what she must do for her family.

ternative versions (the story is found also in Luke and John), Matthew most closely aligns with Mark's version (Mark 14:3–9). The settings are the same (the house of Simon, "the one suffering leprosy"), the woman is unnamed and there is no indication that she is a sinner and is seeking forgiveness from Jesus, and the dialogue of Jesus and those who oppose her actions is nearly identical in both texts. Both incidents are also brief. The focus is on the meaning of the anointing as a foreshadowing of Jesus's death and thus a symbolic preparation for his burial. And like Mark, Matthew ends the scene with an emphasis on the worthiness of her actions: *what she has done* will be remembered and will be regarded as an integral component of preaching the good news (*ho epoiēsen hautē*, 26:13).

Matthew's audience is clearly meant to admire what the woman has done for Jesus. Three separate times Jesus calls attention to her actions (26:10, 12, 13). The fact that she is given no name and no label turns the audience's focus to her actions, which are the primary aspect of her identity in the text.[62] But the story also sheds light on the gospel's presentation of discipleship: while the woman gets it right, the disciples who are with Jesus get it all wrong. Some unique features of Matthew's version highlight this. Matthew is more specific than Mark about the source of the protest toward the woman's actions. The *disciples* are the ones who are angry by her "wasteful" actions (*hē apōleia*, 26:8). And by leaving out Mark's description of their complaints as internal, Matthew implies that their protest is more openly confrontational and that they have expressed their logic publicly—that money derived from the sale of the ointment could have been given to the poor (26:8–9). This places them in direct opposition to the woman, and ultimately to Jesus, as the meaning of her action has been lost on them. They regard it as a waste, while Jesus views it as essential because it anticipates his burial.[63] At the very least, this clash of views displays a continuation of the theme of the Twelve's misunderstanding that runs through the gospel, a misunderstanding made even more egregious by the fact that Jesus has just told them of his upcoming crucifixion (26:2).[64] By missing the connection between her actions and

62. See also M. Eugene Boring, "The Gospel of Matthew," in *The New Interpreter's Bible*, vol. 8, ed. Leander E. Keck (Nashville: Abingdon, 1995), 466.

63. Perhaps Matthew's audience would recall Jesus's recent criticism of the scribes and Pharisees, who practice showy and inauthentic piety that shows no care for others and who would interpret the disciples' response as an attempt to distance themselves from the religious authorities in this way (Matt 23:1–36).

64. Anderson, "Gender and Reading," 17. Wongi Park, "Her Memorial: An

Jesus's burial, the disciples put themselves in the position of criticizing the woman for doing the very thing that would be regarded as a proper and pious custom.[65] And given the potential in the cultural landscape for increased social status through benefaction, the Twelve's response would likely have been interpreted by Matthew's audience as motivated by the desire for public recognition ("Look at us and how we care for the poor!") rather than any real concern for the less fortunate.[66]

Moreover, Matthew's adaptation may imply a closer relationship between the disciples' rejection of the woman's action, Jesus's positive response, and Judas's decision to work with Jesus's enemies to betray him (26:14–16). While the sequence of these narrative events is identical to the Gospel of Mark, Matthew replaces the simple "and" that connects the two passages in Mark with "then"—a more specific marker of time (*kai*, Mark 14:10; *tote*, Matt 26:14).[67] Perhaps it is Jesus's reaction to the woman that prompts Judas to go through with his betrayal. This is even more likely given that Matthew uses *tote* just two verses later to emphasize that it is the payment from the chief priests that prompts Judas to begin looking for an opportunity to betray Jesus (26:16). The emphasis on these verses, then, is on the sequence of events that build tension and lead directly to Jesus's arrest. In addition, both passages are about money, one contrasting the woman's generous act with the disciples' outward selflessness, the other revealing that this is a facade of piety for at least one of them. The actions of the woman and the actions of Judas are in some way connected to money, but one clearly makes use of her resources to honor Jesus while the other seeks payment to betray him. Ultimately, the woman's actions anticipate the suffering of the Messiah, the disciples as a whole fail to understand it, and Judas's resultant actions put that suffering into motion.[68]

Alternative Reading of Matthew 26:13," *Journal of Biblical Literature* 136 (2017): 140, also sees a contrast between the woman and the disciples in that they have been earlier criticized for failing to remember (*oude mnēmoneuete*, Matt 16:9).

65. Park, "Her Memorial," 137, argues that Jews at this time would have regarded the act of burial more important than almsgiving, since it could not be repaid.

66. Cf. Matt 19:13–14.

67. BDAG, "tote," 1012, describes *tote* as a "special favorite of Matthew," and counts upwards of ninety instances of the term in the gospel.

68. *Pace* Kopas, "Matthew," 19: "While the others are baffled, Jesus and the woman saw it as connected with his messiahship of suffering. She, a woman, recognized what the others did not." Park, "Her Memorial," argues against read-

The Women at the Cross and Tomb (Matthew 27:55–56, 61; 28:1–10)

Jesus's female disciples figure most prominently at the end of Matthew's narrative.[69] Here, as in the other canonical gospels, women are within viewing distance of his crucifixion (27:55–56), witness his burial and return to the tomb to care for his body (27:61; 28:1), and are the first to hear that Jesus has risen from the dead (28:5–7).[70] In the following discussion we will look at the ways that Matthew adds unique elements to the finale of the gospel story and discuss how these elements help shape his portrayal of female discipleship.

In Matthew 27:55–56 the audience is told that Jesus did not die entirely alone without any friends. While they are watching from a distance, some women are present at his crucifixion. In fact, "many" of them are there (*pollai*), and we are even told the identity of some of them: Mary Magdalene, Mary the mother of James and Joseph, and the mother of the sons of Zebedee. The two Marys will show up again later, witnessing the burial of Jesus's body and going to the tomb after the Sabbath.

Although Matthew does not apply the term *mathētēs* to the women, two key indications suggest that they should be regarded as such. First, they are described as women who had *followed* Jesus from Galilee and had *served* him (*ēkolouthēsan, diakonousai*, 27:55).[71] We

ing *eis mnēmosynon autēs* in Matt 26:13 as an objective genitive, where the woman is the object of the memorial. Instead, Park argues that it is *what she has done* that is memorialized.

69. Sheila E. McGinn, "Why Now the Women? Social-Historical Insights on Gender Roles in Matthew 26–28," *Proceedings: Eastern Great Lakes and Midwest Biblical Societies* 17 (1997): 109, underscores the increase in the passion narrative, not only in mention of women, but in the focus on their actions: "When one takes into account the question of the *active* presence of women, as compared to the discussion of women as objects, then the trend is even more striking. Of the eighteen scenes with active women in Matthew's entire gospel, fully one third of them are found in these last three chapters, which comprises only 10.7% of the gospel."

70. There are, however, different women in each gospel scene.

71. Contra Kingsbury, "Index," 61, who argues that use of the term for the women in 27:55 is literal rather than metaphorical (they accompanied him from place to place), and so does not consider them disciples: "The appended notation that they were 'waiting on him' is not meant to characterize them as

have already seen that both descriptors are used to refer to the actions of those who would have been considered disciples of Jesus. Following and serving Jesus are actions that function as the primary descriptor for the women and are the two things that bind them together as a group. Second, immediately after this passage, Joseph of Arimathea, who *is* called as a *mathētēs*, is introduced by the phrase "who *also* was a disciple of Jesus" (*hos kai autos emathēteuthē tō Iēsou*, 27:57). This wording indicates that Matthew regards the women as part of the group of disciples to which Joseph of Arimathea also belongs (they are the immediate antecedent in 27:56). This association is reinforced by their presence together with Joseph of Arimathea at Jesus's tomb.

Mary Magdalene and the other Mary are present at Jesus's tomb twice in the story. The first time they are there is the night Jesus is buried, and they witness his burial by Joseph of Arimathea. The way Matthew describes the scene leaves the impression that the women linger longest at the tomb. Rather than simply state that they were present, Matthew's account emphasizes the sequence of events: Joseph asks Pilate for the body; Pilate gives the order; Joseph takes the body and wraps it in linen, lays it in his tomb, rolls a large stone in front of it, and then leaves (27:58–60). The very next thing he tells the audience is that the women were there, sitting opposite the tomb.[72] It is possible that Matthew's audience would have interpreted their movement to the tomb and their sitting opposite it as an indication of their posture as mourners—a practice that was common among Jews at the time and was expected to be done by family members.[73] Perhaps, then, this serves as further evidence that the women were seen as belonging

---

disciples of Jesus in the strict sense of the word but instead explains why they had been in his company." However, the fact that they have traveled with him all the way from Galilee suggests some type of following in the metaphorical sense—a discipleship that indicates a level of commitment that goes beyond the crowds or a temporary following. This is even further supported by their presence at the tomb.

72. Contra Rick Strelan, "To Sit Is to Mourn: The Women at the Tomb (Matthew 27:61)," *Colloquium* 31 (1999): 34, 38, I do not think that their role as mourners would replace their role as witnesses—it is because of their mourning that they are able to witness to the resurrection of Jesus! Carolyn Osiek, "The Women at the Tomb: What Are They Doing There?," in Levine and Blickenstaff, *Feminist Companion to Matthew*, 214–17, sees the women's roles as both mourners and witnesses.

73. Cf. 1 Macc 1:27; Job 2:8; Ezek 8:14; Luke 10:13; Matt 4:16.

among the disciples (as Jesus's family members), and that they are again doing what the eleven should have been doing—mourning the loss of their family member, Jesus. By narrating Joseph's departure, and then only afterward telling the audience that the women were there and ending the scene with that image (we are not told that the women depart), Matthew leaves the impression that the women were the last ones standing (or in this case sitting) by Jesus's side—even in death.

After the Sabbath, the two Marys return to the tomb. Matthew does not tell us why they return—they are simply coming back to the place that they left.[74] His account is also unique in that it includes the spectacle of the angel's grand entrance (with an earthquake). And the women are there to witness it! While the guards at the tomb panic and pass out, the women do not—their fear and joy at the news that Jesus is risen is channeled into action (28:8). They are commissioned to notify the disciples of Jesus's resurrection and his promise to meet them in Galilee,[75] and they run quickly to carry out the angel's command. Just as suddenly as the appearance of the angel, however, Jesus also appears to the women (28:9). This happens while they are on their way to tell the other disciples about him. This extra scene provides no new information for the women to share with the disciples. Jesus is simply repeating what the angel has already told them (28:7). The scene thus indicates that the importance of Jesus's appearance to the women *is that he appeared to them*—that they were the first believers to witness Jesus's resurrected body.[76] For our purposes, it is also crucial to recognize that they experienced this epiphany because they obeyed the instructions to go and tell the disciples of Jesus's resurrection. Their faith that Jesus did indeed rise from the dead is borne out in their immediate response (they do not stand around and deliberate with each other or ask for further proof from the angel). It is also expressed in their worship of Jesus when they encounter him. As in the other gospel accounts, the women's eyewitness testimony is considered trustworthy and reliable, indicating that his resurrection has a direct bearing on their lives as women. Jesus's appearance to them on their way to give that testimony reinforces this.

74. Osiek, "Women," 208, interprets this as their return to the vigil that was interrupted by the Sabbath.

75. Matt 26:32.

76. Osiek, "Women," 208, sees this as primarily reinforcing that Jesus has risen.

Matthew's emphasis on the actions of the Marys is also borne out in the details he does not give in his version of the resurrection story. Unlike in Luke's Gospel, for instance, we are not told anything about the meeting that the women had with the eleven disciples. No information is given about their response to the women's news. The emphasis, rather, is on the movement of the women to go and tell, and the presence of the eleven in Galilee shortly thereafter indicates that the women followed through with their task. Ironically, while it is unclear whether women are present at the Great Commission (or whether there are any disciples other than the eleven),[77] in Matthew's resurrection narratives only the women actually "go" anywhere on behalf of the gospel!

Conspicuously absent at the cross and tomb are Jesus's closest male companions—the eleven remaining apostles. None of them are anywhere near the cross.[78] None of them go to the tomb. By their inclusion in the crucifixion scene—if only tangentially, from a distance—the women are connected to Jesus's death in a way that the absent apostles are not. Considering that one of the requirements of discipleship is the willingness to suffer and take up the cross, these women are much closer to that kind of commitment than the apostles (Matt 16:24–26).[79]

Before the women share the good news with them, the last place the audience has seen the disciples is in Gethsemane when most of them fled to avoid arrest (26:56), at the courtyard of the high priest when Peter denies Jesus three times (26:69–75), and alongside Judas when he returns his blood money and commits suicide in his grief (27:3–5). Moreover, when the eleven do appear at the end of

77. McGinn, "Why Now?," 113, argues that the women are not commissioned to the gentiles like the eleven because Matthew is redefining the public and private sphere, where the private (the household) is now Israel (so the women can go and tell the disciples because they are Jewish) and the nations are now public. But Matthew distinguishes between the women and the *eleven*, rather than the women and male disciples, and thus it is not clear that he places any restrictions along strictly gendered lines.

78. Ironically, while James and John are absent, their mother is there (27:56). Emily Cheney, "The Mother of the Sons of Zebedee (Matthew 27.56)," *Journal for the Study of the New Testament* 68 (1997): 13–21, argues that she demonstrates model discipleship because she is present apart from her sons and therefore demonstrates the requirement to commit to the new family of believers. See also Wainwright, *Feminist Reading*, 329.

79. See also Shin, "Matthew's Designation," 408.

the narrative, it is not an entirely flattering picture. When they first encounter the resurrected Jesus, some worship him as the women did, but some doubt (28:9, 17). This mixed response of belief and unbelief is the last word in the gospel on their actions. Although they are given the Great Commission, Matthew does not recount their response. While the discipleship of the eleven disciples is left ambiguous at best, the women in the story do not fail to act on their belief in Jesus's resurrection and on his promises.[80]

Conclusion

As we have seen, although Matthew most often reserves *mathētēs* for the apostles, it is clear from the narrative that there were more than just twelve men who followed Jesus. Among these are women, and their presence increases as the narrative climaxes in Jesus's death and resurrection. By punctuating his patrilineal genealogy with women, Matthew sets the tone for the remainder of his gospel. The audience is prepared to expect that women will have an important role to play in the story of salvation, beginning with Mary and ending with the Marys who become the first witnesses to the risen Jesus. In between, he depicts women as models of faith and understanding, often in contrast to the Twelve. In all of their stories, the actions of these women are portrayed as models of the kind of discipleship that Jesus calls for—a discipleship that is faithful, risky, persistent, and willing to embrace suffering as the cost of following him.

80. Kopas, "Matthew," 19, argues that the roles that women play in the passion narrative in contrast to their male counterparts are a consistent theme in Matthew. Examples apart from those we have studied include the maidservant who identifies Peter (26:69–75) and Pilate's wife (27:19).

Four

Female Discipleship in the Gospel of Luke

The Gospel of Luke stands out from the other canonical gospels because it is essentially volume one of the two-volume work commonly referred to as "Luke-Acts." Whereas the Gospels of Matthew, Mark, and John conclude at the resurrection or at the ascension, Luke continues his story of Jesus beyond the ascension, recounting the ways in which "the good news" takes hold of the Roman Empire ("in Jerusalem, in all Judea and Samaria, and to the ends of the earth," Acts 1:8). From Luke's perspective, then, we will get an extended view of female discipleship.[1]

For the past fifty years, scholarly discussion on Luke's views of women has gone back and forth, with some interpreting the gospel as depicting a favorable portrait of women, while others argue that he silences their impact on Jesus's ministry. The twists and turns of opinion on this subject have resulted in quite the debate. Much of the discussion is prompted by the fact that in the Gospel of Luke (volume one) women feature fairly prominently and plentifully in Jesus's ministry, while in Acts (volume two) much more focus is on certain male leaders of the early church.[2] For decades, interpreters of the Third Gospel saw the sheer number of stories about women as a sign that

1. Because this narrative extends into the beginnings of the church and the early gentile mission, I will save my reflections on female discipleship in Luke-Acts for chapter 5.

2. As I will discuss in chapter 5, I think the drop-off in Acts has less to do with Luke's interest on restricting women per se, and more to do with Luke's focus on Peter and Paul as particularized examples of the gospel outline given in Acts 1:8.

Luke was pro-woman (the gospel has several stories of women not included in the other canonical gospels).[3] Other clues that point to a positive portrayal of women in the Gospel of Luke may be found in the pairing of male and female characters (indicating the shared roles of men and women in the gospel story)[4] and in the crucial focus on women at the beginning of the gospel. But even with the additional stories involving women, there is some question as to the nature of Luke's treatment of these women and what level of impact women actually have on the narrative and on Jesus's ministry. Accordingly, some scholars argue that he presents their stories in such a way as to provide support for restricting their roles or leadership within the community, or that their characters often have little impact on his narrative.[5]

3. See Robert J. Karris, "Women and Discipleship in Luke," in *A Feminist Companion to Luke*, ed. Amy-Jill Levine (Sheffield: Sheffield Academic, 2002), 24–27, and Barbara E. Reid, "The Gospel of Luke: Friend or Foe of Women Proclaimers of the Word?," *Catholic Biblical Quarterly* 78 (2016): 3–4, for helpful timelines and bibliographies of both views. Proponents of the gospel's "positive" views on women include Jane Kopas, "Jesus and Women: Luke's Gospel," *Theology Today* 43 (1986): 192–202, and Marla J. Selvidge, "Alternate Lifestyles and Distinctive Careers: Luke's Portrait of People in Transition," *Sewanee Theological Review* 36 (1992): 91–102. Dorothy A. Lee, *The Ministry of Women in the New Testament: Reclaiming the Biblical Vision for Church Leadership* (Grand Rapids: Baker Academic, 2021), argues that the Gospel of Luke is more positive toward women while Acts is less so.

4. See Constance Parvey, "The Theology and Leadership of Women in the New Testament," in *Religion and Sexism*, ed. Rosemary R. Ruether (New York: Simon & Schuster, 1974): 117–49, on these character pairings and their function. William E. Arnal, "Gendered Couplets in Q and Legal Formulations: From Rhetoric to Social History," *Journal of Biblical Literature* 116 (1997): 75–94, argues that these pairings reflect a concern with legal formulas rather than gender inclusivity. His conclusions are influenced by his source-critical methodology. As we will see below, however, a focus on the narrative leads the audience to see a comparison and contrast between the actions of the male and female in the pairing.

5. Many have credited Elisabeth Schüssler Fiorenza, "A Feminist Critical Interpretation for Liberation: Martha and Mary: Lk. 10:38–42," *Religion and Intellectual Life* (1986): 21–36, for breaking ground on this interpretation. Mary Rose D'Angelo, "Women in Luke-Acts: A Redactional View," *Journal of Biblical Literature* 109 (1990): 441–61, and Jane Schaberg, "Luke," in *The Women's Bible Commentary*, ed. Carol A. Newsom and Sharon H. Ringe (Louisville: Westminster John Knox, 1992), 275–92, have also had a significant impact on this view,

The focus of this study—active female discipleship—will provide the lens through which we will tackle these issues in the Gospel of Luke. We will see that the author portrays the women who follow Jesus positively. Their actions contribute to the audience's understanding of what it means to be a disciple of Jesus. As in other gospels, they provide examples of faithful and active discipleship while more prominent male disciples do not. Thus, the following two chapters are not meant to function as a general survey of the treatment of women in Luke-Acts. Rather, I will examine the texts that deal specifically with those women who are obedient to God when they embrace Jesus as the Messiah, some of whom Luke offers as exemplars of active faith in him. In the process, I will focus primarily on the stories that either are found only in the Gospel of Luke or include uniquely Lukan content and perspectives that are crucial to his presentation of discipleship.

Limiting the study to discipleship specifically does not mean that my observations in the following chapters have nothing to contribute to the larger discussion of Luke's treatment of women. While scholars have combed through the Lukan stories for clues as to his views on women and their roles in the ministry of Jesus and later in the leadership of the church, there is an additional aspect to consider. Examining how Jesus interacts with women, what they do as a response to him, or even how he receives their actions are important enterprises. But the *manner* in which women engage in discipleship is also crucial. We will consider (a) whether their actions are consistent with the gospel's understanding of what it means to be a disciple in the first place, and (b) whether they are doing any better at achieving that than their fellow male disciples. This approach also pushes back against a misreading that assumes that male disciples fare better than they actually do in the

as well as Barbara E. Reid's earlier works (*Choosing the Better Part? Women in the Gospel of Luke* [Collegeville, MN: Liturgical Press, 1996]; "'Do You See This Woman?' Luke 7:36–50 as a Paradigm for Feminist Hermeneutics," *Biblical Research* 40 [1995]: 37–49; and "Luke: The Gospel for Women?," *Currents in Theology and Mission* 21 [1994]: 405–14), which she has since extensively critiqued in Reid, "Friend or Foe." Somewhere in the middle is Turid Karlsen Seim, *The Double Message: Patterns of Gender in Luke-Acts* (Nashville: Abingdon, 1994), who argues that Luke is ambiguous in his treatment of women. See also Amy-Jill Levine and Ben Witherington III, *The Gospel of Luke*, New Cambridge Bible Commentary (Cambridge: Cambridge University Press, 2018), whose commentary includes a dialogue between Witherington (who sees Luke as an advocate for women) and Levine (who sees Luke restricting women's roles to ancillary ones).

Gospel of Luke. In fact, the male disciples that follow Jesus are actually quite underdeveloped characters who do little to affect the narrative trajectory.[6] Repeated concerns that Luke depicts women in ways that are consistent with perspectives of the first century that place limitations on women may be addressed when readers attend to his portrayal of a version of female discipleship that is held up as exemplary and is presented alongside and against his portrayal of male discipleship. By presenting women as persons who act in ways that are consistent with what it means to follow Jesus, Luke is subverting the very patriarchal values that undergird the Greco-Roman and Jewish cultures of the first century and are often assumed and acted on by other characters in his narrative. At the very least, his treatment of women is best viewed in the context of a particular concern of this gospel: to present the story of Jesus as a story that belongs to the marginalized—gentiles, the poor, and those with less social capital and power.[7]

The Women Who Begin the Gospel (Luke 1–2)

The first clue to Luke's attitude toward women is found in the gospel's opening two chapters. Almost all of the material in his infancy narrative is absent in Matthew, and the bulk of the action revolves around two women: Elizabeth and Mary.[8] An additional important female character is Anna, a prophetess who has devoted her life to waiting in expectation for the coming of the Messiah and who joins Elizabeth and Mary in rejoicing in the birth of Jesus.

6. With Reid, "Friend or Foe," 13, who rightly observes that Peter (the premier male disciple) has only a few lines in the gospel and that the only other male disciples who speak are James and John. While the lack of "speaking parts" does not necessarily indicate their *un*importance, the male disciples are not elevated above the few other speaking characters in Luke by getting more airtime (Martha and Zacchaeus). In fact, they are given even less dialogue than Jesus's enemies (Reid is right to note that their words are meant to set up Jesus's own [16–17]).

7. Selvidge, "Alternate Lifestyles," 94: "None of the synoptic writers advocates one particular lifestyle for anyone, especially women. More than any other synoptic writer, Luke writes stories about women who choose alternate lifestyles."

8. Richard Bauckham, *Gospel Women: Studies of the Named Women in the Gospels* (Grand Rapids: Eerdmans, 2002), 47, calls this a "gynocentric" text, noting that Mary has been given more words in these chapters than any other character.

The gospel begins with a double birth narrative: that of John the Baptist and of Jesus. Both stories give background to the boys' miraculous conceptions. Elizabeth and Zechariah are an elderly couple with a priestly pedigree. Luke describes them as righteous, but they have no children because Elizabeth is infertile—a devastating circumstance that could eventually leave her without protection and resources (1:6–7).[9] Mary, on the other hand, is a young woman who is betrothed to Joseph. As was expected of Jewish women at the time, she is a virgin and so also "cannot" have children (1:26–27). Yet both couples receive unexpected news. Through the angel Gabriel, God informs both Zechariah and Mary that they will have sons who will play a key role in what God is doing in the world: John will prepare a people for the Lord (1:17), and Jesus will be the Messiah who will rule God's long-awaited kingdom (1:31–33).[10] While Zechariah doubts this announcement by the angel and is made mute as a punishment for his unbelief (1:18–20), Mary accepts her news (1:34–38). Once she learns of her own pregnancy, she travels to see Elizabeth, who erupts in praise and blessing toward Mary, her unborn child, and the God who has orchestrated it all (1:41–45). Mary responds with the Magnificat, a song of praise and prophecy that connects what God is doing through her pregnancy ("the lowly state of his servant") and what he has done and will continue to do for those who are lowly (*tapeinōsin, tapeinous*; 1:48, 52) and hungry (*peinōntas*, 1:53)—just as he has done for his people, Israel (1:54–55).

After Mary returns home, Elizabeth delivers a baby boy, and while bringing him to be circumcised, she publicly voices what Zechariah cannot: that the baby should be called John. When Zechariah confirms this in writing, his punishment is removed, and he is able to praise God and testify to John's future role in preparing the way for what God will do through Jesus (1:57–79). The infancy narratives end climactically with the birth of Jesus—a mixture of humble and awe-

9. See Candida R. Moss and Joel S. Baden, *Reconceiving Infertility: Biblical Perspectives on Procreation and Childlessness* (Princeton: Princeton University Press, 2015), 70–102, who argue that infertility in Scripture should not be regarded as a curse but is the "way of the world" (102).

10. Although Luke only recounts Gabriel's visit to Zechariah (and not to Elizabeth), the fact that she knows this is from "the Lord" (1:25) and later is well informed as to Gabriel's commands to name him John (1:60) suggests the possibility that she also received a visit that is not recorded in the gospel.

inspiring circumstances, in many ways anticipating the kind of life he will live on earth (2:1–7).[11] Just like in the case of John's circumcision, Jesus's later dedication at the temple is an opportunity for public recognition of his importance—this time by Simeon, who has been waiting to lay his eyes on the Messiah (2:25–35), and the prophetess Anna, who has lived at the temple since being widowed (2:36–38).

In these opening chapters, then, we see Luke's emphasis on the divine orchestration of the events that have led to Jesus's presence on earth and that have anticipated the great things he will do in carrying out God's salvation for his people. These are crucial passages. In them we see the stories of three women—women who have faith in what God is doing (and *how* he is doing it), women who demonstrate that faith through their active response to him. Elizabeth, Mary, and Anna stand out in these first chapters, sometimes as a foil to unbelief (Zechariah doubts, while Elizabeth and Mary accept and rejoice). The women in the partnerships act as the vocal parent. Zechariah is made mute as a punishment and cannot fully carry out his tasks as priest and new father. Joseph is a "mute" character in the story, having no speaking parts. By contrast, the verbal responses of Elizabeth and Mary have profound impact on the narrative as they anticipate in miniature what God will accomplish through Jesus in Luke's Gospel. The mothers physically participate in God's plan by birthing the children of promise. And Anna joins her male counterpart in testifying to the coming of the Messiah (Simeon's speech is recorded, while Luke describes Anna as praising God and "speaking about him to all who were looking for the redemption of Jerusalem," 2:38).

But should we regard these women as "disciples"? Do their stories have something to say about female discipleship in the Gospel of Luke? The answer is yes. While they are not portrayed as following Jesus in the same way that women will later follow him during his ministry, Luke's portrait does suggest that they are disciples, because they see what God is doing through Jesus and follow him in active response.

One of the ways that their discipleship is indicated is through their words and actions. And these actions are significant given that all

11. The Son of God will perform healings, exorcisms, resurrection, and control over the natural order, but he will also "have no place to lay his head" (Luke 9:58).

three women find themselves in various degrees of impossible situations. Elizabeth, in her response to her sudden and unexpected pregnancy, testifies to the prior shame that she has borne as an infertile woman (1:25).[12] Mary is a young, poor, and unwed mother who must give birth in less than ideal circumstances.[13] Anna has been widowed for decades and has chosen the unconventional path of dedication to God rather than remarrying and bearing children.[14] Both Mary and Elizabeth respond positively to the news of their pregnancies, and both understand and embrace the role that their sons will play in God's work in ways that go above and beyond their partners.[15] As kin, they naturally rejoice in each other's blessing, but they also recognize

12. It may also be the reason that she goes into seclusion for five months—until roughly the time it would be clear to her community that she was, indeed, no longer infertile. Cf. Joel B. Green, *The Gospel of Luke*, New International Commentary on the New Testament (Grand Rapids: Eerdmans, 1997), 81. Denise Powell, "Elizabeth's 'Seclusion': A Veiled Reference to Her Bold Belief?," *Bulletin for Biblical Research* 29 (2019): 488–98, argues that Elizabeth's seclusion indicates her faith that what Gabriel said would indeed take place (as she was postmenopausal and would have no physical marker that she was pregnant until she started to show).

13. Bauckham, *Gospel Women*, 58, argues that Mary's story belongs in other tales of infertility and birth stories (like Sarah's and Elizabeth's) because, as a virgin, she would not have been able to have a child without miraculous intervention. See Natalie Webb, "Overcoming Fear with Mary of Nazareth: Women's Experience alongside Luke 1:26–56," *Review and Expositor* 115 (2018): 101, who argues that the term "lowliness" (1:48, *tapeinōsis*) used by Mary as a self-description in the Magnificat is found in the LXX to connote sexual humiliation (e.g., the rape of Dinah in Gen 34, the incestual rape of Tamar in 2 Kgs 13, the violation of the Levite's concubine in Judg 19–20, and the sexual assault of the women of Zion and Judah in Lam 5). If applied here, this would underscore just how socially precarious Mary's position is and that she knows that the path she treads on is a dangerous one.

14. For discussion on the ambiguous language concerning Anna's age and years of widowhood in Luke 2:37–38, see Green, *Gospel of Luke*, 151, and Bauckham, *Gospel Women*, 99–101. Both suggest that there may be echoes of Judith's story (Jdt 16:23). Regardless of her exact age, Anna was very old, indicating her level of dedication to God (see also Bonnie Thurston, "Who Was Anna? Luke 2:36–38," *Perspectives in Religious Studies* 28 [2001]: 49).

15. Yet acceptance and understanding is a process for Mary. That she is initially troubled is a testament to her willingness to embrace her circumstances despite the difficulties it may bring her (1:29). Cf. Webb, "Overcoming Fear," who speculates that one of the ways that Mary overcomes any fear she might have had in her circumstances was to find strength in her relationship with Elizabeth.

that there is something going on that is bigger than the miracle of their conceptions: God is using their sons for his purposes.[16] Thus, by embracing and rejoicing in their sons, Mary and Elizabeth embrace God's plan and commit to their role in following him, a prerequisite for discipleship that Jesus later makes clear (8:21). Additionally, Mary not only responds to the news of her pregnancy positively but proceeds to *bear the Messiah*, a fact that is emphasized by the prevalence of language in this section that calls attention to her actions and agency: it is time for *her* to deliver *her* child, *she* gives birth, *she* wraps him in cloth, and *she* lays him in a manger (2:6–7). Later, her actions become the sign to which the angels point in their announcement, and the one that the shepherds will use to recognize Jesus (2:12).[17]

In many ways, the words and actions of these women indicate their willingness to follow God as prophetic messengers. Not only is the Magnificat concerned with the themes that are so prevalent among the prophets in the Scriptures (e.g., God's actions on behalf of the poor, the fulfillment of his promises to Abraham, and the humbling of God's enemies), but it demonstrates a concern for others that is self-sacrificial (in the sacrifice of their bodies, reputations, and, ultimately, the lives of their sons)—a fundamental element of Jesus's own actions and prayers, which his disciples are meant to follow (22:42).[18] Elizabeth spontaneously responds to being filled with the Holy Spirit and pronounces a blessing on Mary, which echoes Gabriel's announce-

16. Green, *Gospel of Luke*, 51.

17. F. Scott Spencer, *Salty Wives, Spirited Mothers, and Savvy Widows: Capable Women of Purpose and Persistence in Luke's Gospel* (Grand Rapids: Eerdmans, 2012), 81–82, calls Mary the "generative subject of all the action." Later, Spencer argues that Mary functions as a "fully embodied human agent" rather than simply a "womb-container that carried and delivered God's Son," which is demonstrated in her very realistic reaction to losing Jesus in Jerusalem in Luke 2:48 (98, 100).

18. Contra D'Angelo, "Redactional View," 451–52, the fact that these women ultimately serve the prophet Jesus does not denigrate or subtract from their role as prophets themselves. From the perspective of the gospel writers, *no one* compares to Jesus. He is the focal point, not because he is a man and they are women, but because he is the Son of God. Thus, their prophetic roles in service to Jesus—who is the ultimate prophet—make them exemplars of discipleship for the community.

The Magnificat also shares many similarities with Hannah's song (1 Sam 2:1–10), which is a prophetic text. See Bauckham, *Gospel Women*, 60–67, for a helpful discussion of the parallels between them.

ment (1:28, 30, 42).[19] Even the manner in which she pronounces the blessing highlights her role as a prophet: she does so "with a loud cry" (*kraugē megalē*, 1:42). Elizabeth's greeting of Mary and her baby is very similar to the response by the crowd of Jesus's disciples who welcome Jesus into Jerusalem at the end of the gospel (*phōnē megalē*, 19:37).[20] Elizabeth is doing what disciples should do—she is welcoming the Son of God. She is also committed to following God's commands, even when it invites dismissal among her people, much like the experiences of so many of God's prophets. When Elizabeth is obedient to the commands of God to name her son John, her relatives deny her "right" to name him, instead calling on Zechariah to do so (1:60–62). Anna eschews a more traditional path of remarriage to remain at the temple, fasting and praying. In this way she is ready to receive Jesus and promptly tells others who have likewise been anticipating God's redemption (2:38). And even though we lack the words of Anna's prophecy, women are still the overwhelming focus of this passage, as even Simeon's prophecy serves to reinforce the message of the Magnificat and speaks to Mary's destiny, not Joseph's.[21] In fact, we learn more *about* Anna in this passage than we do Simeon, giving her role as prophet and follower of God additional credibility.[22] This credibility may have been further enhanced in the eyes of Luke's audience because of her position as a prophetess. She is a *univira*, and as such she demonstrates a loyalty to her deceased husband that would have made her a trustworthy religious figure—the kind of person whom God would use to communicate his message.[23]

Another way that Luke presents Elizabeth, Mary, and Anna as disciples is to highlight their faithfulness by pairing them with male counterparts, sometimes to draw the audience's attention to the woman's

19. See also Lee, *Ministry of Women*, 40. See Reid, "Friend or Foe," 8, who argues that Elizabeth's proclamation also anticipates Jesus's own qualifications for blessedness in Luke 11:27, which "affirms the importance of hearing and acting on God's word, something that Jesus' mother exemplifies." This also becomes a fulfilled prophecy within this section of the gospel, through the words of Mary (1:48b).

20. Barbara E. Reid and Shelly Matthews, *Luke 1–9*, ed. Amy-Jill Levine, Wisdom Commentary 43A (Collegeville, MN: Liturgical Press, 2021), 37.

21. F. S. Spencer, *Salty Wives*, 90–91.

22. See also Green, *Gospel of Luke*, 150.

23. Susan E. Hylen, *Women in the New Testament World*, Essentials of Biblical Studies (New York: Oxford University Press, 2019), 90; Thurston, "Who Was Anna?," 50.

faithful action as it stands in contrast to the man, and sometimes to highlight their parallel roles in proclaiming the presence of the Messiah. In an intriguing intertextual role reversal, it is the wife who believes the heavenly messenger's announcement of the coming birth of her son, while her husband does not: Elizabeth serves as the "Abraham" of the story, while Zechariah becomes the "Sarah" (Gen 18:9–15).[24] In fact, Elizabeth's faith surpasses that of Abraham, providing a model for Mary's own response.[25] The Genesis account makes no mention of Abraham's response—only that Sarah reacted to the announcement with derision.[26] Even in the face of dismissal by her own relatives, Elizabeth is obedient to God's instructions and testifies to John's name, while Zechariah must follow her lead and support her publicly before he can witness to God's acts in his own words (1:63–64).[27] Moreover, not only is Elizabeth depicted as one who believes God's word over against her own husband, but Mary is perhaps even more clearly presented as a foil for his unbelief. It is Mary who, like Zechariah, receives a personal visit from the angel Gabriel. But unlike Zechariah, Mary accepts the news, even as she has questions about the mechanics of it all ("How can this be, since I am a virgin?," 1:34 NRSVUE).[28] She is not doubting *that* these things will happen as Gabriel says they will; she is won-

24. Green, *Gospel of Luke*, 81, refers to Elizabeth's response as "open-handed acceptance."

25. Reid and Matthews, *Luke 1–9*, 36–37, describe Elizabeth as a wise mentor for Mary.

26. The admirable quality that Abraham possesses in this account is his hospitality to strangers, not his belief in their promise. In fact, while Sarah often gets a bad rap for laughing in this story, Abraham has the *exact* same response when God communicates the promise directly to him in the previous chapter (17:17).

27. Green, *Gospel of Luke*, 61–63, argues that Luke is deliberately drawing on the audience's concept of status to "turn the tables on Zechariah," who is presented as a priest (high status) but who rejects God's message (low status), while his wife who is barren (low status) is restored to honor with her answered prayer (high status).

28. See Brittany E. Wilson, *Unmanly Men: Refigurations of Masculinity in Luke-Acts* (Oxford: Oxford University Press, 2015), 79–112, who argues that through his forced silence Zechariah is "unmanned"—i.e., the power and privileges he would receive as a father are removed from him. By contrast, "Mary emerges as an exemplary disciple in the birth narrative, who responds to Gabriel (1:34, 38), delivers the Magnificat (1:46–55), and speaks on behalf of herself and her husband (2:48)" (111).

dering *how* they could happen.[29] Once Gabriel explains that she will conceive by the Holy Spirit, she responds as a faithful prophet called to service—her version of Isaiah's "Here am I, send me" (1:38), one that linguistically mimics Gabriel's announcement of her conception of Jesus (*idou*, 1:31, 38).[30] Anna, on the other hand, is not contrasted with her male counterpart but joins Simeon as one who has been waiting for the Messiah and who immediately recognizes and proclaims it when she encounters him.[31] Further, Anna's constant presence in the temple is similar to that of the apostles in the beginnings of the early church (Luke 2:37; Acts 2:46), and her constant praying is reminiscent of the widow who models determined prayer by crying out to God "day and night" (*hēmeras kai nyktos*, Luke 18:7).[32]

We should not underestimate the impact that these narratives of Elizabeth, Mary, and Anna have on the Gospel of Luke precisely because of their *place* in the narrative. Beginnings matter. The opening words of any text set the tone and expectations for the audience about everything else that follows. By beginning his story with episodes that depict faithful women who act in accordance with and alongside God's divine plan, Luke is setting up the audience's acceptance and expectation that women are an important part of what God is doing.[33] God is orchestrating the birth of John and Jesus at a turning point in Israel's story.[34] Who will be on board with what he is doing, and

29. F. S. Spencer, *Salty Wives*, 69, helpfully distinguishes between Zechariah's misplaced focus on the circumstances and Mary's focus on the content of the message that is being delivered to her: "Mary attends to the angel's message from the start, whereas Zechariah becomes stuck initially on the spectacle." See also Brendan J. Byrne, *The Hospitality of God: A Reading of Luke's Gospel* (Collegeville, MN: Liturgical Press, 2000), 23: "Where Zechariah had been troubled by the angelic apparition, what troubles Mary is the content of this greeting."

30. Isa 6:8–9. See also Lee, *Ministry of Women*, 41–42.

31. Thurston, "Who Was Anna?," 48, follows Raymond E. Brown, "The Presentation of Jesus (Luke 22:22–40)," *Worship* 51 (1977): 5–6, who sees parallels between Anna and the women who ministered at Shiloh and are depicted positively as ones who are committed to fasting and praying in Exod 38:8 LXX and Tg. Ps.-J. Exod 38:8. Thurston also sees Anna's proclamation forming an *inclusio* with that of the women at the tomb in Luke 24:10 (50).

32. See also Thurston, "Who Was Anna?," 51.

33. See Reid, "Friend or Foe," 9, who rightly observes that the Magnificat contains many themes that will become important in Luke-Acts and anticipates Jesus's own actions.

34. Bauckham, *Gospel Women*, 55 and 28: "Mary's song is similarly program-

therefore join Elizabeth and Mary in the type of behavior that is later expected of those who follow Jesus? Who will recognize the coming of Jesus and go and tell others about him just as Anna does?

The Woman Who Loves Jesus (Luke 7:36–50)

All four canonical gospels tell a story about a woman who anoints Jesus.[35] In Matthew, Mark, and John, the event takes place toward the end of Jesus's life—as tensions are escalating and it looks inevitable that Jesus will be arrested and executed. In the Gospel of Luke, however, the story comes much earlier—toward the beginning of Jesus's ministry. Each gospel story has singular features that contribute to its respective interests and emphases, and so we will examine how the elements of this particular anointing story aid our understanding of Lukan discipleship.

Jesus has been active up to the moment of the anointing. He has healed the slave of a centurion from afar (7:1–10), raised a widow's dead son to life (7:11–17), allayed the doubts of John the Baptist and his disciples by reminding them of the "proof" of his messiahship that he has demonstrated in his miracle-working (7:18–23), and then used that opportunity to teach the crowds about John's role as the messenger who has prepared the way for him (7:24–35). In the immediate context of the woman's anointing, then, Luke has emphasized Jesus's extraordinary power as a miracle-worker, his authority to teach, and the content of that teaching: that Jesus is the one whom God has sent. He ends this section by teaching that there are two possible reactions to what God has done: a rejection of John the Baptist indicates a rejection of what God is doing through Jesus (represented by the Pharisees and experts of the law, 7:30), and an acceptance of John the Baptist constitutes an acceptance of what God is doing through Jesus (represented by "all of the people, including the tax collectors," 7:29).

In the next scene Luke contrasts two reactions to Jesus—this time in a more intimate meal scene. A Pharisee named Simon invites Jesus to eat with him at his house. Given what Jesus has just said about those who reject and accept him, the fact that Jesus is being hosted

matic for the story of her son that the rest of Luke's Gospel (and even the Acts of the Apostles) narrates."

35. Matt 26:6–13; Mark 14:3–9; John 12:1–8.

by a Pharisee should strike the audience as unexpected—why would a Pharisee extend such hospitality to Jesus?[36] Perhaps Simon will prove to be an exception to the rule Jesus has just stated? As an artful storyteller, Luke has crafted the narrative to create an opportunity for the hospitable Pharisee to defy expectation by testifying to Jesus's identity as Messiah and honoring him. Yet it is not Simon who honors Jesus but an outsider—a woman from the city who is known, not by her name, but by her reputation as a "sinner" (7:37). While the invited guests are dining, she crashes the party, approaching Jesus with a jar of ointment and using the combination of her tears and the ointment to anoint Jesus's feet, drying them with her hair (7:38). When Simon observes that Jesus makes no move to stop this nonsense, he interprets Jesus's lack of action as proof that he cannot possibly be a prophet from God (7:39). Jesus divines Simon's thoughts. He responds by telling a parable of two debtors, asking the Pharisee to acknowledge which of the debtors will "love" the creditor more—the one who has been forgiven the larger amount of debt or the one who has been forgiven the lesser amount (7:40–42). When Simon declares that the one who is forgiven most will be the one who loves the most, Jesus proceeds to identify that hypothetical debtor with the woman who has just anointed him—the woman from whom Simon thinks Jesus should distance himself.[37] While doing so, he takes the opportunity to contrast the minimal hospitality Simon showed him with the extravagant honor the woman shows (7:44–46). Her actions indicate that her many sins have been forgiven—she has shown "great love" (*ēgapēsen poly*, 7:47), while Simon has not. Jesus reiterates the relationship between her active love and her forgiveness by crediting her faith and pronounces a blessing of peace on her (7:50).

Much of the discussion of this passage has centered on the identity of the woman who is described as "sinful" (7:37, 39) and whose many sins are forgiven (7:47). Unlike Simon the Pharisee, she remains nameless, and so this description serves as her primary identifier until

36. Rachel L. Coleman, "Boundary-Shattering Table Fellowship as a Defining Mark of Discipleship in Luke-Acts," *Wesleyan Theological Journal* 54 (2019): 133.

37. The added "I suppose" (*hypolambanō*) may indicate Simon's desire to leave room for doubt here—i.e., a reluctance to choose the larger debtor. The qualifier may indicate that he can already see where this conversation with Jesus is headed!

Jesus overturns it at the end.[38] While some scholars interpret this label and her corresponding action of wiping Jesus's feet with her hair as a hint that she has been a prostitute or that her sins are to be understood as sexual, there is no clear evidence from the text to support this assumption.[39] Rather, Luke is being deliberately ambiguous (he could have labeled her a prostitute if he wanted to, and were that his goal, he would have).[40] Since he refuses to divulge what kind of sin she has participated in, if the audience assumes it is sexual or tries to pass judgment on her, they will find themselves on the side of Simon, who questions Jesus's competency as a prophet because he does not react to her notoriety in the way that the Pharisee thinks he should.[41] Instead of inviting further sleuthing as to the nature of her sins, the description of her as a "sinful woman" serves to locate her in a group

38. Hence the title of this subheading: "The Woman Who Loves Jesus." Jesus relabels her, and I have followed his lead by rejecting the use of her former label (as the "sinful woman"). See also Levine and Witherington, *Gospel of Luke*, 208–16.

39. Dorothy A. Lee, "Women as 'Sinners': Three Narratives of Salvation in Luke and John," *Australian Biblical Review* 44 (1996): 1–15, argues that she is likely a prostitute. Green, *Gospel of Luke*, 307–10, sees her actions as being initially perceived as sexually erotic, but thinks that this would be mitigated by her weeping. Sun Wook Kim, "A Discussion of Luke's Portrayal of Women and the Eschatological Equality between Men and Women in Luke 7:36–50," *Korean Evangelical New Testament Studies* 12 (2013): 721–22, sees her actions not as erotic but as an indication of her sincerity in the face of Simon's apathy. After a helpful discussion of possible interpretations concerning her unbound hair, Charles H. Cosgrove, "A Woman's Unbound Hair in the Greco-Roman World, with Special Reference to the Story of the 'Sinful Woman' in Luke 7:36–50," *Journal of Biblical Literature* 124 (2005): 687–88, argues that a first-century audience would not initially interpret her actions as sexually provocative because (a) the host did not "supply" her as entertainment for his guests, (b) the context is at a Pharisee's house (not a Greco-Roman party), and (c) she is weeping. He argues that because of her weeping, and knowing that it was common for women to unbind their hair to grieve, it is unlikely that Luke's audience would interpret this as a sexual display.

40. Reid, "Do You See," 42, criticizes scholarly speculation on the subject by rightly observing that no one discusses what type of sinner Peter might have been when he refers to himself as a "sinful man" in Luke 5:8! And remember that there is no shortage of male authors willing to use accusations of sexual practice and lack of sexual self-control as ammunition to ridicule women at the time (e.g., Ben Sira).

41. Yet Cosgrove, "Unbound Hair," 689, is right to point out that Simon's assumption that Jesus is not a prophet precisely because he does not know "who or what kind of woman (she) is" (7:39) likely indicates that Simon does not think her actions are obviously sexual. See also Reid, "Do You See," 43.

that has already been introduced earlier in the chapter: those people who are counted among the tax collectors (7:29, 34; see also 5:30; 15:1; 18:13).[42] She, then, is an outsider because she is unwelcome when she enters, but she will leave an insider because of what she has done. She demonstrates what it looks like to recognize the mercy of God.[43]

Another ambiguity of the passage has to do with the timing of the woman's forgiveness. On the one hand, she could have entered Simon's home prepared to anoint Jesus as a grateful response for a forgiveness she had already received. On the other, the act of forgiveness could have been a result of her anointing of Jesus. Jesus tells Simon that she has shown great love because (*hoti*) her sins are forgiven (7:47). From a chronological standpoint, however, Jesus makes an announcement that her sins are forgiven after she anoints him (7:48). Given the emotional nature of her encounter with Jesus (indicated by her weeping), I think it likely that she is responding to forgiveness that she has already received.[44] An action of response

42. Lee, *Ministry of Women*, 44.

43. Green, *Gospel of Luke*, 307, argues that the fact that a woman described as "sinful" enters a *Pharisee's* house makes this insider/outsider dynamic all the more striking and would result in pressure on Simon to respond appropriately: "The woman who enters Simon's house, whose sinful state is evident to all, comes into this scene like an alien, communicable disease; given Pharisaical view of holiness, the propriety of Simon's response to the spectacle transpiring before him would be assumed." Reid, "Do You See," 44, also notes that a prostitute would be a participant at the banquet, but she is clearly an interloper. *Pace* Levine and Witherington, *Gospel of Luke*, 212, however, there is no indication that Simon is concerned about purity laws. Rather, the focus of his criticism is on whether Jesus is a prophet (7:39). See also Joseph Sievers and Amy-Jill Levine, eds., *The Pharisees* (Grand Rapids: Eerdmans, 2021), for a collection of essays that explore how Pharisees and Jews came to be regarded as synonymous and in turn have been vilified throughout Christian history, and especially Amy-Jill Levine, "Preaching and Teaching the Pharisees," 403–27 in that collection, who offers a corrective for preaching and teaching on the Pharisees that avoids harmful stereotyping and anti-Semitism.

44. Green, *Gospel of Luke*, 313, describes this literary device as a "gap" in the story line. It is not an unusual move in Luke's Gospel because it includes several characters who have already begun their "journey of discipleship" before their appearance in the narrative. Another example is found immediately following in Luke 8:1–3. See also Reid, "Do You See," 41, who argues that the imperfect *ēn* in 7:37 has the connotation "used to be" and indicates that she is no longer the sinner she once was because she has been forgiven. Another example might be Zacchaeus, whose statement suggests that he has already been in the practice of paying back those he had cheated in the past (Luke 19:8). This is how Green,

would also make the most sense of the parable, as Jesus's emphasis in the story is on the proper response of the debtors to forgiveness: they should show love.[45] If this is the case, the woman's actions are born out of the gratitude that comes from someone who has been forgiven—it is a response to what has already been done.[46] The timeline of her forgiveness is not really the point of the story, however.[47] The point is that she responds appropriately to what she has received, just as the one who was indebted most will do.[48] Jesus's pronouncement of forgiveness, then, is more performative in nature—for the benefit of Simon and his guests, and even Luke's audience—because the very actions that are lauded by Jesus are criticized by the Pharisee.

The contrast between the woman's actions and Simon's is a focal point of the narrative. In many ways he functions as an antithesis to her. He responds to Jesus with doubt and scorn, while she responds to Jesus with gratitude. Despite the fact that he is the host of the meal, the hospitality he offers Jesus is lacking when compared to hers.[49] In fact, her above and beyond hospitality, as demonstrated

---

Gospel of Luke, 671–72, interprets the use of the present here—as a progressive present that indicates that he is already and continuing to be in the practice of giving to the poor. And, as in the woman's story, the witnesses to Jesus's treatment of Zacchaeus also protest because he is a "sinner" (19:7).

45. This would also be consistent with *apheōntai* in 7:48, a perfect tense that indicates a past action with enduring present effects. See also Reid, "Do You See," 41–42.

46. Dorothea H. Bertschmann, "Hosting Jesus: Revisiting Luke's 'Sinful Woman' (Luke 7.36–50) as a Tale of Two Hosts," *Journal for the Study of the New Testament* 40 (2017): 39, rightly observes that the standard terms for repentance and guilt are absent from this story. She reads it through the lens of mutual giving and receiving: Jesus gives forgiveness and receives the anointing, and the woman anoints Jesus because she has experienced forgiveness.

47. Kim, "Discussion," 723, believes the *hoti* in 7:47 is functioning primarily as a connector of the parable and the woman's story, rather than indicating whether her love or her experience of forgiveness came first.

48. See Kent A. Van Til, "Three Anointings and One Offering: The Sinful Woman in Luke 7.36–50," *Journal of Pentecostal Theology* 15 (2006): 73–82, who argues that Luke's version of the event differs from the other canonical gospels because the woman is giving an offering to Jesus (rather than anointing him). This is consistent with Luke's emphasis on generosity as a response to the gospel, particularly from those who have been viewed as "other" (e.g., Zacchaeus, 19:8).

49. Green, *Gospel of Luke*, 308, notes that his neglectful hosting is further

by the acts of anointing Jesus and drying his feet with her hair, corresponds to the above and beyond response that Jesus gives in publicly testifying to her forgiveness.[50] In this way she acts more like Jesus than anyone else in the narrative, a required feature of discipleship.[51] Socially and religiously, Simon the Pharisee is an insider, while the woman has been known as a "sinner" and is thus an outsider.[52] Yet, despite his social advantage, Simon is the one who receives public correction from Jesus, while she receives forgiveness and acceptance.[53] As a result, she draws closer to Jesus, while the distance increases between him and Simon. Furthermore, the way that Luke withholds information on Simon's lack of hospitality until after the woman has demonstrated hers, combined with the absence of any final positive response from Simon, places Simon's shortcomings in sharp relief to the woman's willingness to embrace Jesus, and it underscores even more clearly the honor toward Jesus that this woman publicly displays—even while knowing it could come with an embarrassing public spectacle.

---

amplified by the fact that Luke twice calls him a host (7:36, 39) but never includes any narration of him actually hosting.

50. Lee, *Ministry of Women*, 45, sees in her actions the implication that she has now taken over as host: "Her hospitality and ministry arise out of self-knowledge and recognition of Jesus's identity as Savior, knowledge that Simon lacks in both respects." Bertschmann, "Hosting Jesus," 41–43, argues that the woman's actions are so over the top with regard to cultural expectations of hospitality that it would have been seen as overboard to the point of awkwardness—until Jesus redefines them as expressions of great love.

51. In response to Schaberg, "Luke," 285–86, who argues that Luke's version of the anointing story deliberately removes the woman's prophetic insight included in the Gospel of Mark (14:3–9), see Lee, "Women as Sinners," 11, who argues that Luke 7:36–50 provides a corrective to Jesus's opposition and is presented as a model of service that is later exemplified in the ministry of the women who follow Jesus (8:1–3).

52. Pharisaic opposition to the way that Jesus interacts with "sinners" is a common theme in the gospel. See the parable of the Pharisee and the tax collector (Luke 18:9–14). Monika Ottermann, "How Could He Ever Do That to Her?!' Or, How the Woman Who Anointed Jesus Became a Victim of Luke's Redactional and Theological Principles," in *Reading Other-wise: Socially Engaged Biblical Scholars Reading with Their Local Communities*, ed. Gerald O. West (Atlanta: Society of Biblical Literature, 2007), 108.

53. Coleman, "Boundary-Shattering," 134, observes that Jesus's physical orientation remains toward the woman after the parable, even as he addresses Simon.

The Women Who Follow, Serve, and Learn (Luke 8:1–3; 10:38–42)

At the center of his gospel, Luke highlights the role that women had in Jesus's ministry, including them among those who followed him, supported him, served him, and learned from him. Of the canonical gospels, Luke is the only one explicitly to state that women were among Jesus's committed followers who went along with him in his ministry and even contributed to its funding (8:1–3).[54] Later he recounts that, after emphasizing the urgency of following him even if it meant giving up familial obligations (9:57–62), Jesus sent out a large group of followers in pairs to places he wanted to go (10:1–12) to preach the coming of the kingdom. At the end of chapter 10, Luke tells another meal story—this time about Jesus's encounter with a pair of sisters who differed in their priorities when it came to following him. Given the density of the discipleship motif in these three chapters and the prominent role that women have in them, they should be understood as critical evidence of Luke's understanding of the place that female disciples had in the ministry of Jesus.

Immediately following the encounter with the woman who anointed Jesus, Luke includes a summary statement of what Jesus was doing, where he was going, and who was with him. In Luke 8:1–2 he mentions two groups that accompanied Jesus: the Twelve and some women who had been cured of evil spirits and physical ailments. Although this is the first explicit reference to women in Jesus's entourage, that women would be traveling with Jesus would not necessarily have raised eyebrows in the first century. Other contemporary Jewish groups had female followers who participated in travel with male followers or who lived with the men in community.[55] Like the Twelve who had already been listed in the narrative (6:14–16), some of the women are listed here: Mary Magdalene, Joanna the wife of Chuza, and Susanna.[56] Un-

54. The other Synoptics mention the women who were with Jesus only after the fact, at the crucifixion scene (Mark 15:40–41; Matt 27:55–56).

55. E.g., the families at Masada, the Bar Kokhba rebellion, and the Essenes all included women. Lynn H. Cohick, *Women in the World of the Earliest Christians: Illuminating Ancient Ways of Life* (Grand Rapids: Baker Academic, 2009), 310, also notes that the expectations of hospitality at the time would have eliminated or greatly reduced the difficulties for women to find appropriate shelter when on the road.

56. Although Luke only mentions three names, they are part of a much larger group of women (8:3).

like the Twelve, however, their primary function in the group is stated: they "provided for them out of their resources" (8:3).

These women reappear at the end of the gospel—they watch Jesus being crucified (23:49), see where Jesus is buried (23:55), prepare spices for his body and bring them after the Sabbath to the tomb (23:56–24:1), become the first to witness the empty tomb (24:2–3), encounter the "men" at the tomb and receive the first announcement of Jesus's resurrection (24:4–7), and "remember" Jesus's prior teachings that they received while in Galilee with him (24:6–8). We will look more closely at the passion and resurrection narrative at the end of the chapter, but for now we highlight the through line in the narrative. The same women involved in Jesus's ministry are also there when that ministry culminates in his resurrection. By naming some of them so early in the narrative and then calling back to them at the end of it (with shout-outs to Mary Magdalene and Joanna in both passages), Luke portrays them as always in the background of the story.[57] Their presence is further accentuated by the fact that Luke includes these women alongside the Twelve—he thinks of them as part of the larger group of disciples.

More, Luke highlights their actions, while the Twelve are simply "there" with Jesus. In 8:1–3, Luke credits them with supporting the very ministry that is described as so urgent in 10:1–12.[58] Unlike some, I see no reason to assume that the kind of actions with which the women are credited were limited to traditional female roles involving food.[59] While "providing" for the ministry would have most certainly

57. See also Bauckham, *Gospel Women*, 110. Likewise, Karris, "Women and Discipleship," 32, sees these verses functioning as more than a summary statement, but as a "concise narrative statement that describes a prolonged situation or portrays an event as happening repeatedly within an indefinite period of time." Including their names may also be an indication that Luke's audience either knew them or knew of them.

58. Some manuscripts differ as to whether the women provide for Jesus (singular *autō*) or the whole group (plural *autois*). Lee, *Ministry of Women*, 48, argues that the singular reading makes more sense of the passage because Luke emphasizes two groups of disciples: male and female. I am not convinced that either reading makes a substantive difference, as Jesus makes it clear that discipleship (following him) involves serving others (22:26–27).

59. Contra Ben Witherington III, "On the Road with Mary Magdalene, Joanna, Susanna, and Other Disciples—Luke 8:1–3," *Zeitschrift für die neutestamentliche Wissenschaft und die Kunde der älteren Kirche* 70 (1979): 243–48; E. Jane Via, "Women, the Discipleship of Service, and the Early Christian Ritual

involved the day-to-day necessities for a traveling community such as food and shelter, the language of *diēkonoun* can carry with it elements of leadership (see Acts 6:2).[60] It was primarily an economic term connoting financial support, and it was possible for wealthy women to be benefactors, supporting the people and causes that interested them both financially and socially.[61] The disadvantages and restrictions of their gender could be trumped by their higher social status, and it appears that at least some of these women had the means to support the ministry with their patronage.[62] Joanna's accompanying description as the wife of Herod's steward Chuza highlights her elite status by virtue of being married to a man who held political influence. That she is presented as the decision-maker of her finances (*she* is Jesus's benefactor, not Chuza) might indicate that she is in a *sine manu* marriage, or even that she was a widow at the time.[63] Either way, she has control

---

Meal in the Gospel of Luke," *St. Luke's Journal of Theology* 29 (1985): 37–60; Jennifer Halteman Schrock, "'I Am among You as One Who Serves': Jesus and Food in Luke's Gospel," *Daughters of Sarah* 19 (1993): 22. If one accepts the argument that it was unusual for women to follow a rabbi without mention of their husbands with them, why would we assume that they would be concerned with maintaining traditional roles of table service in the context of an already untraditional practice? See also David C. Sim, "The Women Followers of Jesus: The Implications of Luke 8:1–3," *Heythrop Journal* 30 (1989): 58, who rightly observes that when the gospels explicitly address issues of food supply for Jesus's followers, it is Jesus and the Twelve who are responsible for it.

60. Green, *Gospel of Luke*, 319, who also lists Luke 4:39; 10:40; 12:37; 17:8; and 22:26–27.

61. Amanda C. Miller, "Cut from the Same Cloth: A Study of Female Patrons in Luke-Acts and the Roman Empire," *Review and Expositor* 114 (2017): 205, argues that Luke's audience would not have assumed that the women were simply "uninvolved donors," given the influence female patrons could have on their clients. See also Richard I. Pervo, "Unnamed Women Who Provide for the Jesus Movement," in *Women in Scripture: A Dictionary of Named and Unnamed Women in the Hebrew Bible, the Apocryphal/Deuterocanonical Books, and the New Testament*, ed. Carol Meyers, Toni Craven, and Ross S. Kraemer (Grand Rapids: Eerdmans, 2001), 442, who argues that "out of their own resources" (*ek tōn hyparchontōn autais*; 8:3) was an established benefaction formula. Also see Sim, "Women Followers," 51–52, who argues that *diēkonoun* is an economic term here, but that these women would not have been wealthy, and Bauckham, *Gospel Women*, 110–21, for his critiques of Witherington and Sim.

62. Cohick, *Earliest Christians*, 22–23.

63. Cohick, *Earliest Christians*, 311–14. I agree with Cohick that there is no reason to assume that Joanna had to give up her prior wealth to follow Jesus.

of her wealth and has chosen to give it to the ministry. Their actions in giving to Jesus's ministry recall the generosity of the woman who loved Jesus (7:36–50) and locates them with others whose faithfulness is exemplified by their generosity.[64]

Luke describes the women as being "with" Jesus (*syn autō*, 8:1) and alongside the Twelve, a phrase that is shorthand for discipleship and attributed to those who have also made sacrifices to follow Jesus and formed a "willing attachment" to him (8:38; 9:18; 22:56).[65] Moreover, the immediate context—both in the summary and later in Luke 10:1–20—is that of proclaiming the good news of the kingdom of God throughout Galilee. Since we have already been told that women are actively involved in following Jesus, there is no reason to assume that they are absent from the seventy who are sent out by him shortly thereafter.[66] Luke 8:1, then, functions as a programmatic statement

---

Rather, it is more likely that she kept it to help serve as a patron of the community, with the added contribution of her political and social connections. Hylen, *Women*, 108: "If modern readers understand that women could own property and serve as patrons, we may notice them doing so in the New Testament. Likewise, if we do not assume all women were inferior to all men, we may notice women with significant social and political influence." Joanna would be one such example of this.

64. Luke 19:1–10; 21:1–4.

65. Schuyler Brown, *Apostasy and Perseverance in the Theology of Luke*, Analecta Biblica 36 (Rome: Pontifical Biblical Institute), 83. Note that in Luke 22:56 Peter denies being *with* Jesus—a rejection of his discipleship (*syn autō ēn*). Green, *Gospel of Luke*, 318, suggests that the nature of their healing might indicate that they would have already been ostracized from their community and so would consider other disciples as their new kinship group.

Lee, *Ministry of Women*, 47, thinks it noteworthy that Mary Magdalene is first in the list of female disciples, functioning much like Peter in the list of the Twelve, and that this placement indicates her leadership role in the community. It may also be implicit at the end of the gospel, where Mary Magdalene is again mentioned first, and Peter functions in that passage as the representative apostle (24:10, 12).

66. Contra Barbara E. Reid, "Luke: The Gospel for Women?" *Currents in Theology and Mission* 21 (1994): 409–10, I do not find an argument from silence compelling here. Just because Luke doesn't explicitly list women as members of the missional group does not mean that they were not. Moreover, Cohick, *Earliest Christians*, 312, rightly observes that *diēkonoun* is "tightly connected with the idea of serving under orders, or functioning as a go-between, an emissary." This function, then, involves a commissioning by another person (Jesus) and a carrying out of that commission by the one who receives it (Acts 6:1–2).

for Jesus's ministry, and so the implication is that these women were active participants in what he is doing.[67] It is also significant narratively in that 8:3 is the first substantive description of the activity of any of Jesus's followers in the gospel. Up to this point the focus has been on Jesus's activities, and it is only after this that the actions of the Twelve begin to be included.

Shortly after Jesus sends out the seventy disciples, he is welcomed into the house of a woman named Martha (10:38). While there, Martha busies herself with the many tasks (*pollen diakonian*) of hosting, while her sister, Mary, sits at Jesus's feet to listen to his teaching. Flustered, Martha appeals to Jesus to compel her sister to help her with the work (10:39–40), but Jesus refuses, correcting instead Martha's anxiety and distraction while lauding Mary for her choice in listening to him (10:41–42).

This episode presents two women who follow Jesus—one who expresses her discipleship by serving Jesus as a host, and the other who does so by learning from him.[68] Scholars often attempt to glean from the story clues about Luke's perspective on women's roles or to discern which sister had correct priorities—both options that focus on limitations.[69] But an effort to choose one sister's actions over the other lands us in the very same trap in which Martha found herself in the first place. Jesus did not dismiss her activities in hosting him as irrelevant, useless, or unnecessary (Luke already emphasized the importance of proper hospitality toward Jesus in 7:36–50). Moreover, we have seen that it was expected that a virtuous woman would care for and manage the work in the home, and so Martha's assumption that Jesus would prioritize the work she is doing over Mary's action makes sense in that cultural context.[70] It was *Martha* who framed the

67. See also Lee, *Ministry of Women*, 47.

68. If original, the textual variant *hē* in 10:39 ("Mary, who *also* sat") suggests that Martha also sat at the feet of Jesus at first (before she became distracted), indicating that both sisters were disciples. See Tommy Wasserman, "Bringing Sisters Back Together: Another Look at Luke 10:41–42," *Journal of Biblical Literature* 137 (2018): 457, and Mary Rose D'Angelo, "Women Partners in the New Testament," *Journal of Feminist Studies in Religion* 6 (1990): 65–86, who argue for this reading.

69. E.g., D'Angelo, "Women Partners"; Schüssler Fiorenza, "Feminist Critical Interpretation."

70. Hylen, *Women*, 60.

sisters' choices in terms of either-or: in her view, Mary must choose to help her with the tasks *rather than* sit at the feet of Jesus. Jesus prioritizes listening to him, but he does not limit Martha or Mary's activity to one thing or another.[71]

This distinction is made clearer by the longer reading of 10:42a, which is Jesus's response to Martha's request to make Mary help her. Rather than "Martha, Martha, you are anxious and distracted about many things, *but only one thing is necessary*" (*henos de estin chreia*), Tommy Wasserman has convincingly argued that the longer reading is preferred: "Martha, Martha, you are anxious and distracted about many things, *but few things are necessary—or indeed only one*" (*oligōn de estin chreia ē henos*).[72] This reading resists an interpretation that pits one sister's actions against the other (listening over serving). Instead, Jesus prioritizes the "one thing" (discipleship) over the "few things" (meal)—all of which are legitimate actions for his followers.[73] Any correction that Jesus has for Martha, then, is due to her choosing one aspect of discipleship over another, to the point where the choice causes comparison, distraction, and anxiety (10:41).[74]

This passage says more about what female discipleship *can* be than about what it cannot. Martha is not a failed disciple because she is engaged in serving Jesus. Quite the opposite is true: Jesus has just recently stated that those who welcome and set food before his disciples are indicating their readiness to be receptive toward the good news (10:8) and are therefore acting as if they are receiving Jesus too

71. Adele Reinhartz, "From Narrative to History: The Resurrection of Mary and Martha," in *"Women Like This": New Perspectives on Jewish Women in the Greco-Roman World*, ed. Amy-Jill Levine (Atlanta: Scholars Press, 1991), 169, argues that Jesus's critique of Martha is directed toward her prioritizing of physical needs instead of hearing the word.

72. Wasserman, "Bringing Sisters Back," 460.

73. As Gordon Fee, "'One Thing Is Needful'? Luke 10:42," in *New Testament Textual Criticism: Its Significance for Exegesis: Essays in Honour of Bruce M. Metzger*, ed. Eldon Jay Epp and Gordon D. Fee (Oxford: Clarendon, 1981): 61–75, has argued, the "few things" emphasizes the body. It therefore highlights the anxiety that Martha feels at being overwhelmed in providing for the physical needs of her guest. Jesus recognizes the need for the provision but also recognizes the mistake that Martha makes in choosing that over what Mary is doing.

74. Lee, *Ministry of Women*, 52, is right to point out that Jesus's repetition of her name ("Martha, Martha," 10:41) indicates his sympathetic posture toward her, which would be a helpful response to her anxiety.

(10:16).[75] Moreover, in her hosting and serving Jesus, Martha joins other female disciples who serve in different ways (*diēkonoun*, 8:3; *diakonian*, 10:40).[76] Likewise, Mary is not inactive by sitting at the feet of Jesus.[77] She is listening and learning from him, inhabiting the posture of a disciple.[78] Thus, serving and listening are two sides of the same coin of discipleship.

75. Warren Carter, "Getting Martha Out of the Kitchen: Luke 10:38–42 Again," *Catholic Biblical Quarterly* 58 (1996): 266–67, argues that this receiving language is meant to be understood primarily as eschatological.

76. Contra Schüssler Fiorenza, "Feminist Critical Interpretation," 30–31, who limits the term's meaning here to "preaching" and sees in the episode evidence of Luke's resistance to female leadership in the church. See Luke 4:39; 8:3; 12:37; 17:8; and 22:26–27—which indicate a broader meaning of "serving." See also John N. Collins, "Did Luke Intend a Disservice to Women in the Martha and Mary Story?," *Biblical Theology Bulletin* 28 (1998): 104–11, and André Lemaire, *Les Ministères aux origins de l'Église, naissance de la triple hiérarchie: évêques, presbytres, diacres* (Paris: Cerf, 1971), for in-depth studies on the term.

77. This is the fundamental difficulty I have with Schüssler Fiorenza's ("Feminist Critical Interpretation," 29) understanding of the sisters' actions and Jesus's critique. I do not see Luke attempting to limit the role of women in the church by calling on the sisters to be passive because I do not understand listening to be a passive activity in the gospel. In fact, Kopas, "Jesus and Women," 198, rightly connects Jesus's response to the woman's exclamation in Luke 11:27–28 ("Blessed rather are those who hear the word of God and obey it!" [NRSVUE]) as further evidence that Mary was not passively listening but rather was acting as a model of the type of behavior expected of followers of God.

Nor do I see Jesus's role here as a representative of male authority/leadership. Although Jesus is a male, he is also divine, and so whatever Luke says about Jesus is primarily *Christo*centric, not necessarily androcentric. See also Reinhartz, "Narrative to History," 171, and Mary Ann Beavis, "Mary of Bethany and the Hermeneutics of Remembrance," *Catholic Biblical Quarterly* 75 (2013): 743; contra Schüssler Fiorenza, "Feminist Critical Interpretation," 29–30.

78. Craig S. Keener, *Acts: An Exegetical Commentary*, vol. 1, *Introduction and 1:1–2:47* (Grand Rapids: Baker Academic, 2012), 601, notes that this posture for disciples was usually taken by men as a way of training for their own future teaching roles. Green, *Gospel of Luke*, 435, also sees Mary's position as countercultural. Carter, "Getting Martha Out," 268, sees in Luke's presentation of Mary as one who is "listening" (*ākouen*) to Jesus a callback to 10:16 (as an antonym for rejecting the disciples—and therefore Jesus—and so functions here as a synonym for receiving him): "This response suggests that the term 'sister' points beyond a relation of kinship with Martha to denote their joint participation in the community of the disciples of Jesus."

The Women Who Model Kingdom Priorities (Luke 15:8–10; 18:1–8)

Our study of female discipleship in the Gospel of Luke is not limited to the women who actually followed Jesus. One of the features of this gospel is the prominence of women who model kingdom priorities. This happens within two parables: the woman who lost a coin (15:8–10) and the widow who pleads her case before an unjust judge (18:1–8). Jesus tells these parables in order to teach truths about right action that reflects the values of the gospel.

The parable of the lost coin is located between two other parables: the parable of the lost sheep (15:1–7) and the parable of the lost son (15:11–32). All three deal with lost valuables, and the cost of the loss increases with each story, upping the tension in the narrative. The lost sheep constitutes a 1 percent loss, the lost coin makes up 10 percent of the woman's wealth, and the father loses 50 percent of his progeny. Each parable invites the audience to join in the increased anxiety of the one who is looking for or is worried about the thing or person that is lost.[79] Moreover, all three parables teach that God rejoices greatly when "sinners" come back to him, inviting the audience to join in the celebration as the source of the tension is finally removed.[80]

Just like the shepherd and the father of the parables that frame it, the woman who has lost a coin represents a God who is relentless in pursuing, embracing, and rejoicing over those who have returned to him. This brief story paints a vivid picture of a God who does everything possible—who looks high and low—to find the lost. The emphasis of each parable is on the actions of the protagonist, and in the case of the parable of the lost coin, we see a woman who not only goes to great lengths to seek out the coin but also invites her neighbors to come and celebrate once she has found it. The scene Jesus paints of the woman hosting a party after finding the coin suggests that the monetary value of the coin is not what is most important (surely she would spend a great deal of the coin's worth in hosting such a party). Rather, it is the finding of the coin itself that is the cause

79. Lyn Kidson, "The Anxious Search for the Lost Coin (Luke 15:8–10): Lost Coins, Women's Dowries and the Contribution of Numismatics and Phenomenology to Gospel Research," *Australian Biblical Review* 68 (2020): 87.

80. Kidson, "Anxious Search," 87.

for celebration. The woman's actions, then, indicate that God is not concerned with the social status, wealth, or even religious piety of a person, whose "value" comes simply from the fact that they belong to him—a theme that runs throughout the Gospel of Luke.[81]

Similarly, in the parable of the widow and the unjust judge, we see a woman who is also lauded for her persistence (18:1–8). Rather than waiting until the end to give the punchline, Luke introduces the parable by telling the audience its purpose, to underscore the need to pray unfailingly and to not give up (*mē enkakein*, 18:1). Thus, from the beginning the audience knows that the protagonist of the story will model determination and persistence in the face of circumstances that would otherwise tempt someone to give up.

It is fitting, then, that the protagonist of the story turns out to be a widow.[82] Knowing that widows were at a severe disadvantage in the patriarchal world of the first century if they had no man to provide for them, the audience would not be surprised to learn of the circumstances in which she finds herself. Her "opponent" is trying to take advantage of her in some way, and so she must appeal to the courts for help—a situation that would be especially likely for a person who belongs to the most vulnerable group in society and therefore one who would have to rely most on the justice of those in power (18:3).[83] She is a widow who has very little social capital, and she finds her fate resting in the hands of a powerful (male) judge who has no morals or scruples (he "neither feared God nor had respect for people," 18:2 NRSVUE).[84] What *would* be unusual to the audience is the way in which this au-

81. In fact, there are clues in the parable that suggest the woman (i.e., God) identifies most closely with the poor: she has no window (hence the need to light a lamp) and her "wealth" is not disposable income (the coins suggest the savings of the family). See also Green, *Gospel of Luke*, 576.

82. Luke has a penchant for using widows as exemplars and recipients of God's favor or intervention (cf. 2:37; 4:25–26; 7:11–17; 20:45–21:4; Acts 6:1; 9:39–41). Seim, *Double Message*, 230–31, calls Luke's presentation of widows a "bifocal perspective," noting that they represent the most poor and vulnerable of society and yet are often presented as autonomous.

83. Stephen Curkpatrick, "'Real and Fictive' Widows: Nuances of Independence and Resistance in Luke," *Lexington Theological Quarterly* 37 (2002): 216: "The use of a widow is indicative of the theme of justice that is intrinsic to the kingdom of God in Luke."

84. Green, *Gospel of Luke*, 640, who notes that her situation might also suggest that she is poor, as she must resort to persistent requests rather than bribing the judge with money so as to secure a favorable ruling.

dacious widow will not take no for an answer.[85] Even with all that is against her and while having no advocate but herself, her sheer will brings about the desired outcome: the unjust judge acts justly, not because he feels morally compelled to do so, but because of her persistence (18:4–5).[86] The widow, then, represents those who cry out to God continually (18:7), and because God is not an unjust judge but a righteous one, he will quickly grant justice to them (18:8). Jesus closes the parable by wondering aloud if this type of persistence—which he understands to be evidence of the faith (*tēn pistin*)—will be found when he returns again (18:8).[87]

Both of these parables depict women as protagonists who model right action in the face of undesirable circumstances. Although hypothetical disciples, both of these women are determined to do what is right, seeking out what is valuable and what is just, and persisting in their petitions to God.[88] These actions are consistent with God's own work in the world and are a hallmark of what it means to follow him.

The Women at the End of the Gospel (Luke 23–24)

At the end of the gospel, the women who have followed Jesus consistently and funded his ministry—women who have been in the background of the narrative since 8:1–3—find themselves in the middle of the events of Jesus's passion. Luke locates these women at a distance

85. Curkpatrick, "'Real and Fictive' Widows," uses the adjective "audacious" to describe the widow throughout his article. The word perfectly captures the social disadvantages that she must overcome, as well as her personality.

86. Green, *Gospel of Luke*, 641, and F. S. Spencer, *Salty Wives*, 266–67, observe that the language used in 18:5 draws on the image of a boxing match.

87. Green, *Gospel of Luke*, 637, underscores that this "faith" is not a general reference to faith but is rather the kind of faith demonstrated by the widow in the parable. This is indicated by the use of the definite article, which might also implicitly refer to active faith in the Son of Man—i.e., discipleship.

For an alternative reading, see Amy-Jill Levine, *Short Stories by Jesus: The Enigmatic Parables of a Controversial Rabbi* (New York: HarperOne, 2014), 239–65, who argues that neither the judge or the widow comes off looking good in the story, as they both utilize the same system of injustice and act on vengeance. While she raises many thought-provoking points, in both the larger context of Luke and in the way he begins and ends the parable, he is presenting the widow as one who embodies the characteristics of the faithful.

88. The parable of the widow and the unjust judge is directed at the disciples (17:22), indicating that the closing question of 18:8 is also directed at them.

from the crucifixion, but close enough to watch as Jesus dies. While the other Synoptics mention just the women, Luke indicates that they were part of a larger group ("all who knew him," 23:49) that was there.[89] Yet only these women "who had come with him from Galilee" continue to follow in order to observe Jesus's hurried burial.[90] Luke adds that once they've seen where his body has been laid, they go back to the city and prepare spices and ointments in anticipation of their return to the tomb to care for Jesus's body properly after the Sabbath (23:55–56). In the early Sunday morning hours, the women come to the tomb but find the stone rolled away (24:2). Going into the tomb, they see that it is empty, and while they are in a state of utter confusion, two angels appear to them to announce that Jesus has risen from the dead (24:3–5). To help them make sense of it all, the messengers remind them of Jesus's prophetic teachings on what would happen to him. Upon remembering this, the women immediately go back to the remaining eleven and the other disciples and tell them what they have just witnessed (24:6–9). Their story is met with immediate disbelief, although Peter does go to see for himself. Seeing the discarded clothes in the empty tomb, he returns home amazed (24:12).

Although women are present at the crucifixion and at the empty tomb in the other canonical gospels, there are some features that only Luke includes. He has taken care to reiterate the continuity between the group of women who followed Jesus throughout his ministry and funded it (8:1–3) and the women who witness the death and burial of Jesus and plan to honor him in his death by taking care of his corpse.[91] This continuity is further accentuated by the command to "remember"—the women must have been in Jesus's presence as he was giving these passion-resurrection predictions in order to be able to recall them and act on them (9:18–22 and 17:22–37). Not only that, but "remembering" involves more than just thinking about a past event.[92] The previous command to remember comes in the context of the Last

89. Matt 27:55–56; Mark 15:40–41.

90. Green, *Gospel of Luke*, 828, observes that Luke intentionally draws attention only to the women disciples.

91. Lee, *Ministry of Women*, 55, observes that there are seven women who are named among the disciples in Luke, and suggests that this may be a symbolic number (much like the Twelve) signifying completeness or abundance and so may be representative of a much larger group.

92. See also Reid, "Friend or Foe," 21.

Supper and thus is associated with an action that invites the group to participate in the event alongside Jesus (22:19).[93] And more recently, the criminal executed next to Jesus expects that his plea to Jesus to "remember" will result in Jesus acting on his behalf (23:42). It is no accident, then, that the women who have just "remembered" what Jesus had said immediately act on it. On their own initiative they go and tell what they have just witnessed.[94] This testimony is confirmed when a different set of disciples repeats it.[95] In the uniquely Lukan episode of Jesus's appearance to two disciples on the road to Emmaus, the travelers recount the scene at the empty tomb for the "stranger" who has joined them in their travels. Luke does not give the identity of the other disciple with Cleopas (24:18), but it is possible that it is a woman (and perhaps his wife)—a possibility increased by the presence of multiple pairings of couples in Luke-Acts.[96] The stranger they encounter turns out to be Jesus, and he corroborates the women's testimony by connecting the events of his death and resurrection with the prophets and God's fulfillment of the Scriptures (24:25–27).

The role of the women in witnessing to the reality of the resurrection is at the forefront of Luke's account. As we have seen in chapter 2, women acting as witnesses in the first century was fairly unusual, but it was not unheard of. Women were more likely to be asked to testify if the circumstances to which they were testifying were deemed to be directly relevant to them in some way.[97] Luke's resurrection narratives have no indication that the women's testimony was rejected because they were women.[98] Even if this were hinted at in the apostles' initial reaction (that their words were "nonsensical," 24:11), it is almost immediately subverted by the reactions to the testimony of Jesus him-

93. Lee, *Ministry of Women*, 54, argues that remembering for Luke is a mark of faith and is used to demonstrate the trustworthiness of God in the gospel. Karris, "Women and Discipleship," 38, argues that in Luke-Acts remembering also indicates a transformation (e.g., Luke 22:61 and Acts 11:16).

94. Unlike in the other Synoptic Gospels (Matt 28:7; Mark 16:7), they are not instructed to do so.

95. Luke has a penchant for repeat narrations of events that he deems are crucial to the gospel (see also the account of Saul's Damascus-road experience in Acts 9:1–19; 22:6–16; 26:12–18).

96. Selvidge, "Alternate Lifestyles," 98.

97. Karris, "Women and Discipleship," 41–42.

98. Contra Green, *Gospel of Luke*, 839–40.

self.[99] Instead, Luke emphasizes the male disciples' disbelief in the *content* of the message, not the trustworthiness of the messengers per se. The apostles and other disciples do not believe that Jesus has risen from the dead, thus rejecting the testimony of the women.

So while the women diligently follow Jesus even in death, witness the empty tomb, experience the revelation of his resurrection, and tell the apostles the truth of what they have witnessed, neither the remaining eleven apostles nor the disciples on the road to Emmaus respond so positively. In fact, in comparison to the women, their disbelief, lack of understanding, and inaction stand out starkly in the narrative and even prompt correction from a frustrated Jesus (24:25). When the women go to tell the apostles, the men do not believe the word that they receive—a word that aligns with Jesus's previous prophecies and that will be corroborated when he appears to them (24:25, 45–46). Luke is the only gospel writer to include the apostles' negative reaction to (rejection of) the women's witness.[100] Ironically, the sent ones do not believe those who have taken their own initiative to go and tell.[101] The most prominent members among the disciples, then, effectively dismiss the word of the women, of the angelic messengers, and of Jesus himself. Even when the audience anticipates that Peter will at last believe the women, he merely confirms that the tomb is empty—Luke does not indicate that he believes that Jesus is

99. Cf. Miller, "Same Cloth," 206: "To be sure, the male disciples do not believe it, and dismiss it as idle talk—the gossip and ramblings of hysterical women (24:11). But I think we must lay the responsibility for that misjudgment at the feet of the disciples, not the author of the Gospel." Miller also sees in the apostles' reaction a parallel to the dismissal of Rhoda's news about Peter (Acts 12:15)!

100. Contra Reid, "Luke," 407, I do not believe that the negative reaction by the male disciples means that the women are depicted negatively in the narrative. On the contrary, the audience knows that the women's words are true because it has been "with" the women at the empty tomb. Therefore, the women do not look nonsensical—the men do!

101. Reid, "Friend or Foe," 20, sees the strong verbal links between Luke 1–2 and 23:44–24:12 as evidence of the women's prophetic role alongside Elizabeth and Mary: "When the two are connected, the poor reception of the women's words at the tomb can be seen not simply as Luke's disregard for women's witness but as a typical response to the words of a prophet. . . . From this angle, the rejection of the words of the women who were at the tomb can be seen as a confirmation of the truthfulness of their declaration and an affirmation of their ability to proclaim the word faithfully."

risen. He acts no differently upon his return from the tomb, and he certainly does not witness to the other apostles (24:12). His doubt is further emphasized by the morosity of the two disciples who are traveling on the road to Emmaus. They are not joyful but are disappointed and confused, not knowing what to make of the women's testimony or the reality of the empty tomb. It is only after Jesus has instructed them in the Scriptures and has finally broken bread with them (Luke deliberately patterns this scene after the Last Supper in 22:14–23) that they recognize him as their Lord. Even then, the apostles and other disciples who are with them still have lingering doubts—so much so that they do not believe their own eyes when they see Jesus appear among them, and they continue to lack belief until Jesus eats food with them (24:36–42). Thus, we have male disciples who do not "see" Jesus for who he is even when he is in their presence, while the women believe, go, and tell before having seen the risen Jesus at all.

The witness of these female disciples does not end once they share the good news of Jesus's resurrection. There is no reason to think that they are absent from the larger group of disciples whom Jesus commissions in Luke 24:49.[102] Their presence among this group is implied in the narrative in several ways. First, since the last scene to mention them explicitly was with the apostles, it seems likely that they are among their "companions" in 24:33.[103] Second, the primary role of the women has been to witness to the resurrected Jesus—a resurrection that both the angels and Jesus have confirmed is a fulfillment of his own prophecies and the Scriptures—and this is exactly the role that the newly commissioned disciples will have when they are empowered. Thus, their label as *martyres* (witnesses) in 24:48 would recall the women who have already functioned as such, more so than even the apostles who initially rejected the content of their testimony. Third, Jesus promises that he will send "upon" the disciples what God has promised, and that they will be "clothed with power from on high" (*endysēsthe ex hypsous dynamin*, 24:49). This is a foreshadowing of the outpouring of the Holy

102. Contra Luis Menéndez-Antuña, "Male-Bonding, Female Vanishing: Representing Gendered Authority in Luke 23:26–24:53," *Early Christianity* 4 (2013): 490–506, who argues that the women "vanish" during Jesus's resurrection appearances because they are at the cross, burial, and resurrection but not mentioned explicitly after that.

103. See also Lee, *Ministry of Women*, 56.

Spirit that will be narrated in Luke's second volume, the recipients of which will be women as well as men (Acts 2:1–4, 17–21).[104]

Conclusion

The Gospel of Luke starts and ends with women who have central roles in telling the good news about Jesus. Elizabeth and Mary embrace their positions as mothers of John and Jesus and, along with Anna, testify to the divine fulfillment that is taking place in the birth of their children. At the end of his life, women who have faithfully followed Jesus continue to do so, even in his death, and are there to be the first to witness to the community that he is risen from the dead. And in the center of the narrative are women who demonstrate their extravagant love for Jesus, are committed to following Jesus in his ministry and providing for him and his community out of their own resources, show him hospitality in their homes, listen at his feet, and are even presented as narrative examples of the kinds of kingdom priorities that should be embraced by all who profess Jesus as Messiah. These women are followers who put their money where their mouth is—who engage in the kind of active discipleship that demonstrates their embrace of God's offer of salvation to the whole world through his Son.

104. Mikeal C. Parsons, *The Departure of Jesus in Luke-Acts: The Ascension Narratives in Context,* Journal for the Study of the New Testament Supplement Series 21 (Sheffield: JSOT Press, 1987), 58, argues that it also functions as a call-back and conclusion to the farewell discourse at the Last Supper.

Five

Female Discipleship in the Acts of the Apostles

In his first volume, the author of Luke-Acts portrays women as active disciples of Jesus—faithful and committed followers who anticipate Jesus's role in the kingdom of God, support his ministry, honor him with extravagant gifts, learn at his feet, exemplify godly attributes, and announce the good news of his resurrection. But in the second volume the setting changes. After only a few verses, Jesus ascends into heaven (Acts 1:9–11). As the early church begins to form and to take on the ministry of Jesus in his place, women will continue to have as great an impact as they did while they were in his presence. There will be a place for the type of female discipleship that was demonstrated and celebrated in the Gospel of Luke.

There is a strand of scholarship that sees Luke's portrayal of women in Acts as a subversion or an "undoing" of the positive portrayals of women in the Gospel of Luke. Much of this discussion is comparative: the Gospel of Luke is seen as "pro-woman," while Acts seems to reverse those gains. Some scholars point to the clear focus on the leadership of the Twelve[1] and of Paul at the expense of female leadership in the church.[2] Some see in Acts an early anticipation of

1. The Twelve are reconstituted by the addition of a male disciple who replaces Judas in Acts 1:21–26.

2. E.g., see Barbara E. Reid, "The Gospel of Luke: Friend or Foe of Women Proclaimers of the Word?," *Catholic Biblical Quarterly* 78 (2016): 1–23. Mary Rose D'Angelo, "Women in Luke-Acts: A Redactional View," *Journal of Biblical Literature* 109 (1990): 449–50, attributes this to Luke's concern for the gospel's message of the resurrection to be acceptable in the public forum. If this were Luke's primary concern, however, it seems strange that he would underscore

the prophetic role of women in the church at Pentecost, but then a deliberate failure to actually show women engaging as prophets.[3] Others draw their negative conclusions in large part from a reduction of the number of stories that center women in Acts.[4]

We will see, however, that women have more of an influence in the early Christian community than might appear on the surface. It is true that no women in Acts get the kind of airtime that male leaders, particularly Peter and Paul, receive. As the original leader of the Twelve and the most outspoken of all the apostles, Peter takes the helm in the first third of the narrative, beginning with the replacement of Judas and the Pentecost event (Acts 1–2). As Peter's prominence in the story comes to a close, the exploits of the missionary to the gentiles, Paul, dominate the narrative. Peter and Paul get almost all the speaking roles in Acts, particularly in the form of sermons and speeches.[5] I am convinced that this lack of attention on women has less to do with these two figures being *male* (and therefore a moratorium on female leaders) and more to do with their being *Peter and Paul* and the singular roles that they fill in their respective communities. As the de facto leader of the apostles, Peter takes a leadership role in the inchoate church. Likewise, it is primarily through Paul's experiences that Luke tells of the gentile mission. The narrative arc of Acts itself hints that their stories are not ultimately about them—both of their stories end abruptly with loose ends dangling.[6] Rather, the Peter and Paul storylines are vehicles by which Luke takes his audience on the

---

the role that women played in first announcing the resurrection in his own public document on Jesus's life (Luke 24:1–12)! Rikk E. Watts, "Women in the Gospels and Acts," *Crux* 35 (1999): 31, cautions against the assumption that the replacement of Judas with another male apostle or the selection of seven males in Acts 6 was theologically motivated (i.e., that God required males to lead), rather than reflecting cultural and social realities.

3. D'Angelo, "Women in Luke-Acts."

4. E.g., Jacob Jervell, "The Daughters of Abraham: Women in Acts," in *The Unknown Paul: Essays on Luke-Acts and Early Christian History*, trans. Roy A. Harrisville (Minneapolis: Augsburg, 1984), 147, describes the women in Acts as "retreating" and argues that the stories of women in Acts do not affect the narrative in any substantive way—that they could be extracted and Luke's work would be the same (150).

5. Reid, "Friend or Foe," 18.

6. The Peter-dominant thread drops after his dramatic deliverance in Acts 12, and Luke never tells us what happens to Paul once he is placed under house

journey laid out in Jesus's words in Acts 1:8: to spread the gospel from Jerusalem to Judea and Samaria and to the ends of the earth (i.e., Rome). This focus may be one reason why there are fewer stories of women in Acts than there are in the Gospel of Luke.[7]

A decrease in stories on female discipleship does not mean that Luke relegates the impact of women on the next phase of the Jesus movement to the shadows. Nor can we simply declare that the Gospel of Luke is "pro-woman" and that Acts is "anti-woman."[8] As in the first volume of his work, the *manner* with which women engage in discipleship in Acts is key—they demonstrate a discipleship consistent with Jesus's teachings on the subject, and they function as his representatives. One of the subtle ways that Luke emphasizes women's contribution in the early church is to shift his terminology for followers of Jesus. While in Luke he prefers to use the term *mathētēs* for the Twelve, in Acts he uses "brothers and sisters" (*adelphoi*)[9] and *mathētēs* interchangeably and thereby widens the reference beyond the Twelve.[10] Richard Longenecker suggests that the change indicates an emphasis in equality among Jesus's followers, downplaying any subordination that might be implied by maintaining a special title for the Twelve. The result of this shift in language is to bring together the Twelve and the remaining followers of Jesus into one family.[11]

---

arrest in Rome in Acts 28. Were these meant primarily to be about Peter and Paul, Luke has failed his audience by not addressing how their stories end.

7. Luke is drawing intentional parallels between Jesus's ministry with his disciples and Peter and Paul's ministry. E.g., Richard N. Longenecker, "Taking Up the Cross Daily: Discipleship in Luke-Acts," in *Patterns of Discipleship in the New Testament*, ed. Richard N. Longenecker (Grand Rapids: Eerdmans, 1996), 52.

8. *Pace* Turid Karlsen Seim, *The Double Message: Patterns of Gender in Luke-Acts* (Nashville: Abingdon, 1994), whose work balances the tensions here in helpful ways, and who concludes by rejecting the framing of the question to begin with: "It is a preposterous simplification to ask whether Luke's writings are friendly or hostile to women. Luke's version of the life of Jesus and of the first believers cannot be reduced either to a feminist treasure chamber or to a chamber of horrors for women's theology" (249).

9. Although it is the masculine plural form, it is best translated as "brothers and sisters" to recognize the presence of women believers in the community.

10. E.g., Acts 1:16.

11. Longenecker, "Taking Up the Cross," 72–73, also suggests that the term *adelphoi* would be more understandable to a Hellenistic audience than *mathētēs* would. The apostles themselves refer to their Jewish audiences in this familial

In this chapter, then, we will see the ways in which women are engaged in the ministry of the early church, are presented as leaders in their communities, and serve as exemplars of faithful discipleship. Rather than asking, "Where are the women who matter?" we will ask, "What do followers of Jesus *do* in Acts?" We will see that women are doing the sorts of things that disciples are expected to do, both in Jesus's teachings (from the Gospel of Luke) and in his instructions and stated expectations of what God is doing (Pentecost). Their actions align with and reflect the priorities of the early church community (Acts 2:42–47). While Luke does not continue to present the Twelve as foils for faithful discipleship in Acts as he does in the gospel, we will see that women join them as active participants in the community, and sometimes even stand out from the male leaders around them.

Our study of female discipleship in Acts will show that women are neither absent in the story of the early church nor inconsequential. Women engage in prophetic activity that demonstrates God's movement among his people and out in the world. Although often unseen, they are companions and coworkers in the ministry, and they are full members of the community. They benefit from the mutual care that defines the Way and recognize God at work in the world and among his people. They are leaders in their communities—women such as Tabitha, Lydia, and Priscilla who are exemplars of faith, generosity, hospitality, and wisdom. These characteristics and virtues awarded women in Acts reflect the "ideals of the early Church."[12]

Women Who Prophesy (Acts 2, 21)

Following the account of Jesus's ascension in Acts 1:6–11, three major events set the trajectory for Luke's second volume. In addition to their place at the beginning of the narrative, these elements of the story are important as they help shape the audience's understanding of the early church and its expectation of God's movement within it. First is the task of replacing Judas so that the Twelve are reconstituted (1:12–26). Shortly afterward, the events of Pentecost take place (2:1–41).

---

language (Acts 2:29; 3:17; 7:2; 13:26, 38; 22:1; 23:1, 6; 28:17), and in Acts 6:1–7 both terms are used interchangeably to refer to the larger body of believers.

12. Teresa J. Calpino, *Women, Work and Leadership in Acts*, Wissenschaftliche Untersuchungen zum Neuen Testament 361 (Tübingen: Mohr Siebeck, 2014), 2.

Last, Luke describes what life was like in the early church—how the new community of believers engaged with each other in worship and in service (2:42–47).

These opening scenes are not without some ambiguity, particularly regarding women's presence. The ambiguity carries over from the ending of the Gospel of Luke, where it is likely—but not made explicit—that there are women among the "companions" of the apostles, and that it is this same group that experiences multiple appearances of Jesus, eats with him, receives the promise of the Holy Spirit, and witnesses Jesus's ascension. In his overlapping account of the ascension in Acts 1:6–11, Luke again lacks specificity about who witnesses it. Most likely he is referring to the last group mentioned in the gospel (Acts 1:6). Adding to the ambiguity are the two men in white who suddenly appear when Jesus ascends in Acts 1:10. While clearly a call back to the resurrection scene in Luke 24:4–9 (the audience would interpret the two men as the same two characters the women encounter at the tomb), this time Luke has the men address the "men of Galilee" (*andres Galilaioi*, 1:11) rather than the women. In the same way, although only certain males are considered as replacements for Judas in Acts 1:12–26, there is an emphasis on the involvement of women—with particular attention to Mary the mother of Jesus—in prayerful preparation for the selection of the apostle.[13] Thus, these women have a profound impact on the trajectory of leadership among the believers (1:14).

Women are also likely to be part of the larger group of 120 to whom Peter gives his speech about the necessity of replacing Judas (1:15–22). While some scholars argue that the male term "brothers" (*adelphoi*) refers to both men and women,[14] Turid Karlsen Seim notes that the addition of "men" (*andres*) makes that assumption more complicated (1:16).[15]

13. That their prayers are directed toward such a task is implied by the sandwiching of this account with the list of the remaining apostles (1:13) and then the selection of Matthias (1:15–26).

14. Alfons Weiser, "Die Rolle der Frau in der urchristlichen Bewegung," in *Die Frau im Urchristentum*, ed. Gerhard Dautzenberg, Helmut Merklein, and Karlheinz Müller, Quaestiones Disputatae 95 (Freiburg: Herder, 1983), 163.

15. Seim, *Double Message*, 136–37, does not think this is an indication that Luke is trying to make women "completely invisible," but rather that it is a reflection of the early Christian belief that the role of an apostle was considered "almost programmatically restricted to men."

However, while she interprets the presence of this masculine term as an indication that Luke is excluding women from among the 120, other elements of the text challenge this reading. For example, Luke describes the 120 as a "crowd," which, in the Gospel of Luke and in Acts, overwhelmingly refers to a group of men *and* women and would be interpreted as such by his audience.[16] Moreover, Luke describes those involved in the choosing of Matthias as praying during the process (1:24). It would be strange if some of the believers just portrayed as constantly devoting themselves to prayer *among the apostles* are now to be understood as excluded from that activity in the selection of the newest apostle (1:14). The narrative rather suggests that these women were also engaged in the process of apostolic selection. This is reinforced in the following chapter when Luke describes them "all" gathered on the day of Pentecost, surely referring back to the 120 (*pantes*, 2:1). And there is no doubt that women have a crucial role to play in this next event.

Luke describes the day of Pentecost in terms that underscore the comprehensive activity of the Holy Spirit: they, both men and women, were *all* together in one place (*pantes*, 2:1), the Holy Spirit filled the *entire* house (*holon tov oikon*, 2:2), a tongue rested on *each* of them (*eph hena hekaston autōn*, 2:3), and they were *all* filled with the Holy Spirit (*pantes*, 2:4).[17] The coming of the Holy Spirit takes place in a house, rather than the temple, and thus is active in a sphere of society where women had the highest measure of responsibility.[18] Female in-

16. Of the sixty-three total uses of the term *ochlos* in Luke-Acts, none specifically describes a crowd as all male in the gospel (only the crowds at the trials of Jesus were most likely composed of all males as the trials involved the Jewish council; Luke 22:47; 23:4). In Acts, the only all-male "crowd" is made up of priests, which functions narratively as a foil to the religious authorities who reject God by having Stephen murdered (6:8–8:1). Conversely, Luke explicitly describes women as part of the crowds in several places, and they are part of the larger groups coming to the faith in the beginnings of the church (Luke 8:42, 45; 11:27; Acts 11:24–26).

17. The emphasis on "all" also connects to Joel's promise that all who call on the name of the Lord will be saved (Joel 2:32; Acts 2:21).

18. Seim, *Double Message*, 137–46: "When women in the story appear in the house, they are therefore not on the periphery, but are in a central position in relation to the place where the community of faith has much of its life. . . . At the same time, the public sphere retains its importance as the place of power" (146). Here Seim sees another element of the "double message" where culturally the house is restricted as private, yet it becomes central to the early Christian

volvement in the activity of the Holy Spirit is further emphasized by Peter's speech, in part comprising Joel's prophetic words (Joel 2:28–32; 3:1–5 LXX).[19] For our purposes, the key aspect of Peter's use of Joel is twofold: (1) he cites this prophecy to explain the believers' speaking in tongues and the crowd's ability to understand what is being said, and (2) he highlights that within the prophecy itself is the promise that both men and women will prophesy. Thus, Peter interprets Joel's anticipation that the prophetic activity of men *and* women will be an indication that the day of the Lord has come and is being fulfilled *at the precise moment that he is speaking to the crowd.* By placing these words on Peter's lips amid the flurry of the Holy Spirit, Luke validates the prophetic activity of women alongside men *that is already taking place.*[20]

Peter is not citing Joel's prophecy to predict some future event. One of the pieces scholars sometimes give as evidence of Luke's antifeminist thread in Acts is that Luke here gives the women no direct speeches or prophetic words. However, Acts 2 *is* depicting female disciples as engaging in prophetic activity during Pentecost. Furthermore, Luke restricts the designation "prophecy" to just a few utterances in Acts. Apart from the fulfillment of Joel's prophecy in Acts 2, the only other instances where Luke describes speech as prophetic activity are when twelve disciples engage in prophecy after receiving the Holy Spirit from Paul in Acts 19:6 (their gender is not indicated, and the content of their prophecy is not included) and when Agabus accurately predicts Paul's looming imprisonment in Acts 21:10–11 (his prophetic words are included).[21] Thus, a lack of female speeches

community and so the women's influence would be felt there in that community. Perhaps, however, this is Luke's way of redefining power. We have already seen that the strict division of public and private was not consistently practiced in the first century (see chapter 1). Instead, it might be helpful to think of the focus of power within the community being diverted to the household—a place in which women could have significant influence and responsibility.

19. *Pace* Seim, *Double Message*, 136.

20. Seim, *Double Message*, 167, helpfully points out that throughout his speech Peter continually directs the crowd's attention to the activity (done by men *and women*) that is going on around them. Lora Angeline B. Embudo, "Women Vis-à-Vis Prophecy in Luke-Acts: Part 2," *Asian Journal of Pentecostal Studies* 20 (2017): 134, argues that Luke's insertion of *ge* in Acts 2:18a emphasizes the impartiality of the gift of prophecy on both men and women.

21. Other speeches and sermons might fall under the broad category of prophecy, but Luke does not describe them in this way, and so it must be

specifically designated as prophecy does not in itself indicate Luke's dismissal or dilution of their prophetic activity after all.[22]

Since Pentecost serves as the programmatic vision for God's community in Acts (followed by summary statements about church life), the role of women on that day should be understood as part of that vision for the church. Luke indicates that some women are still engaging in prophecy long after the day of Pentecost. In Acts 21:8–9 he reintroduces Philip the Evangelist to the narrative. Among Philip's household are his four daughters, whom Luke describes as having the gift of prophecy. Although we are not given additional information about the content of their prophecies (Luke does not include direct prophetic utterances by the women), he does suggest that their prophetic activity is a continual practice.[23] The practice of prophecy is further accentuated by the Agabus account immediately following, which demonstrates that prophecy is alive and well among the believers, that the prophetic utterances of these disciples is trustworthy and accurate (Paul does indeed end up in chains as Agabus predicted in 21:11), and that female disciples have an active role in the prophetic activity of the church and are even known primarily by that prophetic activity.[24] Themes found in Joel 2 such as the presence of the

---

inferred (for example, Stephen's speech before his martyrdom could be considered a prophetic condemnation of the Jewish opposition who seized him; Acts 6:8–8:1). Luke avoids describing the slave girl's actions as prophecy, instead ascribing them to a spirit of divination (*pneuma pythōna*, 16:16).

22. Working with a much broader definition of prophecy, F. Scott Spencer, "Out of Mind, Out of Voice: Slave-Girls and Prophetic Daughters in Luke-Acts," *Biblical Interpretation* 7 (1999): 136, argues that the presence of Mary in Acts 1:14 and the prophecy from Joel in Acts 2 prepare the audience to anticipate a revitalized female prophetic voice, only to be disappointed with failures such as Sapphira. However, Sapphira is presented as a foil to true discipleship, not a representative of it, and she is not condemned because she is a woman, since she does exactly what her husband does (Acts 5:1–11).

23. The use of the present participle, *prophēteuousai*, connotes ongoing action. Contra D'Angelo, "Women in Luke-Acts," 453, who argues that they are not depicted as prophets in Acts because "they are not explicitly named as prophets, nor are any prophecies attributed to them." However, by this definition, only Agabus would be considered a prophet, which is simply too narrow a definition, considering how many others are engaged in prophetic activity in Luke-Acts. Moreover, it appears that they were well-known as prophets in early church tradition (Eusebius, *Historia ecclesiastica* 3.31).

24. Embudo, "Women," 136, believes Luke includes the content of Agabus's

Holy Spirit, the prophesying and proclamation of God's salvation, and the offer of that salvation to all are key features of the early church and of those who follow Jesus.[25]

Unseen Women (Acts 1–2, 6, 12)

Counting the number of stories of women in Acts and comparing the result with the number of stories of women in Luke might lead to the conclusion that women were less important at the beginnings of the early church than they were during Jesus's ministry. But this approach to Acts inevitably misses the sense of the whole. Often women should be assumed to be present in the narrative, even when their presence is not explicit—what we might call the "unseen" women. In this section we will look at ways in which female disciples are there in the mix of things, actively engaged in discipleship along with the men and serving as valued members of the early Christian community. We will also look at the story of Rhoda as an example of an unseen woman—a disciple who becomes the first in her household to "see" how God has saved Peter, even as she is ignored and dismissed by her fellow believers.

We have already seen that women are in the new community of believers. Acts 1:14 singles out Mary the mother of Jesus and certain women as participants alongside the remaining apostles and Jesus's brothers who have now come to their postresurrection faith. Luke depicts them as devoting themselves to prayer as a group with a single-minded focus. Although the spotlight quickly shifts to the male apostles who need to be reconstituted and who will lead the fledgling community, if we are looking for active female discipleship, we have

---

(and not Philip's daughters') prophecy because it propels the narrative forward. But that does not explain why Luke calls attention to the four female prophets as well. Since what is said about them does not technically move the narrative forward, the impact seems to be to consider their importance as part of the larger group of Christians who were being moved by the Holy Spirit and could see where Paul's actions would take him, even when he could not (Acts 21:12). They help bolster the credibility of the consensus and contribute to the foreboding turn of the narrative.

25. Longenecker, "Taking Up the Cross," 71–72, lists "the major themes of discipleship" in the gospel that recur in Acts, such as the shaping of the apostolic tradition, dependence on God in prayer, ultimate allegiance to Jesus, and a concern for the outcast.

found some. Mary and these women have influence as insiders who are considered important enough to be engaging in prayer alongside the apostles (the emphasis is on the "togetherness" of their activity). Given that this second volume of a two-volume work picks up from and overlaps with the ending of the gospel, it seems likely that Luke's earliest audience would have assumed that these women were the same women who discovered Jesus's empty tomb and were the first to share the gospel message that he had risen from the dead.[26] As I argue in the previous chapter, these women were privy to more than one of Jesus's appearances; they were also recipients of Jesus's commission along with their fellow male disciples (Luke 24:33, 36–53).[27] With regard to the activities of the Holy Spirit at Pentecost, these women are likely to be prophesying, fulfilling Joel's promise even as Peter speaks to the crowd. A careful reading of these opening chapters, then, involves seeing women as integral participants in the events of Acts 1–2, even if they have no speaking parts.

Female disciples are also active beyond Pentecost. In Acts 6:1–6, the plight of the Hellenistic widows presents the second greatest internal threat to the thriving of the community of Jesus followers.[28] Their inclusion at this crucial juncture (after the internal crisis of

26. Keener, *Acts*, 748. On the addition of *kai teknois* (and children) in the Western text of Acts 1:14, see Walter Thiele, "Eine Bemerkung zu Act 1,14," *Zeitschrift für die neutestamentliche Wissenschaft und die Kunde der älteren Kirche* 53 (1962): 110–11, who argues that this is evidence of the "anti-feminist tendency" of the text because it denigrates the women by lumping them together with children; and Curt Niccum, "A Note on Acts 1:14," *Novum Testamentum* 36 (1994): 196–99, who argues that this was added to make sense of the numeric discrepancy between the 120 mentioned in Acts 1:15 and the much smaller list of apostles, women, and brothers.

27. See also Acts 10:41, where the "chosen" witnesses to which Peter refers, and the witnesses mentioned by Paul in Acts 13:31, would have been understood as the same group of believers, which would have included the women. See also Richard Bauckham, *Gospel Women: Studies of the Named Women in the Gospels* (Grand Rapids: Eerdmans, 2002), 306–7.

28. The first is the deception of Ananias and Sapphira (Acts 5:1–11). As she is clearly not a model of discipleship, I will not devote space to Sapphira's story here. However, (1) Sapphira's actions prove that not all female disciples are exemplars of faithfulness in the gospels, and (2) Luke presents the husband and wife as equal partners-in-crime. Her determination to carry on with the lie even when her husband is not around indicates that she had just as much ownership of the plot as he did.

Ananias and Sapphira's deception and before Stephen's martyrdom and the aftereffects of organized persecution against the church) draws attention to the priority of their plight. Luke considers these women to be a vital part of a community that is literally fighting for its life. Their story in Acts 6 is yet another indication that women are in the background as active participants in the Way.[29] And there is no indication that Luke portrays them or the ministry from which they will benefit as somehow less important than other types (and thus the recipients) of ministry. Just as I have argued in the previous chapter that Luke does not prioritize the listening of Mary *over against* the service of her sister Martha in Luke 10:40–41, I think that a similar dynamic is at play in Acts 6:1–6.[30] The apostles are not denigrating the ministry of table-waiting (*diakonein trapezais*, 6:2) in favor of a more superior task (preaching the word of God, *ton logon tou theou*).[31] They are delegating responsibility in a way that makes the most sense of the roles that they already play in the community. Several clues in the narrative indicate that this is the case. First, the apostles *themselves* call the meeting once the need is brought to their attention. If the matter were too trivial a matter for them to address, why would they bother with any part of it? Second, the emphasis is on the problem of *neglect* (*paretheōrounto, kataleipsantas*, 6:1, 2). The apostles want to

29. Joel B. Green, *The Gospel of Luke*, New International Commentary on the New Testament (Grand Rapids: Eerdmans, 1997), 639, observes Luke's penchant for using widows as examples of piety or the recipients of God's goodness. Eben Scheffler, "Caring for the Needy in the Acts of the Apostles," *Neotestamentica* 50 (2016): 154, argues that the concern for widows also reflects Luke's positive attitude toward women.

30. Contra Elisabeth Schüssler Fiorenza, "A Feminist Critical Interpretation for Liberation: Martha and Mary: Lk. 10:38–42," *Religion and Intellectual Life* (1986): 30.

31. See Adele Reinhartz, "From Narrative to History: The Resurrection of Mary and Martha," in *"Women Like This": New Perspectives on Jewish Women in the Greco-Roman World*, ed. Amy-Jill Levine (Atlanta: Scholars Press, 1991), 169, who argues that the use of *diakonia* elsewhere in Luke-Acts indicates a broad concept of serving (Luke 4:39; 8:3; 10:40; 12:37; 17:8; 22:26–27). See Warren Carter, "Getting Martha Out of the Kitchen: Luke 10:38–42 Again," *Catholic Biblical Quarterly* 58 (1996): 264–80, and John N. Collins, "Did Luke Intend a Disservice to Women in the Martha and Mary Story?," *Biblical Theology Bulletin* 28 (1998): 104–11, who discuss the range of meanings of the term in Luke-Acts, from table service to leadership and proclamation (which would make it quite odd, then, for the apostles to use the term to describe a second-tiered ministry).

avoid the neglect that threatens either of the ministries: the neglect of the Hellenistic widows is wrong, as would be the neglect of their own ministry of preaching the word of God.[32] The wording suggests that their concern was that they simply lacked the time to do both, and that the preaching of the word was the better fit for them because they had had the most exposure to Jesus's teachings.[33] Third, Luke continues to validate the importance of the ministry to the Hellenistic widows by listing the names of the men who will lead it, mimicking the list of apostles he gives in Acts 1:13, and depicting the transference of responsibility and blessing from the apostles to the seven by the laying on of hands (6:6).[34] All of these details indicate that the apostles gave the ministry to these widows high priority because they were regarded as important members of the community. The importance of this ministry is accentuated in the following pericope, which focuses on Stephen, the man who sits atop the list of the seven and who serves as the spokesperson for the group. So committed to preaching the word, he will die for it, and it is his death that sparks a diaspora of believers who flee Jerusalem but continue to preach the word (8:4). Because both men and women are the targets of this persecution (8:3), we know that both men and women are among those who are preaching the word as they go.[35] Not only, then, are female disciples deeply

32. See Joel B. Green, *Practicing Theological Interpretation: Engaging Biblical Texts for Faith and Formation* (Grand Rapids: Baker Academic, 2011), 56–70, who argues that Luke's concern is not merely a practical one (Do the widows have enough to eat?), but that the problem with the neglect of the widows is a symptom that reflects a deeper theological problem within the church of the apostles' failure in allowing fracturing within the community—more evidence of neglect. Thus, he sees in this text an indictment of the apostles and an "authorization of fresh leadership for the mission" (69).

33. The sense of urgency here fits well with Luke's outline to trace the spread of the gospel from Jerusalem to the ends of the earth (Acts 1:8), a process that officially begins in earnest immediately after Stephen's martyrdom in Acts 8.

34. See also Scheffler, "Caring for the Needy," 137. We cannot determine why no women were selected to minister to the Hellenistic widows. I would caution against inferring from the all-male list some evidence of early Christian opposition to female leadership. Luke does not justify the choices that are made. Perhaps the deliberate comparison to the male apostles in Acts 1 has some influence on the choice.

35. William D. Booth, "The Open Door for Women Preachers: Acts 2:17, 18; 21:9; Romans 10:15; Ephesians 4:11," *Journal of Religious Thought* 50 (1994): 110.

involved in the beginnings of the church in Acts 1–2, but they are engaged in the spread of the gospel as it moves out of Jerusalem.

Rhoda is another woman who can be described as "unseen," although in her case she is ignored by characters within the narrative itself. Acts 12:6–19 recounts Peter's dramatic escape from prison. The persecution of Christians is heating up, and some of the apostles are now experiencing the same fate as Stephen. Most recently, Herod Agrippa I executed James the son of Zebedee (12:2), and the positive reaction from the Jewish opposition inspires Herod Agrippa to arrest Peter also (12:3). Luke is an artful storyteller and, as in the Stephen episode, fashions his narrative to draw parallels between Peter's experience here and Jesus's own experience: both arrests happen during Passover; both are done to appease the opposition to him and to his followers; both await their fate while being surrounded by soldiers. But while Jesus and Stephen are both executed, Peter escapes jail miraculously. An angel wakens Peter in his cell, instructs him to get ready, leads him past the guards, and walks him through a gate that opens of its own accord (12:7–10). Only when he is outside is Peter aware that what he has experienced is a reality and not just a good dream (12:9, 11).

Upon that realization, he makes his way to a safe place within the city—the house of Mary the mother of John Mark. Here we have a second Mary who is deeply involved in the gathering of the Jerusalem congregation. No husband is mentioned—it is *her* house that appears to be the centralized meeting place for disciples—and her son John Mark will later become a missionary in Paul's ministry (Acts 13:5). Luke states that "many" were gathered at her house in prayer, presumably for Peter and for all those who were being persecuted for their faith in Jesus (12:12).[36] Peter knocks on the outer gate, and the servant, Rhoda, goes to answer it. Recognizing Peter's voice, she is so overcome with joy that she runs to tell the believers inside the house. But she forgets to unlock the gate to let Peter in (12:13–14). Rather than share in her joy or accept her claim, the believers think that she

36. We cannot know the subject of their prayers, but the context of threatening persecution in the narrative implies that the ever-present threat was their focus. The scene also recalls another time when the believers were gathered together after Jesus's death (Luke 24:33–36), although the resurrected Jesus did not have to wait for someone to let him in—he simply appeared suddenly in the room.

has lost her mind. While Luke does not state that the reason for this dismissal has to do with her lower social status, her household position would not have helped her case.

Rhoda, despite being brushed off, is so insistent that Peter is outside that they must find another explanation: perhaps she has seen "his angel" (i.e., they think he is already dead and that she is seeing his spiritual form; 12:15). Matching Rhoda's persistent exclamations, Peter persistently continues to knock on the gate, prompting some in the group finally to open it. At their "amazement," Peter explains what has happened to him and urges them to tell James and the other believers how God has brought him out of prison (12:16–17). Then he leaves.

In many ways Rhoda functions as the ultimate example of an "unseen" woman. Luke arranges the scene around her and the response to her testimony while leaving Peter outside in the street. He could just as easily have told the story of Peter's escape while leaving out the embarrassing—and in some ways comedic—details of a whole household's disbelief.[37] Rhoda is the only one to immediately believe what she hears—that Peter is alive and standing outside the house. The other disciples dismiss the news by dismissing the messenger—she must be crazy![38] Yet she refuses to give up. The "joke" is on the believers who do not believe! A scene where the female slave knows more about what is going on than her owner would certainly catch the ear of the audience. Despite being disregarded by the very people who should recognize the work of God when they see it or hear of it (remember that they are praying at the very moment she delivers the news), she persists in her story, convincing them that she heard

37. Richard I. Pervo, *Profit with Delight: The Literary Genre of the Acts of the Apostles* (Philadelphia: Fortress, 1987), 12–63, argues that the point of Peter being left outside is to provide humor to hold the attention of the audience.

38. See Patrick E. Spencer, "'Mad' Rhoda in Acts 12:12–17: Disciple Exemplar," *Catholic Biblical Quarterly* 79 (2017): 282–98, for a fascinating study of the Greco-Roman narrative convention of comical scenes that involve a bumbling servant. Spencer argues that Rhoda belongs to a group of "model disciples such as Paul, the women at the resurrection, and the servants in the parable of the watchful servants," and sees her story as one that contrasts with the failure of the Twelve to be watchful (e.g., in Gethsemane). The charge of madness is the same charge Festus levels against Paul (*mainē*, 12:15; 26:24)! Spencer sees the identical responses of the believers who are huddling in the house and Festus as an intentional parallel (294). Note that Paul implicitly accuses Festus of huddling "in a corner" (*ou gar estin en gōnia pepragmenon touto*, 26:26).

something worth checking out, even if they will not concede that it is Peter at their doorstep as she has claimed. Her actions are even more noteworthy because her status as a slave would have been considerably lower than that of the rest of those in the house.

Luke presents her persistence alongside Peter's persistent knocking, which draws a connection between her and Peter and over against the believers who fail to believe. As in Luke 24:11, the disciples' lack of belief reflects poorly on them; it does not reflect poorly on the women who tell the good news, or indicate that Luke is silencing women.[39] Ultimately, Rhoda's testimony is proven true to the disciples (even though the audience knows it all along)—the "insiders" were wrong about Peter and therefore wrong about what God was doing.[40] The scene also allows the audience to see the journey that the believers in the house take from unbelief to confirmation of Rhoda's claim as they move from inside the house to the outer gate. Of all the people in the household, an ignored and underestimated servant girl is the one who believes the miracle of Peter's escape and God's provision and acts accordingly—with joy.

39. *Pace* Amanda C. Miller, "Cut from the Same Cloth: A Study of Female Patrons in Luke-Acts and the Roman Empire," *Review and Expositor* 114 (2017): 206. See also P. Spencer, "'Mad' Rhoda," 288.

40. Contra J. Albert Harrill, "The Dramatic Function of the Running Slave Rhoda (Acts 12.13–16): A Piece of Greco-Roman Comedy," *New Testament Studies* 46 (2000): 150–57, who argues that the theme of the bumbling servant would also include the common negative characteristic of selfishness and opportunism. There is no evidence of this in Rhoda's case. The only emotion or thought that dominates her actions is that of joy at knowing Peter has escaped with his life (Acts 12:14). Harrill underestimates the possibility that a narrative can subvert the audience's expectation of character tropes to prove an entirely different point.

Similarly, that ultimately Peter's words persuade the believers does not take away from Rhoda's voice or cast her in a negative light (contra F. S. Spencer, "Out of Mind," 145). Spencer neglects the interplay between the narrative and the audience who hears it. Much like a play or movie where the audience knows much more than the characters in the story do, so Luke's audience knows that Rhoda is right—she is not crazy, and she has not seen Peter's ghost. Luke tells the story in such a way as to present her as the one who sees what God is doing before the other disciples do. While she may not realize this is God's work at first, Luke's audience surely does. So she is in good company, as Peter also does not immediately recognize what has happened to him in the moment he is released—he considers whether it is a dream (Acts 12:9).

Spiritual Leaders (Acts 9, 16, 18)

Several women in Acts prove to be influential community members. Tabitha, Lydia, and Priscilla stand out for their leadership, their contribution to the church, their model behavior of hospitality, and their exemplary faith. While it is possible to overlook them in favor of other leaders who get more consistent narrative attention (like Peter or Paul), a robust understanding of discipleship must consider the stories and actions of these women.[41]

Tabitha

The first female leader Luke presents with detail in Acts is Tabitha, whom he describes as a disciple (*mathētria*, 9:36).[42] Her story begins with a statement resembling an encomium: Luke introduces her by describing her attributes—she "was full of good works and acts of charity" (9:36). But the audience does not meet Tabitha directly or witness her good works. By the time Luke narrates the scene, she has died from a sickness (9:37). This abruptness has the effect of inviting the audience to feel Tabitha's loss alongside her community. A response of mourning is appropriate: Luke highlights her beloved status within the community by recounting their care of her body (9:37) as well as their emotional reaction to her passing—the widows weep and show Peter the clothing that she had made for them (9:39). Even though she has died, representatives of the disciples at Joppa are sent by her community to Peter, with the request that he come to them (9:38). When he arrives, Peter empties the room, kneels and prays, commands Tabitha to "get up," takes her by the hand to help her now-living body to rise, then summons her community to show them that she is alive (9:40–41).

While Tabitha has no direct speech, her reputation—born of her actions—speaks volumes. One of the most important features of Tabitha's story is that she is the only woman the New Testament

41. Teresa Calpino, "Tabitha and Lydia: Models of Early Christian Women Leaders," *Biblical Archaeology Review* 42 (2016): 20: "When reading Acts, it is easy to dismiss them as 'minor characters,' especially when they appear next to the likes of Peter and Paul. But careful exegesis reveals that it is the women, not the apostles, who draw the focus in the passages in which they appear."

42. Luke also gives her Greek name, Dorcas (9:36).

introduces with the feminine form of the word "disciple"; in fact, in terms of narrative order, we learn that she is a disciple before we learn her name (or names).[43] By way of first impressions, Luke informs his audience that Tabitha is more than just a woman who is beloved in her community. She is one among many disciples in Joppa, and mention of her among a significant contingent of faithful followers suggests that she stands out.[44] Tabitha is known for her care for others, particularly those most socially vulnerable. A tangible reminder of her generosity is the clothing she has made, which the widows in her community show Peter as a way of honoring her.[45] It is possible that she was a widow herself (Luke mentions no husband), but one who had enough resources to be a benefactor.[46] The local widows were the ones to experience the benefit of this generosity and skill, since they are the ones who display the most emotion and show Peter the clothing she has made. But this emphasis on the widows does not mean that her discipleship was valued by that part of the community alone. The larger group of disciples in Joppa take initiative after her death, and it is a pair of men who bring Peter to her house.[47] Tabitha's importance as a disciple in her community might also be indicated by Peter's willingness to come immediately to Joppa. Moreover, the narrative gives no indication that the other disciples expected Peter to raise Tabitha from the dead—they request only that he come to them. That they do not expect a miracle may be an indication, as Teresa Calpino suggests, that their hope is for Peter to come and fill for a time the hole in leadership that she has left in the community.[48]

43. Calpino, *Women*, 2, 144.

44. Mikeal C. Parsons, *Acts*, Paideia Commentaries on the New Testament (Grand Rapids: Baker Academic, 2008), 138, argues that this introduction of "a certain female disciple" (*tis ēn mathētria*, 9:36) suggests that there are more female disciples than just her.

45. And we have already seen that spinning and making cloth (woolworking) was considered the activity of a virtuous and industrious woman.

46. Calpino, *Women*, analyzes Lydia and Tabitha as a pair who share some important qualities, such as being presented as (1) working women who are not dependent on a man, (2) childless, (3) women in primary positions in the narrative, and (4) women in charge of a household. She also observes that both Peter and Paul are strongly urged to enter their households (3).

47. Calpino, *Women*, 141.

48. Calpino, "Tabitha and Lydia," 20–21. This is speculation, but it is plau-

Tabitha's provision for widows certainly contributes to her recognition as a disciple and the community respect she receives. Since Jews regarded dispensing charity (*eleēmosynōn*, 9:36) as enacting God's righteousness, her actions would have been viewed as having an impact that went beyond the benefit of the individuals who received it.[49] The importance of giving is also consistent with Luke's concern for the marginalized as well as the apostles' previous concern for widows recounted in Acts 6:1–6. Thus, we see Tabitha caring for widows just as did prominent male leaders, an indication that the care for widows was a much-needed and widespread ministry within the early church.

Tabitha's story also has clear parallels with the raising of Jairus's daughter in Luke 8:40–42, 49–56.[50] The scenes are remarkably similar, with bodies in the house and a contingent of mourners present. Peter's actions are also like those of Jesus: he sends people out of the room, directly commands her to "get up" (*anastēthi*, Acts 9:40), and takes Tabitha by the hand, as Jesus does Jairus's daughter (Luke 8:40–42, 49–56). With these connections, Luke creates an anticipation from his audience that God will do through Peter what he did through Jesus—raise the woman from the dead.

But there are some significant differences as well. Jairus's daughter is nameless—she is important only insofar as she relates to Jairus, a leader of the synagogue (Luke 8:41). She provides an opportunity for Luke to demonstrate Jesus's power in raising her from the dead. In the case of Tabitha, though, Luke establishes her importance as a disciple in her own right and as a beloved member of her community.[51] In this short episode the focus is first and foremost on Tabitha and not on Peter—on

sible and would be consistent with what we are told of Tabitha's importance and reverence in Joppa.

49. See Ivoni Richter Reimer, *Women in the Acts of the Apostles: A Feminist Liberation Perspective*, trans. L. Maloney (Minneapolis: Fortress, 1995), 36–44, and Calpino, *Women*, 154. See also the link between almsgiving and righteousness in Luke 11:41 and 12:33. Rabbinic sources linked acts of charity to righteousness in their interpretation of Scripture and in their use of the term *tzedakah* (righteousness) for almsgiving—e.g., Sukkah 49b; Bava Batra 9a.

50. James R. Edwards, "Parallels and Patterns between Luke and Acts," *Bulletin for Biblical Research* 27 (2017): 488, also sees parallels between the raising of the centurion's servant in Luke 7:2–10.

51. It is also significant that, in the companion account of the healing of Aeneas immediately before Tabitha's story, no personal or relational details are given of the man that is healed (Acts 9:32–35).

her value within the community and the relief that they experience when she is restored.[52] More importantly for the purposes of the narrative, her resurrection has a ripple effect: the event becomes known throughout Joppa, resulting in "many people believing in the Lord" (Acts 9:42).[53] Thus, a woman with humble ministry to the socially vulnerable becomes the avenue by which the gospel takes hold in the town of Joppa.[54]

Lydia

The second female leader in Acts appears in the middle of the account of the spread of the gospel to the gentiles—during the second of the three Pauline missionary journeys. Lydia's conversion is found in Acts 16:11–15, and she makes a final brief appearance in 16:40.

After revisiting some of the churches he planted on his first missionary journey, Paul sets his sights on Bithynia. Unexpectedly, the Spirit prevents him and his entourage from entering the region (16:7). So they head to Troas. While there, Paul has a vision of a Macedonian

52. Calpino, *Women*, 139: "This story was not a portrait of Peter and his actions, but was instead a narrative of the encounter between the apostle and an important disciple in Joppa who, through her independence, righteousness and service to her community, provided a powerful *exemplum* to the audience of Acts. Even though Peter may have performed the miracle, Tabitha's character carried the pathos and driving concern of the story."

53. In Acts, belief happens most often as a result of hearing the word, and also after some displays of supernatural power (4:4; 5:14; 8:12, 13; 11:21; 13:12, 48; 14:1; 16:34; 17:12, 34; 18:8; 19:18).

54. See Rick Strelan, "Tabitha: The Gazelle of Joppa (Acts 9:36–41)," *Biblical Theology Bulletin* 39 (2009): 77–86, who argues that Tabitha's name is a metaphor for proselytes, and that this episode is best understood in light of Luke's emphasis on gentiles coming to the faith in Acts 10–11 and Acts 15. However, I find more convincing Amy-Jill Levine, "Tabitha/Dorcas, Spinning Off Cultural Criticism," in *Delightful Acts: New Essays on Canonical and Noncanonical Acts*, ed. Harold W. Attridge, Dennis R. MacDonald, and Clare K. Rothschild, Wissenschaftliche Untersuchungen zum Neuen Testament 391 (Tübingen: Mohr Siebeck, 2017), who argues that Luke's audience would not have made the connections to this animal symbolism, and provides convincing evidence that Tabitha is presented as fully Jewish in the narrative. Regardless of her ethnicity or religious affiliation, the primary identifier for Luke is that Tabitha is a *mathētria*. J. David Woodington, "Charity and Deliverance from Death in the Accounts of Tabitha and Cornelius," *Catholic Biblical Quarterly* 79 (2017): 634–50, connects the Tabitha and Cornelius accounts, as both practice charity and are "resurrected" because of it.

man begging him to come to Macedonia and help them (16:9), and he responds immediately, interpreting the vision as God's call to preach the good news to the Macedonian people (16:10). This is how Paul ends up in Philippi, a Roman colony in Macedonia.

On the Sabbath, Paul and his companions go down to the river, where they suspect there will be a place of prayer. There they encounter a group of women engaged in worship. Luke introduces one of these women by name. Lydia is described as a worshiper of God and a dealer of purple cloth (16:14a–b). She listens to the Christians who have joined their prayer group. When the Lord opens her heart (16:14c), she listens eagerly to Paul's message, and the result is that Paul immediately baptizes her and her household. The story ends with her insistence that Paul and his companions stay in her home (16:15).

Much ink has been spilled in an effort to understand who Lydia is in terms of her social and religious status, because it is not common for a woman of the time to have a professional occupation outside the home and apart from any mention of a husband. It is also rare for Luke to mention someone's occupation, so the description of her job should draw the attention of the reader. The discussion of her social status centers on three major areas of Lydia's life: her ethnic background, her occupation, and her marital status. Many interpret Lydia's activity of riverside prayer as an indication that she is a proselyte to Judaism. As we've seen, after first describing her as a worshiper of God, Luke states that Lydia is a merchant: she is a dealer in purple cloth, not a seamstress or maker of the material (*porphyropōlis*, 16:14).[55] Whether she sells the most expensive material or the knock-off purple material used by aspiring lower classes, Luke's description of her occupation has no hint of negativity.[56] Concerning her marital status, Luke makes no

55. Teresa J. Calpino, "'The Lord Opened Her Heart': Boundary Crossing in Acts 16,13–15," *Annali di Storia dell'Esegesi* 28 (2011): 84, observes that Lydia is not identified with typical markers of ideal Roman womanhood (such as being a mother or a nurturer, being modest, and being industrious in the home), and that "worshiper of God" replaces these.

56. Calpino, *Women*, 202. Contra Alexandra Gruca-Macaulay, *Lydia as a Rhetorical Construct in Acts*, Emory Studies in Early Christianity 18 (Atlanta: SBL Press, 2016), who devotes a good bit of her argument debunking the assumption that Lydia was high status, and therefore rejects the argument that Luke's audience would have automatic positive association with her. However, Luke's presentation of Lydia as a convert who acts with urgency produces a combined effect that at least challenges any negative stereotypes that would have been applied to Lydia.

mention of a husband or a male guardian. Lydia's ability to make her own choices about religion (including for "her household") and to offer hospitality from her own home suggests that she was the decision-maker for herself and those who worked for and lived with her.[57]

Although relatively brief, Lydia's story has a profound impact on the depiction of female discipleship in Acts. Luke invites the audience to see that there is a connection between Lydia's response to the gospel and her subsequent actions toward Paul and his coworkers. One of the most important characteristics of the narrative is its sense of urgency. It begins with Paul's vision and the frantic call to "come and help." Once in Philippi, Paul and his companions seek out people who are praying—it is the first action we see them taking in the new city. Lydia's response matches that sense of urgency. Her initial response to the gospel is to listen (16:14a), but Luke soon upgrades it to "listening eagerly" at the prompting of God, who opens her heart (16:14c). This emphasis on listening is reminiscent of Mary's actions in Luke 10:38–42, and we have already seen that listening to the gospel is far from passive.[58] Listening is a sign of discipleship.

Other elements in the story are reminiscent of a call narrative.[59] Lydia's actions are prompted by God, she responds unconditionally to his prompting, and the nature of her discipleship is indicated imme-

57. Calpino, "'Opened Her Heart,'" 86, argues that even were Lydia a widow (and there is no indication in the narrative that she is), it would be unusual for her to be without a tutor and, even more so, to invite male guests into her "unsupervised" home. But if her home served as a house church, it might not have been seen as quite so unusual (16:40). Furthermore, if her occupation indicates her higher social status, we have already seen that this could afford a well-connected woman privileges and exceptions to the (social) rule. Whatever her situation, Luke includes no hint of scandal here.

58. Rosemary Canavan, "Lydia: Open-Hearted to Mission," *Australasian Catholic Record* 96 (2019): 425, refers to Lydia's response as "engaging in the activity of listening." See also Gruca-Macaulay, *Lydia*, 273: "Most significantly, God's direct action of opening Lydia's heart enabled her to perceive Paul's God and thereby accorded her access to the highest standard of discipleship: someone who can 'hear, see, and understand' the meaning of the Christ event. When this divine opening of Lydia's heart is coupled with the Pauline group's affirmation of Lydia's faith, we can see how Luke portrays Lydia within a core scriptural understanding of discipleship." Contra F. S. Spencer, "Out of Mind," 147, who describes Lydia's role as a "passive hearer and helper" (because we are not told that she prophesied, and he is contrasting her with the actions of the slave girl in the following passage).

59. In this way Lydia would join other male leaders such as Matthias (Acts 1:23–26), Cornelius (10:1–6), and Paul himself (9:1–8).

diately afterward by her declaration of faithfulness.[60] Lydia responds to what she hears by being baptized—she and her household. The way Luke constructs these two events suggests causality: she and her household are baptized as a result of the Lord opening her heart and her response to him. It also indicates immediacy: there is no indication that much time passes between her listening by the river and her responding in baptism.[61] This fits the larger motif of people listening to the gospel and being baptized without delay that is woven throughout Acts.[62] All of these factors contribute to the sense of urgency, which leads to her actions toward Paul and his companions: she urges them to stay in her home while they are in Philippi.[63]

Lydia makes their acceptance of her invitation contingent on whether they have judged her to be faithful to the Lord (16:15). What motivates Lydia's statement here? She could be inviting them to scrutinize her newfound faith.[64] She could be challenging them to accept the movement of the Lord in her heart just as she has. Or she could be acknowledging the possible optics of the situation: that it might look improper for Paul and his coworkers to stay at her house. It is difficult to determine exactly what her statement means—Luke does not provide any commentary on her invitation. What we do know is that Lydia regards her offer of hospitality as an outpouring of her newfound faith; she explicitly connects her invitation to what God is doing in her heart. Lydia's hospitality is emphasized even further by the fact that her offer is clearly not a feeble one. Not only does she connect their acceptance to her own faithfulness, but also she insists that they stay *with* her (*parebiasato*), suggesting the passion of her heart and her recognition of the urgency of the mission in the region.[65]

60. Calpino, *Women*, 210.

61. The *hōs* (when) that begins 16:15 ties these two events together sequentially.

62. E.g., Acts 8:36–39; 10:47.

63. Both Beverly Roberts Gaventa, *Acts*, Abingdon New Testament Commentaries (Nashville: Abingdon, 2003), 236–37, and Justo L. González, *Acts: The Gospel of the Spirit* (Maryknoll, NY: Orbis, 2001), 189–90, note how passive Paul is throughout the passage and how active God and Lydia are.

64. Following Daniel B. Wallace, *Greek Grammar beyond the Basics* (Grand Rapids: Zondervan, 1996), 690–94, on conditional sentences which indicate that the truth of the argument is assumed for argument's sake, Gruca-Macaulay, *Lydia*, 96–97, interprets Lydia's phrase: "If you have judged me to be faithful to the Lord, and let us assume that you have, then come into my house and stay."

65. Calpino, *Women*, 219, argues that, while *parabiazomai* can indicate force

Acts makes no mention of a synagogue at Philippi (Paul's pattern is to go directly to the synagogue in any town,[66] and in Philippi he goes to the place of prayer at the river). Whereas in the synagogue often Paul is initially received only to be vehemently rejected, here the passion is directed positively—as a testament to Lydia's faith and the embrace of the gospel by her whole household. Thus, the women's prayer meeting takes the place of the expected synagogue meeting, and the results are wholly positive.

Although Luke does not tell us explicitly that Paul's answer to Lydia's invitation is yes, the abrupt ending of her story, plus the fact that he had already indicated his plans to stay in Philippi "for some days" (16:12), suggests that her insistence paid off. That he answered in the affirmative is further substantiated by the fact that Paul and Silas go to her house after being released from prison (16:40). The abrupt ending to the Lydia account leaves us with her invitation as the last word. It is the hospitality that comes from her faith that motivates her actions, the outcome of which is that her house becomes a meeting place for the believers in Philippi (16:40).[67]

Priscilla

By the time we encounter Priscilla, we have already witnessed the prophesying of women at Pentecost, the resurrection of a beloved and generous Tabitha, the joy and belief of the servant Rhoda, and the conversion and leadership of a hospitable Lydia. Luke introduces another female disciple in Acts 18, and although her episode is not lengthy, she leaves her mark on the narrative.[68]

---

against someone's will, here it is presented positively and is an indication that "the narrator did not consider this to be rude behavior."

66. E.g., Acts 13:5, 14; 14:1.

67. Contra Jervell, "Daughters of Abraham," 152, I believe Acts 16:40 indicates that Lydia was much more than Paul's "landlady."

68. C. K. Barrett, "Is There a Theological Tendency in Codex Bezae?," in *Text and Interpretation: Studies in the New Testament Presented to Matthew Black*, ed. Ernest Best and R. McL. Wilson (Cambridge: Cambridge University Press, 1979), 15–28, interprets the sparsity of information on Priscilla (as compared to Paul's praise of her in his letters) as an indication that Luke was "anti-Priscan," yet he also acknowledges that Luke also pays little attention to her husband, Aquila! He also reads too much into the form of her name, arguing that the diminutive form "Priscilla" indicates an ironic stance toward her. However, the diminutive form indicates familiarity with her (Watts, "Women," 32).

After some time in Athens, Paul enters Corinth. There he meets a husband and wife, Aquila and Priscilla, who were part of the Jewish contingent the emperor Claudius expelled from Rome because of some unrest in the city (18:2).[69] Paul finds a certain kinship in Priscilla and Aquila—they share the same trade, tentmaking—and so he joins them in their work at Corinth and stays with them at their house (18:3). Luke gives no indication that Paul shared the gospel with them, and so it is likely that they were already believers when Paul met them.[70] After some time in Corinth, Priscilla and Aquila accompany Paul on his way to Antioch but end up staying in Ephesus, with a plan for him to return after he has visited Jerusalem and Antioch (18:18–19). While they are in Ephesus, a man named Apollos arrives. He passionately preaches the gospel but falls short in his understanding of baptism. Priscilla and Aquila take him aside and correct his misunderstandings by teaching him "the way of God" (*tēn hodon tou theou*, 18:26).

Luke consistently presents Priscilla in tandem with her husband, Aquila. The order of their names varies: Aquila is mentioned first in Acts 18:2, but every time thereafter Priscilla is listed before her husband (18:18, 26).[71] While one should not press the matter too much, it does appear that the normal way to refer to the pair was "Priscilla and Aquila." The foregrounding of her name *may* indicate that she was considered the preeminent one of the couple.[72] Luke at the very least considered

69. Suetonius, *Divus Claudius* 25.

70. That they were already established believers is consistent with the spiritual maturity they display later in the narrative in correcting Apollos (Acts 18:24–26).

71. In the rest of the New Testament, with the exception of 1 Cor 16:19, she is listed first (Rom 16:3–5; 2 Tim 4:19). See Dominika A. Kurek-Chomycz, "Is There an 'Anti-Priscan' Tendency in the Manuscripts? Some Textual Problems with Prisca and Aquila," *Journal of Biblical Literature* 125 (2006): 107–28, for a discussion of the textual variants that might indicate a scribal attempt to diminish Priscilla's role in the New Testament. Kurek-Chomycz notes that no text reverses the order of their names in Acts 18:18, while others do in 18:26. She argues that the context of teaching in the latter text is likely the reason: "The priority of a woman was more difficult to accept when she was reported to be instructing a learned man than when she was merely traveling" (125). Thus, for Kurek-Chomycz, the order of their names indicates their status within the church, and particularly Priscilla's skill as the principal teacher.

72. Jerome Murphy-O'Connor, "Prisca and Aquila: Travelling Tentmakers and Church Builders," *Bible Review* 8 (1992): 40; Linda L. Belleville, "Women Leaders in the Bible," in *Discovering Biblical Equality: Complementarity without Hierarchy*, ed. Ronald W. Pierce and Rebecca Merrill Groothuis (Downers

her to be an equal to her husband in matters of the faith—both are Paul's companions, and both correct Apollos's knowledge of baptism.[73] Not only is Priscilla a coworker in the faith, but also she participates with her husband in their family occupation. Thus, they share all aspects of family life, a reality that was not uncommon at the time.[74]

In terms of narrative impact, their actions have a far-reaching effect on the spread of the gospel. Luke clearly presents Apollos as a missionary asset even though he gets some things wrong (and Paul must come in and clean up his mess by rebaptizing Apollos's converts in the name of Jesus; Acts 19:1–7). The effort to correct Apollos (both directly in correcting his teaching and indirectly by rebaptizing his converts) serves the greater purpose of equipping him to spread the gospel. Thus, Priscilla and Aquila's role as Apollos's teachers is important because it allows Apollos to use his gifts for the gospel—a matter of primary interest to Acts. Moreover, Luke devotes no space to justifying Priscilla's leadership role. His account is matter-of-fact. Priscilla, alongside her husband, is one of Paul's peers, a coworker in the mission to the gentiles, and a mature Christian who has the ability and responsibility to correct incorrect theology. The outcome of her leadership is the successful spread of the gospel.

Conclusion

In the last two chapters I have traced the important ways that women model faithful and active discipleship in Luke-Acts. In the Gospel of Luke, model discipleship starts at the very beginning, with Mary,

---

Grove, IL: IVP Academic, 2005), 122, argues that when the subject is their occupation, Aquila is mentioned first, but in matters of ministry Priscilla precedes him. See Robert Jewett, *Romans: A Commentary*, Hermeneia (Minneapolis: Fortress, 2006), 955, who argues that she had a higher social status than her husband. While these suggestions are plausible, the narrative impact of her being listed first draws attention to her importance as a coworker in the faith—she is just as active as her husband, if not more so.

73. F. Scott Spencer, *Journeying through Acts: A Literary-Cultural Reading* (Peabody, MA: Hendrickson, 2004), 188, interprets the alternating order of their names as an indication of mutuality in their relationship.

74. Lynn H. Cohick, *Women in the World of the Earliest Christians: Illuminating Ancient Ways of Life* (Grand Rapids: Baker Academic, 2009), 130.

Elizabeth, and Anna's openness and dedication to God's divine orchestration through his Son, Jesus. It is manifested in the grateful embrace and love that the unnamed woman shows in anointing Jesus. Female disciples help fund Jesus's ministry, travel with the larger group of disciples, and are the first to witness the empty tomb and announce it to the believers. Women serve Jesus by showing hospitality and by sitting at his feet to learn from him. They model kingdom priorities by caring for the lost and persisting in their requests for justice. In Acts, women are active participants in the beginning of the early church, engaging in prayer for the selection of the newest apostle and prophesying at Pentecost. Female disciples are often in the background—ever present as the church begins to flourish in the face of persecution. They are vital members of the new community. They are coworkers in the faith. They are disciples who care for the marginalized, lead house churches, and provide corrective teaching and wisdom to others. These women see what God is doing in their midst and join in the work of spreading the gospel.

After all we have observed of female discipleship in Luke-Acts, we can answer the question of whether Luke subverts his positive portrayal of women in the gospel by removing their importance in Acts. The answer is a resounding no. While there are some differences between the two volumes, overall the portrayal of female discipleship is consistent.[75] In fact, as the narrative of Acts progresses, we see women having increasingly central roles in the life and ministry of the church. Tabitha receives healing to continue her ministry. Lydia converts and hosts a house church in Philippi. Priscilla teaches and corrects a male missionary and joins Paul in his mission work to the gentiles. Women are consistent models of faithful discipleship, working alongside the men to advance the good news—from Jerusalem to Judea and Samaria and to the ends of the earth.

75. Luke does not appear to be as interested in comparative discipleship (contrasting female and male discipleship) in Acts as he does in the gospel. Rather, he focuses on the spread of the gospel. This is likely to do with the absence of the physical presence of Jesus to follow. The primary question of discipleship in Acts is not "Who is most like Jesus?" but "Who is joining the work of the Spirit in the church?"

Six

Female Discipleship in the Gospel of John

The Gospel of John gives less attention to the privileged status of Jesus's inner circle of male disciples than do the Synoptic Gospels. John's Gospel lacks an apostles list, never applies the term *apostoloi* to the group, and rarely refers to them as "the Twelve."[1] Moreover, since the bulk of the narrative's attention is on Jesus, John has less to offer in terms of an explicit discussion of discipleship.[2] But the narrative does give important clues as to what it means to follow Jesus faithfully from a Johannine perspective. For example, there is the explicit criticism of those who see the "signs" (*sēmeia*) that Jesus performs but do not believe, or those who require tangible proof in order to believe. According to this gospel, true discipleship is about understanding what those signs are saying about Jesus's identity.

In most of the key stories of the women who encounter Jesus, their actions and interactions with him have something to say about who he is. It is his mother's initiative that inspires Jesus to conduct his first sign at the wedding at Cana (2:3–5). The Samaritan woman's discussion with Jesus at the well prompts her to testify to her community

1. John 6:67, 70, 71; 20:24. His preference for the term *mathētai* can make it difficult to determine exactly who is included in the group at any given point in the narrative. While our default is often to assume it refers to Jesus's closest male disciples, I will use "disciples" to indicate a combined group of males and females where there is some ambiguity or indication that the circle is wider. Otherwise I will specify by using the term "male disciples" or "female disciples."

2. See, however, Rekha M. Chennattu, *Johannine Discipleship as a Covenant Relationship* (Grand Rapids: Baker, 2005), who views the Johannine theme of discipleship through the lens of Israel's covenant with God.

and results in their belief in Jesus as "the Savior of the world" (4:1–42). Martha delivers the most robust confession of Jesus's identity in the gospel (11:27). Mary's act of anointing Jesus with nard anticipates his death (12:1–8). A group of women stand by Jesus as he is crucified (19:25). And Mary Magdalene is the first to discover the empty tomb, the first to encounter the risen Jesus, and the first to proclaim the gospel message that the Son of God is alive (20:1–18).[3] These women have an active role in illuminating and witnessing to the identity of Jesus throughout the gospel, and the author resists a sharp separation between Jesus's inner circle of male disciples and others who follow him, suggesting that the primary aspect of discipleship is not about who people are but about what they do.[4]

Another notable aspect of female discipleship in John is that its depiction is often located in an emotional or dramatic scene, especially toward the latter half of the narrative. While John accentuates Jesus's divinity (what is often called "high Christology") more than the Synoptics do, the gospel contains some intimate moments that display his humanity, proving that his divinity does not preclude emotional encounters with people. When these moments happen, women are almost always there. In John 11, Jesus shares in the deep grief of Martha and Mary at the death of their brother Lazarus. In John 12, Jesus comes to Mary's defense by snapping at Judas when the disciple publicly criticizes her for wasting money on Jesus's anointing. In the death scene in John 19, his mother is at the cross, prompting Jesus to transfer the familial relationship he has with her to the disciple whom he loves. From now on, this disciple will care for the mother of Jesus as his mother, and she will care for him as her son. And in John 20, Mary Magdalene's roller coaster of emotions are on full display as she discovers that Jesus is not dead, nor his body stolen, but that he is standing right in front of her. These dramatic and emotional moments invite the audience to participate in the deepening relationships between Jesus and the women who are committed to him.

3. Given its late addition into the gospel (the earliest manuscripts do not include this story), I will not include the story of the adulterous woman (7:53–8:11).

4. Raymond E. Brown, "Roles of Women in the Fourth Gospel," *Theological Studies* 36 (1975): 690: "The fourth Gospel glorifies the disciple and never uses the term 'apostle' in the technical sense, almost as if the Evangelist wishes to remind the Christian that what is primary is not to have a special ecclesiastical charism from God but to have followed Jesus, obedient to his word."

Several of these women start off misunderstanding or lacking a full grasp of the truth about Jesus. This is not to be understood as a criticism of the women. In John's Gospel misunderstanding is a typical response to Jesus and is an important vehicle for teaching truths about him.[5] It is crucial that a person be receptive to his teachings[6] and then come to a fuller understanding. This movement from misunderstanding to understanding is a key feature of the stories of these female disciples, and that movement always leads to action—a requirement of discipleship (13:17).

Most of these acts of discipleship come immediately after or are in the middle of some sort of failure or lack of action on the part of the men who are with Jesus. In John 2, Jesus's mother is the one who takes initiative at the wedding—not the male disciples who are with Jesus. While in John 3 Nicodemus's encounter with Jesus comes under the cover of night and contains no indication that Nicodemus will respond positively, the Samaritan woman in John 4 meets Jesus out in the open, engages in a theological back-and-forth with him, and responds by telling the townspeople to come and see the man she believes is the Messiah. Meanwhile, the male disciples do not know what to make of the fact that Jesus is talking to this woman, and they miss the deep significance of this encounter as a moment of the harvest of disciples in the area on account of their greater concern for lunch. John 12 recounts that Judas Iscariot, one of Jesus's closest companions, is more interested in lining his own pockets than in honoring Jesus and publicly criticizes Mary for her generosity. And while Peter and the beloved disciple are willing to go see the empty tomb for themselves in John 20, they leave before they have a chance to meet Jesus in the garden as Mary Magdalene does. John presents all of these women positively and in intimate relation to Jesus, often in contrast to the men who are present nearby.[7] These accounts show women acting on their beliefs: whenever these women encounter Jesus in this gospel, their actions speak louder than words.

5. See also Kelli S. O'Brien, "Written That You May Believe: John 20 and Narrative Rhetoric," *Catholic Biblical Quarterly* 67 (2005): 287–90.

6. O'Brien, "Written," 291: "Receptivity is rewarded by further revelation and greater understanding."

7. Sandra M. Schneiders, "Women in the Fourth Gospel and the Role of Women in the Contemporary Church," in *The Gospel of John as Literature*, ed. Mark Stibbe, New Testament Tools and Studies 17 (Leiden: Brill, 1993), 129.

The Initiative of Jesus's Mother (John 2:1–12)

Our first encounter with a woman in the Gospel of John comes at the very beginning of Jesus's public ministry. By not including a birth narrative as Matthew and Luke do (Matt 1:18–25; Luke 1:26–38), John lacks an initial reason to mention Jesus's mother. Yet, rather than appearing at a random moment in the midst of Jesus's ministry as she does in Mark (3:21, 31), the mother of Jesus in this gospel shows up in his story in two key places: at the first "sign" that Jesus performs, and at the end of his life, as he dies on the cross (John 2:1–12; 19:25–27).[8] Thus, the presence of his mother forms an *inclusio*, bookending the beginning and ending of Jesus's earthly mission.

The careful reader will also note that John never refers to Jesus's mother as Mary, unlike the Synoptic Gospels. By calling her "the mother of Jesus" (*hē mētēr tou Iēsou*) on each occasion, he places her maternal role at the forefront of both of the passages in which we find her. Her actions are to be understood as the actions of a mother to a son—a mother who follows him in his ministry.

Jesus's first public work has been to call the first of his disciples. By the time we get to John 2, he has collected nearly one-half of the men who will constitute his closest companions (1:35–51).[9] The scene now shifts to a wedding celebration in the Galilean town of Cana. Along with his mother, Jesus and his disciples have been invited to the party, where, unbeknownst to those in charge of the feast, the wine has quickly run out. Jesus's mother, aware of this problem (we do not know how), tells her son that there is no more wine (2:3). Despite Jesus's less than promising initial response ("Woman, what is that to me and to you? My hour has not yet come," *Ti emoi kai soi, gynai; oupō hēkei hē hōra mou*, 2:4), she urges the servants to do whatever Jesus instructs them to do (2:5), a foreshadowing that Jesus will indeed fix the problem.

8. These texts are also linked by the theme of Jesus's "hour" (*hōra*), which refers to his death on the cross. See Christian P. Ceroke, "Jesus and Mary at Cana: Separation or Association?," *Theological Studies* 17 (1956): 1–38, who advocates for a broader understanding of *hōra* as the time when Jesus performs *all* the signs.

9. Andrew and one other unnamed disciple of John the Baptist (1:40), Peter (1:42), Philip, and Nathanael (1:43–45). John is unique among the gospel writers in that he does not use the more formal term "apostles" (*apostoloi*) for Jesus's inner circle of disciples.

Jesus instructs the servants to fill up six large stone jars with water, draw out a cupful, and take it to the steward to taste (2:6–8). The steward tastes the water that has now become wine and immediately congratulates the bridegroom for unconventionally saving the good wine until the celebration is well underway rather than serving it at the beginning and leaving the inferior wine for later, when the guests are unable to differentiate the good from the bad (2:10). As a result of this first sign, Jesus's disciples begin to believe in him, although John does not elaborate on the extent or content of that belief (2:11).[10]

This story is both playful and perplexing. It is playful in that John lets the audience know that the bridegroom had nothing to do with the surplus of good wine. In fact, he actually failed to secure enough wine for the guests, indicating that he was an incompetent host. Thus, he has come dangerously close to embarrassing himself, his new wife, and his family by failing to provide the hospitality that would be expected at the time.[11] Neither the bridegroom nor the steward nor the other guests at the wedding have any idea how close they've come to a premature ending to their celebration. All of the credit should go to Jesus, who performs the sign, and his mother, who initiates the solution by making him aware of the problem and arranging the servants to aid Jesus in whatever he decides to do about it.

Yet the story is perplexing because the exchange between Jesus and his mother is not as simple as the outcome of the scene might suggest. Much of the scholarly discussion on this passage revolves around the problematic elements. First, Jesus's response to his mother's statement that the wine has run out is enigmatic and, on the surface, seems to be a rejection of her request. Second, despite his seeming refusal, he immediately grants her implied wish. Interpretations of Jesus's response include (a) that Jesus is resisting or even rejecting his mother's role as one with authority over him;[12] (b) that John is emphasizing her role as a headwaiter or leader in the community over against her role as his mother, because her function in the narrative is to be the catalyst for

10. This is the first time the gospel explicitly attributes belief to the disciples, although Jesus anticipates their belief in 1:50–51.

11. Ceroke, "Jesus and Mary," 33–34.

12. E.g., Joseph A. Grassi, "The Role of Jesus' Mother in John's Gospel: A Reappraisal," *Catholic Biblical Quarterly* 48 (1986): 78, 99; Turid Karlsen Seim, "Roles of Women in the Gospel of John," in *Aspects of the Johannine Literature*, ed. Lars Hartman and Birger Olsson (Uppsala: Almqvist & Wiksell, 1987), 60.

the provision of wine to the guests;[13] (c) that Jesus uses a respectful address that addresses her feeling of helplessness, spurs her to action, and ultimately hints at the importance of what he will say next;[14] (d) that Jesus's terse response is an indication that he refuses to be involved in an issue of local honor and reciprocity but is operating on a higher, spiritual level than what his mother first realizes;[15] and (e) that the mother of Jesus is functioning symbolically as the church, whose primary role will not come to fruition until after Jesus's death and resurrection.[16] All of these theories recognize a tension between the dialogue of these two key characters and their attending actions.

We might think of this dynamic as one of push and pull. On the one hand, there are several indications of a certain distance between Jesus and his mother (push), while, on the other hand, John emphasizes her role as a disciple who follows Jesus and whose identity is found in her relation to him (pull).[17] This push-pull dynamic is evident at the beginning of the passage, as John suggests that they came to the wedding separately and that Jesus's presence there is somewhat remarkable (push).[18] Yet, although they enter the celebration from separate directions, after the sign they leave together (pull). For a second example of push-pull dynamics, she approaches Jesus with the problem because she has access to him as his mother (pull), yet she frames her words in such a way as to avoid an outright request, which allows him to respond in a way that indicates a certain autonomy from her (push).[19] She has enough gumption and insight to recognize that

13. E.g., Jean-Bosco Matand Bulembat, "Head-Waiter and Bridegroom of the Wedding at Cana: Structure and Meaning of John 2.1–12," *Journal for the Study of the New Testament* 30 (2007): 55–73.

14. E.g., Ceroke, "Jesus and Mary," 28–29, 36.

15. E.g., Ritva H. Williams, "The Mother of Jesus at Cana: A Social-Science Interpretation of John 2.1–12," *Catholic Biblical Quarterly* 59 (1997): 679–92.

16. E.g., Raymond E. Brown, *The Gospel according to John I–XII*, Anchor Bible 29 (New York: Doubleday, 1966), 105; André Feuillet, "Le Messie et sa Mère d'après le chapitre xii de l'Apocalypse," *Revue biblique* 66 (1959): 55–86.

17. In John 19:25–27, her role as mother is both reinforced and redefined. See discussion below.

18. The mother of Jesus is mentioned first, and Jesus and his disciples are introduced with "but also" (*de kai*). The combined conjunctions can indicate a sense of heightened emphasis—in this case, on the presence of Jesus and his entourage.

19. Ceroke, "Jesus and Mary," 16, calls this "a masterpiece of non-authoritative strategy."

Jesus's response is not an outright rejection of her request and so arranges help for him (pull), but it is not clear that she knows exactly what he plans to do (push). Thus, we see in the passage an indication that Jesus is distancing himself from his mother in terms of her maternal influence,[20] but he is not rejecting her initiative to fix the problem. Rather, he implicitly welcomes her initiative.

Relatedly, and for the purposes of our larger study, this episode says something about her role as a disciple of Jesus, particularly since John emphasizes her initiative and her insistence that he will act in some way. At a minimum, it is clear that the mother of Jesus is with him and later follows him. At the same time, she is not simply his mother; she is a disciple and so belongs to a different sort of family he is creating. This family goes beyond the boundaries of the nuclear or biological one. At the wedding she functions as a leader who instructs the servants to follow Jesus's commands.[21]

There is also a sense that she knows more than the other disciples introduced thus far (Nathanael, for example, doubts whether the Messiah can even come from Nazareth, meeting Jesus with initial skepticism, 1:45). And whether or not she anticipates Jesus's supernatural response when she reports the shortage of wine, she knows he is the person to whom she must take the problem, indicating her belief that he will be able to do something to help the situation. Her actions are in line with a major emphasis of the story and of the Gospel of John as a whole: the signs Jesus performs speak primarily to his identity.[22]

In the end, the mother of Jesus is numbered among the group who travels to Capernaum with Jesus, a group that includes his brothers

20. This distancing is indicated by the term he uses to address her directly: "woman" (*gunai*) rather than "mother" (*mētēr*).

21. Elisabeth Schüssler Fiorenza, *In Memory of Her: A Feminist Theological Reconstruction of Christian Origins* (New York: Crossroad, 1983), 327, argues that because Jesus's retort distances himself from the mother-son relationship and the fact that she is depicted as instructing "the community" to do what Jesus says, the author indicates that her instructions should be kept not because she is Jesus's mother but because she is a female disciple. See also Jey J. Kanagaraj, "The Profiles of Women in John: House-Bound or Christ-Bound?," *Bangalore Theological Forum* 33 (2001): 62: "A leader always takes initiative to act positively at the time of crisis and also influences others to act in the right way. In this sense Mary can be called a model leader and a faithful disciple of Jesus."

22. André Feuillet, "L'Heure de Jesus et le Signe de Cana: Contribution a l'Étude de la Structure du Quatrième Évangile," *Ephemerides Theologicae Lovanienses* 36 (1960): 15.

and the disciples he has called to follow him thus far (2:12). There is no reason to regard her as separate from the other followers of Jesus. The mother of Jesus is the catalyst for his actions at the wedding at Cana, the first of the signs that will indicate who he is and what he has come to do.

The Samaritan Woman's Witness (John 4:1–42)

Jesus's next encounter with a woman comes in John 4, where he engages in a theological discussion with a Samaritan woman. This encounter results in many people from her town believing that he is "the Savior of the world" (4:42). John is fond of incorporating dialogue in his narrative at key moments, and John 4 is the longest dialogue in the gospel. It also provides a good teaching moment for his male disciples, as they are invited to witness the "harvest" that is taking place—a harvest in which they are expected to be a part (4:34–38).

On his way from Judea back to Galilee, Jesus passes through Samaria and stops at the town of Sychar. While his male disciples go into the town to find food for lunch, Jesus rests at the well, a well that is connected to the patriarch Jacob—a fact that becomes a topic of conversation in the dialogue that ensues. As he is resting there, a Samaritan woman comes to the well to draw water, and Jesus asks her for a drink. The woman is shocked on two accounts: that Jesus is a Jew and a male and yet is asking a Samaritan who is a woman to give him something to drink.[23] Jesus's request prompts a lengthy back-and-forth exchange between Jesus and the woman, covering a range of topics (his ability to give her living water, 4:10, 13–15; his superiority over Jacob, 4:12–15; his knowledge of her marital past and current status, 4:16–19; the Jewish-Samaritan dispute over where to worship God, 4:20; Jesus's claim that true worshipers will worship in "spirit and truth," 4:21–24; and his disclosure to her that he is the Messiah, 4:25–26). Their discussion leads to her increased understanding of who Jesus is and ultimately inspires her to tell her fellow townspeople to "come and see" him (4:29).

23. Her response and John's explanation in 4:9 does not imply that Jews had no interactions with Samaritans (the disciples have gone into the city to buy food from, presumably, Samaritans). It seems that her incredulity has to do with him wanting a drink from her jar.

The episode ends with two very different sorts of scenes contrasting the Samaritan woman and townspeople with the male disciples who have come to the town with Jesus. John presents these scenes in an alternating sequence, with the effect of inviting us to compare and contrast the two groups: (1) the male disciples return and are "astonished" that Jesus is speaking with a woman (4:27);[24] (2) the woman leaves to tell the townspeople about Jesus and asks them to come and confirm that he is the Messiah (4:28–30); (3) "meanwhile" the male disciples urge Jesus to eat the food that they have brought and do not understand that the "food" that is most important is to do the will of God, which is the work of the harvest (4:31–38); and (4) the Samaritan townspeople, who display an initial belief in Jesus based on the woman's testimony, invite Jesus to stay with them and confirm their belief in him because of his "word" (4:39–42).

As in the account of the wedding at Cana, parts of this episode are enigmatic. Some see in John 4 evidence of a betrothal type scene—a recognizable literary setting much like those found in Genesis 24:11 and 29:2 and Exodus 2:15–21—and argue for varying effects on its interpretation as a result.[25] Others focus on the marital history and sociocultural status of the woman and discuss whether this indicates an immoral lifestyle.[26] Some seek to explain the abrupt changes in

24. Cf. Seim, "Roles," 59, who notes that the male disciples make no mention of her ethnicity—it is her gender that is of most concern to them. John, on the other hand, repeats the fact that she has "two strikes" against her three times in the space of three verses: she is a Samaritan woman (4:7–9).

25. E.g., Adeline Fehribach, *The Women in the Life of the Bridegroom: A Feminist Historical-Literary Analysis of the Female Characters in the Fourth Gospel* (Collegeville, MN: Liturgical Press, 1998); Lyle Eslinger, "The Wooing of the Woman at the Well: Jesus, the Reader and Reader-Response Criticism," in Stibbe, *Gospel of John*, 165–82.

26. Jerome Neyrey, "What's Wrong with This Picture? John 4, Cultural Stereotypes of Women, and Public and Private Space," *Biblical Theology Bulletin* 24 (1994): 77–91; Jo Ann Davidson, "The Well Women of Scripture Revisited," *Journal of the Adventist Theological Society* 17 (2006): 209–28; Harold W. Attridge, "The Samaritan Woman: A Woman Transformed," in *Character Studies in the Fourth Gospel: Narrative Approaches to Seventy Figures in John*, ed. Stephen A. Hunt, D. Francois Tolmie, and Ruben Zimmerman (Grand Rapids: Eerdmans, 2016), 268–81. Lynn H. Cohick, *Women in the World of the Earliest Christians: Illuminating Ancient Ways of Life* (Grand Rapids: Baker Academic, 2009), 123–28, describes several scenarios that would be more likely to explain her multiple marriages than that she is an immoral woman, and argues that it

topics throughout the conversation between Jesus and the Samaritan woman.[27] Others have speculated as to the tone of her interaction with Jesus and whether this truly indicates her belief in him.[28]

Much more space is required for a thorough treatment of these approaches—space that I cannot spare here. Instead, I would like to focus on the narrative elements that speak directly to the notion of discipleship in the Gospel of John and, in particular, on those aspects of the story that present the Samaritan woman as a follower of Jesus alongside the other disciples in the gospel. There are several clear indications in the passage that the woman models faithful discipleship in action—a discipleship that results in a harvest of belief among the Samaritans of Sychar. To aid this presentation of the woman's discipleship, John invites the reader to compare and contrast the woman with Nicodemus in 3:1–21 and the male disciples with Jesus in Samaria.

The movement from misunderstanding to faith and understanding is a pervasive theme in John. No character gets it completely right from the beginning, but many grow in their faith and understanding of who Jesus is. This growth is apparent for the male disciples. In fact, by John 4 we have already encountered this movement from misun-

was likely a combination of widowhood and divorces (which she would not be able to initiate on her own). Her current nonmarried status might also be an indication that she was a Roman's concubine, who could not marry her if she was below his social rank. Cohick is right to observe that, regardless of her specific circumstances, Jesus refrains from condemning her behavior or her situation. See also Caryn A. Reeder, *The Samaritan Woman's Story: Reconsidering John 4 after #ChurchToo* (Downers Grove, IL: IVP Academic, 2022), who offers a detailed survey of the traditional interpretations of John 4:1–42 as a story about a sinful woman, and then offers an alternative reading with a view toward practical application in the life of the church and its treatment of women.

27. E.g., Eugene Botha, "John 4.16: A Difficult Text Speech Act Theoretically Revisited," in Stibbe, *Gospel of John*, 183–92; Davidson, "Well Women"; Jean K. Kim, "A Korean Feminist Reading of John 4:1–42," *Semeia* 78 (1997): 109–19.

28. Rudolf Bultmann, *The Gospel of John: A Commentary*, trans. George R. Beasley-Murray, Rupert W. N. Hoare, and John K. Riches (Philadelphia: Westminster, 1971), 193; Toan Do, "Revisiting the Woman of Samaria and the Ambiguity of Faith in John 4:4–42," *Catholic Biblical Quarterly* 81 (2019): 252–76. Rose Mukansengimana-Nyirimana and Jonathan A. Draper, "The Peacemaking Role of the Samaritan Woman in John 4:1–42: A Mirror and Challenge to Rwandan Women," *Neotestamentica* 46 (2012): 299–318.

derstanding to understanding among Jesus's closest companions, as Nathanael moves from initial skepticism surrounding Jesus's origins to a willingness to follow him (1:46–51).[29] Several times John notes that these disciples did not understand Jesus's actions or teachings until after he was resurrected (e.g., 2:22; 13:7). In her dialogue with Jesus, the Samaritan woman also appears as someone whose understanding of Jesus's teachings gradually increases, ultimately leading to her understanding of his identity.[30] Even when the topics get difficult (marital history, Jewish-Samaritan disputes on worship), she never leaves and, in fact, deliberately extends the discussion by asking questions and making her own theological observations.[31] A conversation that starts out with "Why are you asking me for a drink?" ends with her hurrying to tell her neighbors about the man she has just met.[32]

29. In 1:50–51 Jesus hints that Nathanael's understanding of who Jesus is has only just begun.

30. Cf. Neyrey, "What's Wrong," 83, who emphasizes her change in status from radical outsider to consummate insider. Also note that this passage contains the first use of the Johannine "I am" formula (*egō eimi*, 4:26), and it is immediately after this statement that she leaves to witness. See also Schneiders, "Fourth Gospel," 132.

31. See also Frank Anthony Spina, *The Faith of the Outsider: Exclusion and Inclusion in the Biblical Story* (Grand Rapids: Eerdmans, 2005), 149: "Even a cursory interaction would have been proscribed, let alone this increasingly involved one. But Jesus has begun the exchange, while she, despite her protestations, has allowed herself to be engaged. And though she could have walked off in a huff at any point, or even have slipped away demurely, she does neither. To the contrary, she not only remains involved, she reveals a genuine curiosity." Spina is overstating the Jewish-Samaritan divide, I think. The fact that the disciples have willingly gone into the Samaritan town to get food (4:8) indicates that there was no proscription of Jewish and Samaritan interaction. Note also that the woman is the one who prolongs the discussion by asking questions and adding more words to the dialogue—she does not display a reluctance to interact with Jesus.

32. I do not interpret her question "He cannot be the Messiah, can he?" (4:29 NRSVUE) as evidence of doubt for three reasons: (1) Up to this point in the narrative, when Jesus reveals something to her, she accepts it. I see no reason why the revelation of his identity in 4:26 would be any different, particularly since the entire episode is one long progression of sight/belief in him. (2) John describes her words to the townspeople as "testimony" (*dia ton logon tēs gynaikos martyrousēs*, 4:39), which always indicates belief when Jesus is the subject (e.g., 21:24). And (3) the townspeople interpret her invitation as belief (4:42).

Thus, as with the male disciples, the Samaritan woman's increased exposure to Jesus leads to an increased understanding, which, in turn, leads her to testify about him.[33]

Prior to his encounter with the Samaritan woman, Jesus had been engaged in another theological conversation. John 3:1–21 recounts a discussion between Jesus and a Pharisee named Nicodemus. Like the Samaritan woman, Nicodemus engages in a back-and-forth with Jesus about his identity and sustains this dialogue by asking questions throughout (3:4, 9). But this is where the similarities end (at least at this point in the narrative). Unlike the woman, Nicodemus comes to Jesus at night, which, coupled with his introduction as someone who is representing a group who has already shown some resistance to Jesus and will become an increasingly hostile opposition group (2:18–20), suggests a negative portrayal of him.[34] Perhaps the clearest contrast, however, comes in how the scenes end. While the two individuals might begin at the same place in terms of their lack of understanding, at the end of their respective conversations the Samaritan woman witnesses to her group.[35] In contrast, we do not know what Nicodemus's response to Jesus's teachings will be.[36] The juxtaposition

33. If the woman had a reputation and was shunned by her community, that same community would not be likely to listen to her when she goes to tell them about Jesus. See also, e.g., Davidson, "Well Women," 225, and Janeth Norfleete Day, *The Woman at the Well: Interpretation of John 4:1–42 in Retrospect and Prospect* (Leiden: Brill, 2002), 174.

34. Nicodemus's representative function is indicated by his introduction as a "leader of the Jews" (*archon tōn Ioudaiōn*, 3:1) and his use of the plural "we" (*oidamen*) in 3:2.

35. Following J. A. du Rand, "The Characterization of Jesus as Depicted in the Narrative of the Fourth Gospel," *Neotestamentica* 19 (1985): 20–21, Fehribach, *Bridegroom*, 30, uses helpful language of "below" and "above" thinking. In this case, while the Samaritan woman and Nicodemus both start out with "below" thinking (taking as literal what is meant to be spiritual), we are told that only the Samaritan woman moves to "above" thinking as her conversation with Jesus progresses.

36. At this point, Mary L. Coloe, "The Woman of Samaria: Her Characterization, Narrative, and Theological Significance," in *Characters and Characterization in the Gospel of John*, ed. Christopher W. Skinner (London: Bloomsbury T&T Clark, 2013), 189, is right to point out that we are left only with "How is this possible?" (3:9). Later we will see Nicodemus's journey toward discipleship progress as he becomes willing to advocate for fair treatment of Jesus (7:50–51) and is ultimately involved in his burial (19:39–42—while Nicodemus is not ex-

of these two stories invites us to weigh the responses of both characters, and at this point Nicodemus is found wanting.

Nicodemus is not the only one who fails to measure up to the type of discipleship that the Samaritan woman displays. I have already noted the alternating sequence of the woman's actions with the response of the male disciples in John 4:27–42. John's use of "meanwhile" (*en tō metaxy*, 4:31) has the effect of emphasizing that *while* she is witnessing and calling people to Jesus, the male disciples are preoccupied with food and are confused about the kind of food that sustains Jesus: doing the will of God (4:34).[37] Not only that, but they are only asking him to eat, while she has been asking him questions that have led her to understanding.[38] Moreover, while the harvest language that Jesus uses to explain his highest priority emphasizes action (it is the labor that makes it possible to reap the harvest, 4:38), these

---

plicitly called a disciple, his identification with Joseph of Arimathea and his contribution to Jesus's burial suggests this). Cf. Winsome Munro, "The Pharisee and the Samaritan in John: Polar or Parallel?," *Catholic Biblical Quarterly* 57 (1995): 710–28, who wants to balance the negative views of Nicodemus by highlighting similarities between him and the Samaritan woman: "The reader is to hold them together, even if in uneasy tension, as two persons fitting into the very varied continuum of those who are to be accounted believers and, thus, part of the messianic community of Jesus" (711). At this point in the narrative, however, the contrasts outweigh the similarities.

37. Deborah C. Inyamah, "Contrasting Perspectives on the Role of the Feminine in Ministry and Leadership Roles in John 4 and 1 Timothy 2:11–15," *Journal of Religious Thought* 60 (2010): 98, observes that the male disciples believe Jesus is speaking about food from the market from which they have just returned, while Jesus is actually referring to the group of Samaritans who are on their way, responding to the witness of the Samaritan woman. These men are looking backward while the woman is moving forward! Contra Kim, "Korean Feminist," 113, who sees the "meanwhile" as a narrative device to shift the focus to the male disciples and victimize the Samaritan woman: "The replacement of the direct response of her people to the Samaritan woman's witness by the dialogue between Jesus and his disciples shows that the woman is not a missionary but a victimized woman whose purpose is to exemplify the role of exchange object between groups of men." Resisting Kim's reading, however, is the fact that the people are already on their way to Jesus as a result of her testimony (4:30), and that John gives credit to her explicitly for the role she plays in the Samaritans' belief ("Many Samaritans from that city believed in him *because* of the woman's testimony [*dia ton logon tēs gynaikos martyrousēs*]," 4:39).

38. They keep their questions to themselves, which indicates a further lack of understanding (4:33) and perhaps even a lack of trust in his judgment (4:27).

disciples have done nothing that leads to eternal life in this episode, while the Samaritan woman's dialogue with Jesus and her resulting actions have led to a harvest of believers.[39]

Martha's Confession (John 11:1–44)

At the center of the gospel, the audience encounters two sisters who interact with Jesus in different ways, both of which indicate faithful discipleship. Martha and Mary are the sisters of Lazarus, Jesus's friend who is the beneficiary of his most impressive sign: the raising of a man from the dead. Although the sign revolves around Lazarus, it is Martha and Mary whom John foregrounds in 11:1–44 and 12:1–8.[40] More specifically, it is their actions that move the plot along and provide insight into Jesus's identity.

Martha's discipleship is the primary focus of John 11:1–44, although Mary plays a small part as well. The story begins with the sisters notifying Jesus that his dear friend Lazarus is sick (11:3).[41] Jesus's immediate response is a foreshadowing of what he will do later: he

39. Ben Witherington III, *Women in the Ministry of Jesus*, Society for New Testament Studies Monograph Series 21 (Cambridge: Cambridge University Press, 1984), 61, argues that the woman is represented by the sower. Cf. Schneiders, "Fourth Gospel," 133, and Brown, "Roles," 691, who notes that the expression that the other Samaritans believed because of her word (*logos*) shows up again in 17:20, when Jesus prays for his future disciples. This indicates that a woman is numbered among his other (male) disciples because she also bore witness to Jesus. See also Peter F. Lockwood, "The Woman at the Well: Does the Traditional Reading Still Hold Water?," *Lutheran Theological Journal* 36 (2002): 19–20.

40. John suggests that his audience is more familiar with Martha and Mary than they are with Lazarus, as he describes Bethany as "the village of Mary and her sister Martha" (11:1). Further, the premature mention of Mary's anointing suggests that she was known to his community (11:2).

41. According to the sisters, Lazarus is the one whom Jesus "loves" (*phileō*, 11:3). Witherington, *Ministry of Jesus*, 106, also sees a similarity between the implied request for healing (in the form of the news that Lazarus is ill) and that of the mother of Jesus in John 2:3. Both prompt Jesus's action. Adele Reinhartz, "From Narrative to History: The Resurrection of Mary and Martha," in *"Women Like This": New Perspectives on Jewish Women in the Greco-Roman World*, ed. Amy-Jill Levine (Atlanta: Scholars Press, 1991), 173, thinks it significant that the sisters are the ones who initiate the action in the story. Because they send notice to Jesus, the sign of their brother's resurrection is made possible.

claims that the illness will lead not to Lazarus's death but rather to God's glory and his own (11:4). John increases the suspense when he describes Jesus's choice to wait to see the family, even though he loves all three of them (11:5–6). Finally, after two days Jesus and his male disciples head to Bethany, with his stated intention to "awaken" the "sleeping" Lazarus—a decision that his companions first meet with resistance and misunderstanding, and then with a sense of resignation (11:7–16). Jesus arrives in Bethany after Lazarus has already been dead and buried for four days, and so belatedly joins the mourning party. When Martha hears that Jesus is on his way, she goes out to meet him while Mary stays home with the guests (11:17–20).

Here we encounter the central dialogue of the story. Martha expresses regret that Jesus has not arrived sooner (and so has missed the opportunity to heal Lazarus), demonstrates her faith that God will still answer any request that Jesus makes, and then responds to Jesus's claim that Lazarus will be resurrected with a statement of her conviction in the general resurrection, that Lazarus will be raised one day in the future (11:21–24). This dialogue provides the setup for Jesus to make one of his "I am" statements, "I am the resurrection and the life," claiming that death will not have the last word for anyone who believes in him (11:25–26). In response to his question "Do you believe this?" Martha proclaims her faith: "Yes, Lord, I believe that you are the Messiah, the Son of God, the one coming into the world" (11:27 NRSVUE).

Immediately after this confession, she goes back to bring Mary to him, because he has remained outside the village at the tomb (11:28–31). Mary falls at Jesus's feet and makes the same statement that Martha made earlier—that had Jesus come sooner, Lazarus would not have died (11:32). Then follows an emotional scene where Jesus joins the group of mourners, a sign of his true friendship with Lazarus and his sisters and an unusual display of his empathy in this gospel (11:33–38). When Jesus commands the stone to be removed from the entrance to the tomb, Martha warns him that there is a stench because Lazarus has been dead for four days (11:39). Jesus responds by reminding her of their prior conversation, prays to the Father aloud to demonstrate to those watching that what he is about to do is evidence that God has sent him, and then commands Lazarus to come out of the tomb—which, of course, he does (11:40–44).

The dialogue between Martha and Jesus anchors a moving and fantastical passage, leading to the last and most impressive of all Jesus's signs in the gospel. Martha shows that she understands more about Jesus's identity than has previously been expressed by any character in the story, and yet she does not seem to grasp completely what Jesus is capable of or what his intentions might be. Once again, we have a dialogue that operates on two levels. As the conversation heads toward her confession in 11:27, Martha understands Jesus to be making one sort of claim (that she will see her brother again when all those who worship God will be raised in the general resurrection),[42] while he is upping the ante (he will raise Lazarus from the dead in mere moments). This is brilliant storytelling, as John frames this dialogue for the audience—a community who already knows of Jesus's capabilities, knows his intention for Lazarus (11:11), has witnessed all Jesus's promises coming true, and already anticipates his own resurrection from the dead. Jesus has been talking on one level (above), while Martha is speaking from another (below), a scenario we have already seen in Jesus's dialogue with his mother (John 2) and the Samaritan woman (John 4).[43] Once again, we have a female disciple whose combination of misunderstanding and belief in Jesus provides the canvas on which the author paints a portrayal of Jesus's identity as Son of God and Messiah.

There has been some discussion about whether Martha's confession constitutes an adequate understanding of Jesus or faith in him.[44]

42. The Pharisees believed in the general resurrection, while the Sadducees did not (see Mark 12:18; Acts 23:8). It seems that most Jews at the time held some belief in life after death.

43. As well as in the Nicodemus episode.

44. E.g., Reinhartz, "Narrative to History"; Harold W. Attridge, "From Discord Rises Meaning: Resurrection Motifs in the Fourth Gospel," in *The Resurrection of Jesus in the Gospel of John*, ed. Craig R. Koester and Reimund Bieringer, Wissenschaftliche Untersuchungen zum Neuen Testament 222 (Tübingen: Mohr Siebeck, 2008). Robert G. Maccini, "A Reassessment of the Woman at the Well in John 4 in Light of the Samaritan Context," *Journal for the Study of the New Testament* 53 (1994): 35–46, argues against A. E. Harvey, *Jesus on Trial: A Study in the Fourth Gospel* (London: SPCK, 1976), that Martha's confession is presented as credible evidence as a witness given its placement in the "narrative apex" about resurrection (36). If Martha's confession would have been viewed as credible witness testimony about Jesus, then John might be subtly indicating that matters of the gospel were perfectly within the purview of female concerns. And while the context of her confession is not a court of law, it still demands the credibility of the person testifying.

In terms of narrative development, Martha's role as the exemplar of faithful discipleship is made clear. First, at this point in the gospel, Martha's statement of faith is the most robust of any other character's expression of faith. While Nathanael, the Samaritan woman, and Peter all make claims about Jesus's identity, Martha's is a three-pronged description, and her belief is more explicitly located in Jesus's identity than the others are because it comes as a response to Jesus's claim that those who "believe in" him will live (11:25, 26).[45] In fact, Martha's combination of titles for Jesus (Messiah, the Son of God) appears elsewhere only in John 20:30–31, the purpose statement of the gospel. John writes the gospel so that the audience will come to believe that Jesus is the Messiah and the Son of God. Martha's confession, then, reflects the type of belief that the gospel is trying to engender. She becomes the model for John's target audience.

Second, Martha's confession prompts action: she goes back to Mary and urges her to go to Jesus.[46] John connects the confession and her "going" with the temporal marker "when" (*kai*) in 11:28. Now both women will be able to witness the sign that demonstrates the truth of what he has told her: "I am the resurrection and the life" (11:25).[47]

Third, it is not clear at all that Martha's warning of the stench of Lazarus's body indicates a lack of faith in what Jesus is able to do (11:39).[48] Rather, Martha's words serve the narrative dramatically by

45. Her confession also contains a combination of elements that are also present in the claims of Nathanael and the Samaritan woman ("Son of God," 1:49; "Messiah," 4:29), and comes before she witnesses a sign to confirm or solidify her belief in Jesus (see also Seim, "Roles," 72).

46. Contra Francis J. Moloney, "Can Everyone Be Wrong? A Reading of John 11.1–12.8," *New Testament Studies* 49 (2003): 515, I do not think Martha's reference to Jesus as "the teacher" (*ho didaskalos*) suggests an inadequate faith or confession on her part.

47. Elisabeth Schüssler Fiorenza, "A Feminist Critical Interpretation for Liberation: Martha and Mary: Lk. 10:38–42," *Religion and Intellectual Life* (1986): 31–32, sees Martha's call to Mary as a parallel to Andrew and Philip's call of Peter and Nathanael in 1:35–51, although Reinhartz, "Narrative to History," 175, points out that Mary was already a disciple of Jesus, and argues that her call to Mary simply serves to transition the narrative to the next scene. These need not be mutually exclusive options. The audience would be reminded of these early instances of going and telling about Jesus and the subsequent discipleship based on belief in him.

48. Contra Moloney, "Can Everyone Be Wrong?," 520.

emphasizing the reality of death: Lazarus isn't just sleeping (11:12)—his body will have started decaying by now. John repeats that Lazarus is dead, even twice in this verse.[49] That Martha does not quite understand what Jesus can and will do has already been made clear in their dialogue, for she is thinking of the general resurrection, not Lazarus's immediate resurrection. And she is not alone. None of the other characters anticipate Lazarus's resurrection, even those male disciples whom Jesus told of his intentions to "wake" him (11:11). Jesus's sign will be a shock to all who witness it, even those who have professed their belief and love for him. This shocking turn is emphasized by the repeated claims of Martha, Mary, and the Jews who have come to mourn their brother: that Jesus could have done something to stop his death from happening (11:21, 32, 37).

While John depicts Martha as a faithful disciple who recognizes who Jesus is, brings others to him, and helps move the narrative along toward the cross and resurrection, Jesus's closest male disciples are another story. While they feature prominently in the lead-up to Jesus's journey to Bethany, they disappear once they arrive in town (11:42), as they are not mentioned at all once Jesus engages with the two sisters. Nor is their presence in the opening scene at all favorable. They express resistance to Jesus's decision to go to Judea because they fear his opposition (11:8; had he listened, the rest of the story would not have happened). Like Martha and the other characters, they do not understand Jesus's metaphor of "sleeping" as death, but unlike Martha, they lack an interest in continuing the conversation and thus do not progress in their understanding (11:12–16). Although Martha does not understand fully what Jesus is going to do until he does it, she does display a certain level of belief in him with her confession that comes *prior* to the sign Jesus performs.[50] By contrast, Jesus states that he will do this sign *so that* the male disciples will believe (*hina pisteusēte*, 11:15). With the mention of Thomas immediately following, John is drawing attention to their lack of belief, in contrast to the ready belief of Martha. More, we later discover that Thomas's claim that he is willing to die with Jesus is empty, as neither he nor any

49. This is the reason John tell us (again) that Martha was "the sister of the dead man" (11:39). See also 11:4 (anticipating Lazarus's death), 13, 14, 17, 21, 25, 32, 37, 44.

50. See also Schneiders, "Fourth Gospel," 136.

of the other male disciples will remain by Jesus when he is arrested and stands trial. Although no one fully gets it in the Gospel of John, the female disciples get closest—as close as human characters in the narrative can get—to the truth of who Jesus is.

Mary's Anointing (John 12:1–8)

The second story involving Martha and Mary comes in the next chapter, and this time the focus is on Mary. While Martha's discipleship centered on her words about Jesus's identity, Mary's story emphasizes actions that model faithful discipleship.[51]

After Martha's confession and Jesus's performance of the sign that proves he is "the resurrection and the life," John notes that some of the Jews who had witnessed Lazarus's resurrection proceeded to go to the Pharisees to report on him (11:45–46). Jesus's enemies are worried about the ramifications of the belief in Jesus that comes as the consequence of his signs. Their concern is that Jesus will gain enough believers to attract the attention of Rome, and that the Romans will respond with violence against the people and the temple (11:48). This worry leads Caiaphas unknowingly to predict the substitutionary nature of Jesus's death: that it is better to have one man die for the people than to have the whole nation destroyed (11:50). While the high priest certainly intends his observation as a motivation for the council to offer Jesus up as a strategy to stave off a potential Roman crackdown on the Jews, the audience knows that, no matter what the intentions of Jesus's enemies might be, Jesus's death is precisely the reason for which God has sent him: to give his only Son so that those who believe will not perish but have eternal life (3:16). Moreover, the members of the Jewish council certainly do not understand that Lazarus's resurrection is merely a foretaste of what God will do through Jesus—that after Jesus dies, he will be raised from the dead.

In John 12:1–8, the story switches scenes once again. We are now at a meal at Lazarus, Martha, and Mary's home, where Jesus is the honored guest.[52] The sandwiching of themes in these three succes-

51. Schüssler Fiorenza, *In Memory of Her*, 330.

52. Reinhartz, "Narrative to History," 181, regards the setting as an important indication that the two sisters were regarded as disciples of Jesus. They host

sive passages (Lazarus's resurrection, the opposition that seeks Jesus's death, and Jesus's anointing, which anticipates his burial) invites us to recognize the connections among them. The narrative is progressing toward the glorification (death) and resurrection of Jesus.

That the dinner is given in Jesus's honor precisely because of his action in resurrecting Lazarus cannot be in doubt.[53] John tells us that Lazarus dined at the table with Jesus while Martha served the meal (12:2).[54] At some point, Mary takes a pound[55] of perfume made from pure nard—a costly ointment—and anoints Jesus's feet and then wipes them with her hair (12:3). John describes the house being filled with the smell of the perfume, much like the fragrance of the incense that fills the tabernacle and temple (Exod 40:27; Lev 16:12–13).[56] It also may serve as a bit of irony, as there has just been a complaint about the stinkiness of Lazarus's preresurrected body (John 11:39), as well as a foreshadowing of the care of Jesus's own dead body with spices and oils (19:39).

This lovely moment is broken by an objection from one of Jesus's male disciples, Judas, who questions Mary's actions by suggesting that it would have been better if she had given the perfume to Jesus so that he could sell it and give the large amount of money (almost a year of wages!) to the poor (12:5). As an aside, John states that Judas made this suggestion not because he cared about the poor but because he was the treasurer of the ministry, and that he had been skimming off

---

the meal with their brother for Jesus and are present among the other male disciples in attendance, suggesting that they were part of—or at the very least close to—Jesus's inner circle.

53. See also Mary L. Coloe, "Anointing the Temple of God: John 12:1–8," in *Transcending Boundaries: Contemporary Readings of the New Testament; Essays in Honor of Francis J. Moloney*, ed. Rekha M. Chennattu and Mary L. Coloe (Rome: Libreria Ateneo Salesiano, 2005), 116.

54. Brown, "Roles," 690, argues that this makes Martha a *diakonos*, an official role that exists as early as Acts 6:1–6.

55. A Roman pound is roughly 11.5 ounces.

56. Coloe, "Anointing," interprets this scene as an indication that Jesus himself is replacing the temple building. See Dominika A. Kurek-Chomycz, "The Fragrance of Her Perfume: The Significance of Sense Imagery in John's Account of the Anointing in Bethany," *Novum Testamentum* 52 (2010): 334–54, for some fascinating insights into the role that the senses play in these anointing stories, which would certainly make the presentation of the gospel a more dynamic experience for John's audience.

the top of Jesus's income for some time (12:6). Responding to Judas's criticism, Jesus defends Mary, connects the ointment with his upcoming burial, and implies that her priorities and sense of urgency are well placed, as the poor will always be with the disciples but he will not (12:7–8).

We have already seen how this episode connects to the two preceding scenes, Lazarus's resurrection and the deliberation and plotting of the opponents that is sparked by this sign.[57] More important, however, is that Mary's action anticipates a following scene in John 13:2–9: Jesus washes the feet of his disciples at his final meal with them. In the passage, Jesus's actions provide an example for his disciples to follow (13:14–15). Not only will he have nothing to do with them if they do not allow him to model servanthood for them (13:8), but he explicitly connects their role as "sent ones" (*apostoloi*, 13:16) to this type of servanthood. This is the only time in the Gospel of John that Jesus uses the term "apostle," and he understands this role to be intimately connected to service—the kind of service that Jesus has just modeled by washing their feet. Thus, Mary and Jesus engage in similar acts of service. Not only is Mary doing what her Lord does, but she does what is required of those who follow him.[58]

The scene at Bethany also includes dissimilar and contrasting actions. While Mary is honoring Jesus by anointing him with costly perfume, Lazarus is again a nonfactor. As in John 11, Lazarus is the reason for all of the action. Here he attends the meal in his own house, but he is only one among several at the table and he lacks any impact on the story (12:2).[59] Much worse than Lazarus is Judas, who actively opposes what Mary does. This episode functions in some important ways in the

57. This connection with Lazarus's resurrection may also explain why John names the woman who anoints Jesus—the Synoptics do not identify her in their versions (Matt 26:6–13; Mark 14:3–9; Luke 7:36–50).

58. J. Ramsey Michaels, "John 12:1–11," *Interpretation* 43 (1989): 289: "Mary of Bethany is a pivotal figure in the Gospel of John. If her anointing of Jesus anticipates the footwashing scene, she is also the first to exemplify the ideal of discipleship to be developed in the farewell discourses of chapters 14–17. It is with Mary and the anointing still in mind that Jesus first sets forth this ideal." It is also noteworthy that Martha is engaging in a different type of service (12:2). Unlike in Luke 10:38–42, these two approaches are not compared or contrasted—each woman serves Jesus in some way.

59. Rather, it is his two sisters who function—in the language of Schüssler Fiorenza, *In Memory of Her*, 330—as "the two ministers at the supper."

larger gospel narrative. John is the only gospel writer to give an early rationale as to why Judas will eventually sell Jesus out to his enemies: he is greedy and shortsighted, interested primarily in his personal gain, and does not display a concern for others whom Jesus loves—either Mary or "the poor" he uses as a pretext for his complaint. And while Mary is willing to make her service public, Judas, in the scene of Jesus's own service in John 13, is noticeably and repeatedly excluded from being regarded as a true disciple, because he has already determined to betray Jesus (13:2), receives no benefit of "cleanness" from the footwashing (13:12–13), and is not numbered among the ones whom Jesus has chosen, because of his anticipated betrayal (13:18).[60] Judas, increasingly portrayed as an unfaithful disciple at best and a nondisciple at worst, lacks the care and humility that Mary demonstrates in her anointing of Jesus, an action that demonstrates priorities that are in line with Jesus's own. Overall, John 11–12 anticipates Jesus's death, burial, and resurrection while placing Martha and Mary at the center as disciples whose actions foreshadow these events.

The Presence of the Women at the Cross (John 19:25–27)

At the crucifixion scene, John places several female disciples in close proximity to the dying Jesus. Although this is not a self-contained story as are the passages we have studied thus far, the women's presence does have an impact on the scene and our understanding of Johannine discipleship. John lists four women at the cross: the mother of Jesus, her sister (unnamed), Mary the wife of Clopas, and Mary Magdalene.[61] Of the four, two figure prominently in the gospel. The mother of Jesus was present and instrumental in Jesus's first sign at the wedding at Cana and has continued to follow him along with the other male disciples he called (2:1–12).[62] Mary Magdalene will play an important role in the resurrection account that follows Jesus's death, and she will be the first to share the news that Jesus is risen (20:1–18).

60. Instead, Judas will "fulfill the scriptures" by betraying Jesus, which is recounted while they are at the meal itself (13:21–30).

61. Cf. Brown, *John*, 904–5, for a helpful discussion of the wording of the list of women and the reasons why it indicates four women.

62. Grassi, "Reappraisal," 71, argues that the seventh sign of the gospel is Jesus's hour (death and glorification). In this case, Jesus's mother is present for the first and the last of his signs.

This scene, then, serves as a sort of hinge between the two women's stories: we find out what will happen to Jesus's mother once her son is dead, and we are introduced to a person who will be a key character in the resurrection story.[63]

Although these women do not seem to be engaged in much activity in the scene (their "doing" is simply to be present at the cross), their position is nevertheless helpful for our understanding of female discipleship in the gospel. First, they are with Jesus at the crucial juncture of the narrative, the moment in which all his actions and teachings culminate: his "hour" has finally come, and they are there to witness it. Along with the anonymous "beloved disciple," they are the only disciples mentioned as being present at the foot of the cross. The other male disciples have either dropped from the narrative since his arrest (18:8–9) or actively denied Jesus (18:17–18, 25–27).[64] Moreover, the language of "standing by" the cross directly contrasts with the actions of some disciples who left early in Jesus's ministry: those who "go away from" him because they do not believe his teaching.[65] Thus, these women represent Jesus's remaining support—they are the last familiar faces he will see before he breathes his last. They are committed to remaining with him until the end.[66]

Second, John focuses on the newly formed kinship between the beloved disciple and the mother of Jesus—a relationship Jesus arranged as one of his last acts before death.[67] The beloved disciple is

63. John does not elaborate on the stories of the other two women—the sister of the mother of Jesus and the wife of Clopas. Narratively, they serve only to swell the ranks of the group that has stood by Jesus's side—an overwhelmingly female group. Given that their mention fails to serve the narrative in any other way, it is safe to assume that his audience was familiar with them.

64. They do not reenter the narrative as a group until 20:19, where they hide from the opposition behind locked doors. It is unclear where Peter is from the moment he denies Jesus (19:27) until we see him running to the tomb with the beloved disciple (20:2). Although outside the typical group of disciples who have been with Jesus throughout his ministry, both Joseph of Arimathea and Nicodemus arrange for the care and burial of his body (19:38–42).

65. Fehribach, *Bridegroom*, 133. See 19:25 (*heistēkeisan . . . para tō staurō tou Iēsou*) and 6:66–67 (*hypagein*).

66. These women are exemplifying the "abiding" that Jesus demands of his disciples in John 15:1–11.

67. The beloved disciple remains by Jesus's side, while his own brothers do not believe in him (7:3–9).

one of the members of Jesus's inner circle, and so Jesus's mother remains in this group as his new mother. The women who are with them would likely be considered part of the family as well. We realize that the mother of Jesus, as part of the household of the beloved disciple, will continue to be involved in the new community of believers.[68]

Third, from a narrative perspective, it is crucial that Mary Magdalene witnesses Jesus's death for herself, as she will soon be confronted with a missing corpse and will later discover that Jesus has risen from the dead. There is no room to entertain the possibility that he avoided death by some deception on the part of his followers.[69]

Mary Magdalene's Proclamation (John 20:1–18)

The final passage that portrays female discipleship in John's Gospel is located in the account of the resurrection of Jesus in 20:1–18. Like the crucifixion scene, this is a key text because it finally recounts the events that have been long anticipated. That a woman features so prominently in the depiction of the resurrected Jesus's first encounters with his followers is remarkably consistent with the positive portrayal of female discipleship that has been a hallmark of the narrative.

In the Fourth Gospel, Mary Magdalene is the first person and the only woman who goes to the tomb on the morning after the Sabbath (20:1).[70] Just days before, she witnessed Jesus's brutal execution. Grief-stricken, she is distraught when she realizes that the stone in front

68. John 14:2–3, 18–20, 28–29. Schüssler Fiorenza, *In Memory of Her*, 331, sees this as an indication of her new role as mother of all the disciples. See also Adriana Destro and Mauro Pesce, "Kinship, Discipleship, and Movement: An Anthropological Study of John's Gospel," *Biblical Interpretation* 3 (1995): 266–84, for a detailed study of the kinship motif at the cross.

69. John emphasizes the testimony of the one who saw the blood and water flow from Jesus's side—a physical indication that he died (19:35). Grassi, "Reappraisal," 73–77, suggests that Jesus's mother would have been an important witness for the community of the crucifixion and of the manner in which he died, as she would be expected to remember her son just as God never forgets his son, Israel (Isa 49:15 NRSVUE: "Can a woman forget her nursing child or show no compassion for the child of her womb? Even these may forget, yet I will not forget you").

70. When she runs to report the empty tomb to Peter and the beloved disciple, she does use the plural "we" (*oidamen*, 20:2), which may suggest that there are other women with her, but John explicitly mentions only her at this point.

of the tomb has been rolled away, and so she runs to tell Peter and the beloved disciple that Jesus's body has been stolen (20:2). At her words, Peter and the beloved disciple run to the tomb, and—in a bit of a competition—the beloved disciple gets to the tomb first. Rather than enter, however, he peeks inside the tomb and confirms that only linen wrappings remain (20:3–5). Once Peter arrives, he enters the tomb and notices that the head cloth is rolled up and has been set apart from the linen wrappings (20:6–7). Following his lead, the beloved disciple goes into the tomb, sees the state of it, and believes (20:8), although John is careful to let us know that neither one of them understood that Jesus had been raised from the dead (20:9).

Abruptly, the two men return home, but Mary Magdalene stays, weeping outside the tomb (20:10–11). While there, she sees two angels sitting in the tomb where Jesus's body had once been. When they ask her why she is weeping, she responds despondently, "They have taken away my Lord, and I do not know where they have laid him" (20:12–13 NRSVUE). At that moment Mary Magdalene encounters the risen Jesus, although she does not recognize him; instead, she mistakes him for a gardener. He, too, asks her why she weeps, and she responds by suggesting that he might have taken the body and that she would take it back if he would just tell her where he put it (20:14–15). Finally, Jesus reveals his identity to her by calling her by name, and she responds with the exclamation "Rabbouni!"—an indication that their primary relationship is that of student and teacher (20:16). Jesus tells her not to hold onto him, because he must still ascend to the Father, and then commissions her to tell the other disciples of his upcoming ascension (20:17). The scene ends when Mary Magdalene goes to the disciples, announces that she has seen Jesus, and delivers the message he has sent with her (20:18).

Mary Magdalene's presence at the tomb continues a narrative thread that we have seen throughout the gospel and emphasized in the previous crucifixion scene: Jesus's female followers desire to remain near him.[71] We are not told why Mary Magdalene goes to the tomb in the wee hours of the morning; it seems that she is simply fol-

71. Martin Hengel, "Maria Magdalena und die Frauen als Zeugen," in *Abraham unser Vater: Juden und Christen im Gespräch über die Bibel, Festschrift für Otto Michel zum 60. Geburtstag*, ed. Otto Betz, Martin Hengel, and Peter Schmidt (Leiden: Brill, 1963), 256.

lowing him once again.[72] Given the effort she makes to be near Jesus, dead or alive, her distress at seeing the tomb open is palpable. Her assumption, that his body has been stolen,[73] causes such panic that she runs and tells Peter and the beloved disciple what (she thinks) has happened. That Mary Magdalene knows exactly where to find these two leaders of Jesus's inner circle of male disciples suggests that she is part of the larger group of disciples who have remained together after Jesus's death (20:19). Although she knows where they are hiding,[74] she is separate from them because she risks her own safety to go and see Jesus's body alone. Later, when Jesus first approaches her, he asks her whom she is seeking.[75] Perhaps her effort to be near him and her initiative in telling the others that Jesus is missing is why she is later rewarded with being the first to see him face to face.[76]

Regarding Mary Magdalene's conclusion that the body of Jesus had been taken, it is important to recognize that *no one* in the story assumes that an empty tomb indicates that Jesus's prophecies have come true—that he has, in fact, been raised from the dead. She draws a logical conclusion: a graverobber has come in the night and stolen Jesus's body, and Peter and the beloved disciple's response to see for themselves indicates that they also consider this possibility likely.[77]

72. Contra Sandra M. Schneiders, "Touching the Risen Jesus: Mary Magdalene and Thomas the Twin in John 20," in Koester and Bieringer, *Resurrection of Jesus*, 163, who believes the timing of her journey to the tomb has a negative import, as darkness usually does in John. Although that is often the case, there are no other indications in the narrative that Mary Magdalene is using the nighttime hour to protect herself or do this in secret (as Nicodemus does in John 3).

73. According to Matt 27:62–64, this was a legitimate concern.

74. Although it is possible that the male disciples do not hide behind locked doors until after Jesus's body goes missing from the tomb (20:19), John implies that they are staying under the radar after Jesus's death, continuing their practice of self-preservation in the face of physical peril (18:25–27; 20:10).

75. Schüssler Fiorenza, *In Memory of Her*, 333, argues that the use of the verb *zetein* in Jesus's question is significant, as it includes the idea of studying and engaging in the activities of a disciple.

76. His appearance to her also fulfills his promise that he will show himself to his disciples (14:21).

77. Cf. Ekaterina Kozlova, "Women and Ancient Mortuary Culture(s)," *Covenant Quarterly* 72 (2014): 159, who considers the prominent role that women had in ancient mortuary culture at the time, which could explain why Mary Magdalene is the one who seems most distraught at the missing body.

Thus, Mary Magdalene does not appear as unbelieving or ignorant among other disciples who know better—all of them believe that something nefarious has happened, despite the fact that Jesus had been speaking of his resurrection in their presence since the beginning of his ministry (2:19–22). At this point, only we know that Jesus is no longer dead but has been raised to life. This is true even of the beloved disciple. Although the gospel says that he "believed" (*episteusen*, 20:8), the context of this statement indicates that his belief is based on his own verification of Mary Magdalene's words (that the tomb is indeed empty), not that he believed that Jesus had been raised.[78] In fact, John says as much in the following verse: they did not yet understand that Jesus must rise again according to the Scriptures (20:9).[79] This is why both men respond to their discovery by returning home. What is there to do, now that even Jesus's dead body is gone?[80]

The theme of "seeing" runs throughout this episode and is key to understanding Mary Magdalene's role, especially in relation to the male disciples. Most of these disciples stay in hiding and see nothing at all. Peter and the beloved disciple see the empty tomb and the discarded wrappings of Jesus's body. Yet they don't really *see* what is going on, at least not in the Johannine sense of understanding (e.g., John 9), and so they go back to join the others.[81] Because they do not stay as Mary Magdalene does, they do not see what she sees: first, two angels who appear in the very place where Jesus's body has disappeared, and second, the risen Jesus himself. The narrative emphasizes that the male disciples who were the closest of all of Jesus's companions just missed the revelation of God's power in the person of the resurrected Christ. Just as at the cross, although Mary Magdalene can do nothing but stay, staying becomes the action that leads to

78. Contra Ken Chan, "John 19:38–20:31: Discipleship after the Death of Jesus," *Conspectus* 15 (2013): 71.

79. Brown, *John*, 1007–8, takes John's statement as an indication of the beloved disciple's belief in the resurrection and suggests as evidence the state of the graveclothes, which Brown thinks would have been a clue either that his body was not stolen or that it had "passed through" them. He does not explain why the beloved disciple would come to this conclusion, but Peter would not have reached the same.

80. And even after they receive the news of Jesus's resurrection from Mary Magdalene, they remain behind locked doors until Jesus visits them personally (20:19). Even after her witness to the resurrection, they still do not *do* anything.

81. Brown, "Roles," 692.

something extraordinary. In the process she becomes the first gospel witness to the resurrection.

Mary Magdalene's conversation with Jesus also indicates her commitment to following him, despite her initial despair in thinking that he is dead and that his body has been stolen.[82] Before Jesus reveals his true identity to her (while she still thinks he is the gardener), she professes her willingness to reclaim Jesus's body from wherever he might have taken him.[83] Unlike the male disciples who are hiding to protect their own lives, Mary Magdalene is not willing to accept that Jesus's body has been stolen and proposes to do something about it. Perhaps her determination to retrieve the body is the reason that Jesus chooses to reveal himself to her, for it is in that moment that he does so. It is quite possible that her display of faithfulness and courage compels him to allow her fully to *see* to whom she is actually talking. And yet, much like the other women we have studied in this gospel, she still has more to learn.[84] Understanding is gained gradually. She responds to this revelation by calling him "Rabbouni," a title appropriate for him during his earthly ministry and indicating her recognition of him as the man she has followed.[85] Although her exclamation does not indicate a lack of faith, it does help explain his

82. Richard Bauckham, *Gospel Women: Studies of the Named Women in the Gospels* (Grand Rapids: Eerdmans, 2002), 284, notes that John's one-on-one resurrection encounter here reflects his penchant for focusing on the stories of interactions between Jesus and individual characters.

83. Although Chan, "Death of Jesus," 66, interprets her inability to recognize Jesus at first as a lack of faith, there is no indication that this is the case. Failure to recognize the risen Jesus is a theme in the Gospel of Luke as well (24:13–32) and here contributes to the typical Johannine movement from misunderstanding to understanding.

84. Dorothy A. Lee, "Partnership in Easter Faith: The Role of Mary Magdalene and Thomas in John 20," *Journal for the Study of the New Testament* 58 (1995): 38, argues that Mary Magdalene and Thomas act in a "narrative partnership," both displaying misunderstanding that should be read positively because "misunderstanding is an authentic marker on the journey of faith."

85. The Johannine Jesus's response is not a criticism of the title she uses per se (as if he were not her teacher any longer). Rather, it functions much like Jesus's accommodation of Thomas's request later in the chapter: a way of emphasizing the continuity between the man they knew and the resurrected Jesus who stands before them (20:24–29). As others have noted, Mary Magdalene recognizes the good shepherd (10:3–5, 14, 27). E.g., Bauckham, *Gospel Women*, 284.

following command, "Do not cling to me" (20:17). He will not go back to his former relationship with his disciples but will soon ascend to the Father. His resurrection has changed the way he will interact with his followers. Moreover, his reaction might anticipate his instructions immediately following. She must go and witness to his resurrection, alerting the other disciples that he is risen.[86]

Mary Magdalene's dedication to Jesus's welfare, even in death, allows her to be the first to *witness* the resurrected Jesus and the first to *witness to* the reality of the resurrection.[87] Her steadfastness and love for Jesus make her the best candidate for sharing the good news that he has risen from the dead. Mary Magdalene's twofold proclamation accurately reflects the illumination she has received from her encounter with the resurrected Jesus: she has seen her Lord, and he will soon ascend to his Father (20:18). In terms of narrative impact, she is the first bearer of the message for which the audience has been waiting, and thus becomes a model for faithful discipleship for the community.[88] A faithful disciple should testify to the good news of Jesus's death and resurrection.

Conclusion

The women who follow Jesus in the Gospel of John provide a model for discipleship through their words and actions. His mother initiates the first sign of his ministry. The Samaritan woman is actively engaged in a conversation that leads to her recognition of Jesus's identity as Messiah, and is prompted by this to tell her neighbors to see for themselves. Martha articulates the climactic confession of the gospel. Mary spends an extravagant amount of money to honor Jesus, and this deed serves as an anticipation both of his own model of service to his disciples and of his burial. His mother, her sister, the wife of Clopas, and Mary Magdalene are all present at the cross to witness his death, when all but one of the male disciples are nowhere to be found. And, finally, Mary Magdalene's dedication to Jesus, even in

86. O'Brien, "Written," 295.

87. Mary Magdalene is often called "the apostle to the apostles."

88. Gerald O'Collins and Daniel Kendall, "Mary Magdalene as Major Witness to Jesus' Resurrection," *Theological Studies* 48 (1987): 632: "The early 'witnesses' of the risen Jesus were the ones who got Christianity going."

death, is rewarded when Jesus gives her the task of proclaiming the first full gospel message: Jesus is alive! While none of the women are presented as perfect, since only Jesus fills this role, even their initial misunderstandings lead to understanding, both on the first level of the narrative as characters in the story and on the second level as examples for the audience of a collective movement that culminates in belief in Jesus as the Messiah who has been sent by the Father for the sake of the world.

Conclusion

Women in the Gospels as Models of Discipleship

In this study we have unearthed a group of disciples whose stories have gone undiscovered—or, worse, been ignored—in most discussions of discipleship. In this process of discovery, we have brought to the surface the ways in which their actions should contribute to our own understanding of discipleship. In a context in which simply being a woman was a disadvantage, the female disciples in Jesus's ministry are portrayed as models of faith. They are people who take initiative. They are disciples who act when all others around them do not. They make good on their commitment to follow Jesus and demonstrate the qualities of discipleship that Jesus demands of his followers.

In the Gospel of Mark, we encounter women who serve: Simon's mother-in-law and the women who have been with Jesus throughout his ministry are present and prepared to serve him at the end, even in death. By bracketing his gospel with these stories, Mark highlights the importance of service in the life of believers. His gospel also contains the stories of women who pursue Jesus and are subsequently lauded for their actions. Representative of these women are the hemorrhaging woman and the Syrophoenician woman—both of whom are desperate and determined to benefit from the healing power of Jesus. In response to their actions, Jesus fulfills their requests. Given his response to their pursuit of him, it is no wonder that he would attract other women who would commit themselves and their resources to his mission. Alongside the women who are constantly in the background of the gospel, Mark spotlights women who demonstrate sacrificial discipleship. The widow who gives up her last coins and the stability that a few coins in her pocket might bring and the woman who showers Jesus with costly ointment represent the kind of discipleship that Jesus demands from his followers. They are lauded for their faith in action—for putting their money where their mouth is. Of the four canonical gospels, Mark makes the strongest contrast between the faithfulness of female disciples in what they do and the twelve male disciples, who often do nothing and sometimes even attempt to thwart Jesus's plan.

In the Gospel of Matthew, through his genealogy the author anticipates the role that women's actions will play in the life of Jesus. The list of Jesus's ancestors includes four women who act in ways that ultimately provide a path for the Messiah. Because Matthew has prepared his audience to expect women to have a crucial part to play in the story of Jesus, it is not surprising that women who encounter Jesus become exemplars of faith. His narratives of the hemorrhaging woman and the Canaanite woman emphasize their faith and the extent to which they are willing to act on that faith to experience healing. Finally, given that women are portrayed as integral parts of Jesus's story, it comes as no surprise that, in the end, it is women who are present to first meet the resurrected Jesus and who are commissioned to be the first preachers of the good news that he has risen from the dead.

In Luke-Acts, the author begins his multivolume work with three women who are centered in the fulfillment of God's promises through Jesus. Elizabeth, Mary, and Anna are prophets of God who anticipate the salvation that Jesus will bring. They display trust in the message they receive from God and embrace their roles in bearing John and Jesus and testifying to the arrival of the Messiah. When others doubt, they believe. The example of this kind of active discipleship is continued in the story of the woman who loves Jesus and shows hospitality to him by anointing him. Moreover, Luke is the only gospel writer to tell his audience early in the narrative that there were women who funded Jesus's ministry—women who had benefited from his healing power and responded with action. As a result of their commitment, they are with him to the very end. Perhaps this commitment is why they are right in the middle of the activity of the Holy Spirit in the new phase of Jesus's ministry. Luke begins his second volume with women engaged in the prayerful selection of a new apostle and with the coming of the Holy Spirit at Pentecost. This activity anticipates the role women will have as prophets and teachers, as leaders of their faith communities, as those who see what God is doing even when they themselves are neglected or overlooked. Throughout Luke-Acts, women such as Martha, Mary, Rhoda, Tabitha, Lydia, and Priscilla serve as exemplars of faithful discipleship in action.

In the Gospel of John, the author highlights Jesus's interactions with women who demonstrate the movement from misunderstanding or lack of understanding to the kind of belief that the gospel aims to engender. Jesus's mother is the catalyst for the first of his signs, and she remains with him until the end of his life. The Samaritan woman engages in a theological discussion that results in the conversion of a whole town. Martha makes a greater confession of faith than any of the apostles. Mary anticipates Jesus's teachings on what disciples should do in serving each other by anointing Jesus. And, because of her presence at the tomb, Mary Magdalene is the first to encounter the risen Jesus and is commissioned to go and tell of his resurrection to the rest of the disciples.

The overwhelming impression from the Gospels is that the women in Jesus's life are women of action. While others around them deliberate, plot, complain, challenge Jesus, or are merely bystanders to the activities taking place around them, a consistent theme of the Jesus story is that there are female disciples who are engaged in what God is doing through him. Jesus's teachings on discipleship are embodied in these women: they serve, sacrifice, demonstrate genuine faith, and are willing to risk their lives for the sake of the gospel. They are *women who do*, and that is something worth recognizing and emulating.

At my university I often end my lectures with a "So what?" moment of reflection. It is my way of acknowledging that I can talk about the gospel stories all day long, but if they don't have some sort of relevance for my students' lives, what's the point? The practice also recognizes that we never just read stories—stories provoke response and affect actions.

So, what is the "So what?" of our study of female discipleship in the Gospels? At a minimum, it urges us to include these stories of women in any discussion of women's roles and leadership in the church. Imagine our study of the topic like the gathering of evidence on a detective's string board. In this analogy, we draw a line from one disparate piece of information to another with yarn so that we can see the connections that might otherwise have been overlooked. In the case of women in the church, our string board should include not only texts such as 1 Timothy 2, 1 Corinthians 11 and 14, and Ephesians 5–6, but also John 4, Mark 7, Luke 8, and so many more gospel stories of Jesus's encounters with women. Including these texts recognizes the importance of allowing the larger scope of Scripture to shape our understanding of discipleship. When we do that, the fact that women are faithful followers of Jesus can be included as a relevant piece of the conversation. There is space to recognize that women are often model examples of discipleship and to admire what they do. Women can receive acknowledgment for their faithfulness and can be entrusted with the kingdom, because Jesus's words apply to them too: "Well done, good and faithful servant" (Matt 25:23).

Bibliography

Allen, Prudence. *The Concept of Woman: The Aristotelian Revolution, 750 B.C.–A.D. 1250*. 2nd ed. Grand Rapids: Eerdmans, 1997.

Anderson, Janice Capel. "Matthew: Gender and Reading." *Semeia* 28 (1983): 3–27.

Arnal, William E. "Gendered Couplets in Q and Legal Formulations: From Rhetoric to Social History." *Journal of Biblical Literature* 116 (1997): 75–94.

Attridge, Harold W. "From Discord Rises Meaning: Resurrection Motifs in the Fourth Gospel." Pages 1–19 in Koester and Bieringer, *Resurrection of Jesus*.

———. "The Samaritan Woman: A Woman Transformed." Pages 268–81 in *Character Studies in the Fourth Gospel: Narrative Approaches to Seventy Figures in John*. Edited by Stephen A. Hunt, D. Francois Tolmie, and Ruben Zimmerman. Grand Rapids: Eerdmans, 2016.

Baffes, Melanie S. "Jesus and the Canaanite Woman: A Story of Reversal." *Journal of Theta Alpha Kappa* 35 (2011): 12–23.

Balch, David L. *Let Wives Be Submissive: The Domestic Code in 1 Peter*. Society of Biblical Literature Monograph Series 26. Atlanta: Scholars Press, 1981.

Barr, Beth Allison. "Faith Adjacent: Beth Allison Barr." *The Bible Binge* podcast, June 17, 2022, https://thebiblebinge.com/bethallisonbarr/.

Barrett, C. K. "Is There a Theological Tendency in Codex Bezae?" Pages 15–28 in *Text and Interpretation: Studies in the New Testament Presented to Matthew Black*. Edited by Ernest Best and R. McL. Wilson. Cambridge: Cambridge University Press, 1979.

Barton, Stephen C. "Mark as Narrative: The Story of the Anointing Woman (Mk 14:3–9)." *Expository Times* 102 (1991): 230–34.

Bauckham, Richard. *Gospel Women: Studies of the Named Women in the Gospels.* Grand Rapids: Eerdmans, 2002.

Beavis, Mary Ann. "Mary of Bethany and the Hermeneutics of Remembrance." *Catholic Biblical Quarterly* 75 (2013): 739–55.

———. "Women as Models of Faith in Mark." *Biblical Theology Bulletin* 18 (1988): 3–9.

Belleville, Linda L. "Women Leaders in the Bible." Pages 110–25 in *Discovering Biblical Equality: Complementarity without Hierarchy.* Edited by Ronald W. Pierce and Rebecca Merrill Groothuis. Downers Grove, IL: IVP Academic, 2005.

Berger, Adolf. *Encyclopedic Dictionary of Roman Law.* Philadelphia: American Philosophical Society, 1953.

Bertschmann, Dorothea H. "Hosting Jesus: Revisiting Luke's 'Sinful Woman' (Luke 7.36–50) as a Tale of Two Hosts." *Journal for the Study of the New Testament* 40 (2017): 30–50.

Black, C. Clifton. *The Disciples according to Mark: Markan Redaction in Current Debate.* Journal for the Study of the New Testament Supplement Series 27. Sheffield: Sheffield Academic, 1989.

Booth, William D. "The Open Door for Women Preachers: Acts 2:17, 18; 21:9; Romans 10:15; Ephesians 4:11." *Journal of Religious Thought* 50 (1994): 108–15.

Boring, M. Eugene. "The Gospel of Matthew." Pages 87–105 in *The New Interpreter's Bible.* Vol. 8. Edited by Leander E. Keck. Nashville: Abingdon, 1995.

Botha, Eugene. "John 4.16: A Difficult Text Speech Act Theoretically Revisited." Pages 183–92 in Stibbe, *Gospel of John.*

Brenner, Athalya, ed. *Are We Amused? Humour about Women in the Biblical World.* London: Continuum, 2003.

Brooten, Bernadette J. *Women Leaders in the Ancient Synagogue.* Brown Judaic Studies 36. Atlanta: Scholars Press, 1982.

Brown, Raymond E. *The Birth of the Messiah: A Commentary on the Infancy Narratives in the Gospels of Matthew and Luke.* Anchor Bible Reference Library. New Haven: Yale University Press, 1999.

———. *The Gospel according to John I–XII.* Anchor Bible 29. New York: Doubleday, 1966.

———. "The Presentation of Jesus (Luke 22:22–40)." *Worship* 51 (1977): 2–11.

———. “Roles of Women in the Fourth Gospel.” *Theological Studies* 36 (1975): 688–99.

Brown, Schuyler. *Apostasy and Perseverance in the Theology of Luke*. Analecta Biblica 36. Rome: Pontifical Biblical Institute, 1969.

Bulembat, Jean-Bosco Matand. “Head-Waiter and Bridegroom of the Wedding at Cana: Structure and Meaning of John 2.1–12.” *Journal for the Study of the New Testament* 30 (2007): 55–73.

Bultmann, Rudolf. *The Gospel of John: A Commentary*. Translated by George R. Beasley-Murray, Rupert W. N. Hoare, and John K. Riches. Philadelphia: Westminster, 1971.

Byrne, Brendan J. *The Hospitality of God: A Reading of Luke’s Gospel*. Collegeville, MN: Liturgical Press, 2000.

Cadwallander, Alan H. *Beyond the Word of a Woman: Recovering the Bodies of the Syrophoenician Woman*. ATF Biblical Series 1. Adelaide: ATF Press, 2008.

Calpino, Teresa J. “‘The Lord Opened Her Heart’: Boundary Crossing in Acts 16,13–15.” *Annali di Storia dell’Esegesi* 28 (2011): 81–91.

———. “Tabitha and Lydia: Models of Early Christian Women Leaders.” *Biblical Archaeology Review* 42 (2016): 20, 60.

———. *Women, Work and Leadership in Acts*. Wissenschaftliche Untersuchungen zum Neuen Testament 361. Tübingen: Mohr Siebeck, 2014.

Camp, Claudia V. “Understanding a Patriarchy: Women in Second Century Jerusalem through the Eyes of Ben Sira.” Pages 1–39 in Levine, *“Women Like This.”*

Canavan, Rosemary. “Lydia: Open-Hearted to Mission.” *Australasian Catholic Record* 96 (2019): 421–30.

Carey, Holly J. “Jesus and the Syrophoenician Woman: A Case Study in Inclusiveness.” *Leaven* 19, no. 1 (2011): 28–32.

———. “Women in Action: Models for Discipleship in Mark’s Gospel.” *Catholic Biblical Quarterly* 82, no. 3 (2019): 429–48.

Carter, Warren. “Getting Martha Out of the Kitchen: Luke 10:38–42 Again.” *Catholic Biblical Quarterly* 58 (1996): 264–80.

———. *Mark*. Edited by Sarah J. Tanzer. Wisdom Commentary 42. Collegeville, MN: Liturgical Press, 2019.

Catchpole, David. “The Fearful Silence of the Women at the Tomb: A Study in Markan Theology.” *Journal of Theology for Southern Africa* 18 (1977): 3–10.

Ceroke, Christian P. "Jesus and Mary at Cana: Separation or Association?" *Theological Studies* 17 (1956): 1–38.

Chan, Ken. "John 19:38–20:31: Discipleship after the Death of Jesus." *Conspectus* 15 (2013): 57–83.

Cheney, Emily. "The Mother of the Sons of Zebedee (Matthew 27.56)." *Journal for the Study of the New Testament* 68 (1997): 13–21.

Chennattu, Rekha M. *Johannine Discipleship as a Covenant Relationship.* Grand Rapids: Baker, 2005.

Clark-Soles, Jaime. *Women in the Bible.* Interpretation: Resources for the Use of Scripture in the Church. Louisville: Westminster John Knox, 2020.

Cohick, Lynn H. *Women in the World of the Earliest Christians: Illuminating Ancient Ways of Life.* Grand Rapids: Baker Academic, 2009.

Coleman, Rachel L. "Boundary-Shattering Table Fellowship as a Defining Mark of Discipleship in Luke-Acts." *Wesleyan Theological Journal* 54 (2019): 128–42.

Collins, John N. "Did Luke Intend a Disservice to Women in the Martha and Mary Story?" *Biblical Theology Bulletin* 28 (1998): 104–11.

Coloe, Mary L. "Anointing the Temple of God: John 12:1–8." Pages 105–18 in *Transcending Boundaries: Contemporary Readings of the New Testament; Essays in Honor of Francis J. Moloney.* Edited by Rekha M. Chennattu and Mary L. Coloe. Rome: Libreria Ateneo Salesiano, 2005.

———. "The Woman of Samaria: Her Characterization, Narrative, and Theological Significance." Pages 182–96 in *Characters and Characterization in the Gospel of John.* Edited by Christopher W. Skinner. London: Bloomsbury T&T Clark, 2013.

Cooper, Kate. "Closely Watched Households: Visibility, Exposure and Private Power in the Roman *Domus*." *Past and Present* 197 (2007): 3–33.

Cosgrove, Charles H. "A Woman's Unbound Hair in the Greco-Roman World, with Special Reference to the Story of the 'Sinful Woman' in Luke 7:36–50." *Journal of Biblical Literature* 124 (2005): 675–92.

Crook, Zeba. "Honor, Shame, and Social Status Revisited." *Journal of Biblical Literature* 128 (2009): 591–611.

Curkpatrick, Stephen. "'Real and Fictive' Widows: Nuances of Independence and Resistance in Luke." *Lexington Theological Quarterly* 37 (2002): 215–24.

D'Angelo, Mary Rose. "Women in Luke-Acts: A Redactional View." *Journal of Biblical Literature* 109 (1990): 441–61.

———. "Women Partners in the New Testament." *Journal of Feminist Studies in Religion* 6 (1990): 65–86.

Danove, Paul. "The Characterization and Narrative Function of the Women at the Tomb (Mark 15,40–41.47; 16,1–8)." *Biblica* 77, no. 3 (1996): 375–97.

Davidson, Jo Ann. "The Well Women of Scripture Revisited." *Journal of the Adventist Theological Society* 17 (2006): 209–28.

Day, Janeth Norfleete. *The Woman at the Well: Interpretation of John 4:1–42 in Retrospect and Prospect*. Leiden: Brill, 2002.

Destro, Adriana, and Mauro Pesce. "Kinship, Discipleship, and Movement: An Anthropological Study of John's Gospel." *Biblical Interpretation* 3 (1995): 266–84.

Dewey, Joanna. "'Let Them Renounce Themselves and Take Up Their Cross': A Feminist Reading of Mark 8.34 in Mark's Social and Narrative World." Pages 23–36 in Levine, *Feminist Companion to Mark*.

———. "Mark as Interwoven Tapestry: Forecasts and Echoes for a Listening Audience." *Catholic Biblical Quarterly* 53, no. 2 (1991): 221–36.

Dixon, Suzanne. "Exemplary Housewife or Luxurious Slut: Cultural Representations of Women in the Roman Economy." Pages 56–74 in *Women's Influence on Classical Civilization*. Edited by Fiona McHardy and Eireann Marshall. London: Routledge, 2004.

Do, Toan. "Revisiting the Woman of Samaria and the Ambiguity of Faith in John 4:4–42." *Catholic Biblical Quarterly* 81 (2019): 252–76.

Downing, F. Gerald. "The Woman from Syrophoenicia and Her Doggedness: Mark 7.24–41 (Matthew 15.21–28)." Pages 129–49 in *Women in the Biblical Tradition*. Edited by George J. Brooke. Lewiston, NY: Mellen, 1992.

Dreyer, Yolanda. "Gender Critique on the Narrator's Androcentric Point of View of Women in Matthew's Gospel." *Hervormde teologiese studies* 67 (2011).

Edwards, James R. "Parallels and Patterns between Luke and Acts." *Bulletin for Biblical Research* 27 (2017): 485–501.

Embudo, Lora Angeline B. "Women Vis-à-Vis Prophecy in Luke-Acts: Part 2." *Asian Journal of Pentecostal Studies* 20 (2017): 111–30.

Eslinger, Lyle. "The Wooing of the Woman at the Well: Jesus, the Reader and Reader-Response Criticism." Pages 165–82 in Stibbe, *Gospel of John*.

Fee, Gordon. "'One Thing Is Needful'? Luke 10:42." Pages 61–75 in *New Testament Textual Criticism: Its Significance for Exegesis: Essays in Honour of Bruce M. Metzger*. Edited by Eldon Jay Epp and Gordon D. Fee. Oxford: Clarendon, 1981.

Fehribach, Adeline. *The Women in the Life of the Bridegroom: A Feminist Historical-Literary Analysis of the Female Characters in the Fourth Gospel*. Collegeville, MN: Liturgical Press, 1998.

Feuillet, André. "L'Heure de Jesus et le Signe de Cana: Contribution a l'Étude de la Structure du Quatrième Évangile." *Ephemerides Theologicae Lovanienses* 36 (1960): 5–22.

———. "Le Messie et sa Mère d'après le chapitre xii de l'Apocalypse." *Revue biblique* 66 (1959): 55–86.

Field, James A., Jr. "The Purpose of the *Lex Iulia et Papia Poppaea*." *Classical Journal* 40, no. 7 (1945): 398–416.

Freed, Edwin D. "The Women in Matthew's Genealogy." *Journal for the Study of the New Testament* 29 (1987): 3–19.

Gaventa, Beverly Roberts. *Acts*. Abingdon New Testament Commentaries. Nashville: Abingdon, 2003.

Gench, Frances Taylor. *Back to the Well: Women's Encounters with Jesus in the Gospels*. Louisville: Westminster John Knox, 2004.

González, Justo L. *Acts: The Gospel of the Spirit*. Maryknoll, NY: Orbis, 2001.

Grassi, Joseph A. "The Role of Jesus' Mother in John's Gospel: A Reappraisal." *Catholic Biblical Quarterly* 48 (1986): 67–80.

Green, Joel B. *The Gospel of Luke*. New International Commentary on the New Testament. Grand Rapids: Eerdmans, 1997.

———. *Practicing Theological Interpretation: Engaging Biblical Texts for Faith and Formation*. Grand Rapids: Baker Academic, 2011.

Gruca-Macaulay, Alexandra. *Lydia as a Rhetorical Construct in Acts*. Emory Studies in Early Christianity 18. Atlanta: SBL Press, 2016.

Gullotta, Daniel N. "Among Dogs and Disciples: An Examination of the Story of the Canaanite Woman (Matthew 15:21–28) and the Question of the Gentile Mission within the Matthean Community." *Neotestamentica* 48 (2014): 325–40.

Gundry, Robert H. *Matthew: A Commentary on His Literary and Theological Art*. Grand Rapids: Eerdmans, 1982.

Hakh, Samuel B. "Women in the Genealogy of Matthew." *Exchange* 43 (2014): 109–18.

Hallett, Judith P. "Women's Lives in the Ancient Mediterranean." Pages 13–34 in Kraemer and D'Angelo, *Women and Christian Origins*.

Hanson, Anthony Tyrrell. "Rahab the Harlot in Early Christian Tradition." *Journal for the Study of the New Testament* 1 (1978): 53–60.

Harrill, J. Albert. "The Dramatic Function of the Running Slave Rhoda (Acts 12.13–16): A Piece of Greco-Roman Comedy." *New Testament Studies* 46 (2000): 150–57.

Hartin, Patrick J. "Disciples as Authorities within Matthew's Christian-Jewish Community." *Neotestamentica* 32 (1998): 389–404.

Harvey, A. E. *Jesus on Trial: A Study in the Fourth Gospel*. London: SPCK, 1976.

Heffern, Andrew D. "The Four Women in St. Matthew's Genealogy of Christ." *Journal of Biblical Literature* 31 (1912): 69–81.

Heil, John Paul. "The Narrative Roles of the Women in Matthew's Genealogy." *Biblica* 72 (1991): 538–45.

Henderson, Suzanne Watts. *Christology and Discipleship in the Gospel of Mark*. Society for New Testament Studies Monograph Series 135. Cambridge: Cambridge University Press, 2006.

Hengel, Martin. "Maria Magdalena und die Frauen als Zeugen." Pages 243–56 in *Abraham unser Vater: Juden und Christen im Gespräch über die Bibel, Festschrift für Otto Michel zum 60. Geburtstag*. Edited by Otto Betz, Martin Hengel, and Peter Schmidt. Leiden: Brill, 1963.

Hooker, Morna D. *Endings: Invitations to Discipleship*. Peabody, MA: Hendrickson, 2003.

Hurtado, Larry W. "The Women, the Tomb, and the Climax of Mark." Pages 427–50 in *A Wandering Galilean: Essays in Honour of Seán Freyne*. Edited by Zuleika Rodgers, Margaret Daly-Denton, and Anne Fitzpatrick-McKinley. Supplements to the Journal for the Study of Judaism. Leiden: Brill, 2009.

Hutchison, John C. "Women, Gentiles, and the Messianic Mission in Matthew's Genealogy." *Bibliotheca Sacra* 158 (2001): 152–64.

Hylen, Susan E. *Women in the New Testament World*. Essentials of Biblical Studies. New York: Oxford University Press, 2019.

Inyamah, Deborah C. "Contrasting Perspectives on the Role of the Feminine in Ministry and Leadership Roles in John 4 and 1 Timothy 2:11–15." *Journal of Religious Thought* 60 (2010): 87–108.

Jervell, Jacob. "The Daughters of Abraham: Women in Acts." Pages 146–57 in *The Unknown Paul: Essays on Luke-Acts and Early Christian History*. Translated by Roy A. Harrisville. Minneapolis: Augsburg, 1984.

Jewett, Robert. *Romans: A Commentary*. Hermeneia. Minneapolis: Fortress, 2006.

Joshel, Sandra R. *Work, Identity, and Legal Status at Rome: A Study of the Occupational Inscriptions*. Norman: Oklahoma University Press, 1992.

Kanagaraj, Jey J. "The Profiles of Women in John: House-Bound or Christ-Bound?" *Bangalore Theological Forum* 33 (2001): 60–79.

Karris, Robert J. "Women and Discipleship in Luke." Pages 23–43 in *A Feminist Companion to Luke*. Edited by Amy-Jill Levine. Sheffield: Sheffield Academic, 2002.

Keener, Craig S. *Acts: An Exegetical Commentary*. Vol. 1, *Introduction and 1:1–2:47*. Grand Rapids: Baker Academic, 2012.

———. "Matthew's Missiology: Making Disciples of the Nations (Matthew 28:19–20)." *Asian Journal of Pentecostal Studies* 12 (2009): 3–20.

Kelber, Werner H. *The Kingdom of Mark: A New Place and a New Time*. Philadelphia: Fortress, 1974.

Kidson, Lyn. "The Anxious Search for the Lost Coin (Luke 15:8–10): Lost Coins, Women's Dowries and the Contribution of Numismatics and Phenomenology to Gospel Research." *Australian Biblical Review* 68 (2020): 76–88.

Kim, Jean K. "A Korean Feminist Reading of John 4:1–42." *Semeia* 78 (1997): 109–19.

Kim, Sun Wook. "A Discussion of Luke's Portrayal of Women and the Eschatological Equality between Men and Women in Luke 7:36–50." *Korean Evangelical New Testament Studies* 12 (2013): 706–33.

Kingsbury, Jack Dean. "The Verb AKOLOUTHEIN ('To Follow') as an Index of Matthew's View of His Community." *Journal of Biblical Literature* 97 (1978): 56–73.

Koester, Craig R., and Reimund Bieringer, eds. *The Resurrection of Jesus in the Gospel of John*. Wissenschaftliche Untersuchungen zum Neuen Testament 222. Tübingen: Mohr Siebeck, 2008.

Kopas, Jane. "Jesus and Women in Matthew." *Theology Today* 47 (1990): 13–21.

———. "Jesus and Women: Luke's Gospel." *Theology Today* 43 (1986): 192–202.

Kozlova, Ekaterina. "Women and Ancient Mortuary Culture(s)." *Covenant Quarterly* 72 (2014): 159–73.

Kraemer, Ross S. "Jewish Women and Women's Judaism(s) at the Beginning of Christianity." Pages 50–79 in Kraemer and D'Angelo, *Women and Christian Origins.*

———. "Monastic Jewish Women in Greco-Roman Egypt: Philo Judaeus on the Therapeutrides." *Signs* 14 (1989): 342–70.

———. "Women's Authorship of Jewish and Christian Literature in the Greco-Roman Period." Pages 221–42 in Levine, *"Women Like This."*

Kraemer, Ross S., and Mary R. D'Angelo, eds. *Women and Christian Origins.* Oxford: Oxford University Press, 1999.

Krause, Deborah. "Simon Peter's Mother-in-Law—Disciple or Domestic Servant? Feminist Biblical Hermeneutics and the Interpretation of Mark 1.29–31." Pages 37–53 in Levine, *Feminist Companion to Mark.*

Kurek-Chomycz, Dominika A. "The Fragrance of Her Perfume: The Significance of Sense Imagery in John's Account of the Anointing in Bethany." *Novum Testamentum* 52 (2010): 334–54.

———. "Is There an 'Anti-Priscan' Tendency in the Manuscripts? Some Textual Problems with Prisca and Aquila." *Journal of Biblical Literature* 125 (2006): 107–28.

Lee, Dorothy A. *The Ministry of Women in the New Testament: Reclaiming the Biblical Vision for Church Leadership.* Grand Rapids: Baker Academic, 2021.

———. "Partnership in Easter Faith: The Role of Mary Magdalene and Thomas in John 20." *Journal for the Study of the New Testament* 58 (1995): 37–49.

———. "Women as 'Sinners': Three Narratives of Salvation in Luke and John." *Australian Biblical Review* 44 (1996): 1–15.

Lemaire, André. *Les Ministères aux origins de l'Église, naissance de la triple hiérarchie: évêques, presbytres, diacres.* Paris: Cerf, 1971.

Levine, Amy-Jill. "Discharging Responsibility: Matthean Jesus, Biblical Law, and Hemorrhaging Woman." Pages 70–87 in Levine and Blickenstaff, *Feminist Companion to Matthew.*

———, ed. *A Feminist Companion to Mark.* Sheffield: Sheffield Academic, 2001.

———. "Gospel of Matthew." Pages 465–77 in *Women's Bible Commentary.* Edited by Carol A. Newsome, Sharon H. Ringe, and Jacqueline E. Lapsley. 3rd ed. Louisville: Westminster John Knox, 2012.

———. "Matthew's Advice to a Divided Readership." Pages 22–41 in *The Gospel of Matthew in Current Study: Studies in Memory of William G. Thompson, S. J.* Edited by David E. Aune. Grand Rapids: Eerdmans, 2001.

———. "Preaching and Teaching the Pharisees." Pages 403–27 in Sievers and Levine, *The Pharisees.*

———. "Second Temple Judaism, Jesus, and Women: Yeast of Eden." *Biblical Interpretation* 2 (1994): 8–33.

———. *Short Stories by Jesus: The Enigmatic Parables of a Controversial Rabbi.* New York: HarperOne, 2014.

———. "Tabitha/Dorcas, Spinning Off Cultural Criticism." Pages 41–65 in *Delightful Acts: New Essays on Canonical and Non-canonical Acts.* Edited by Harold W. Attridge, Dennis R. MacDonald, and Clare K. Rothschild. Wissenschaftliche Untersuchungen zum Neuen Testament 391. Tübingen: Mohr Siebeck, 2017.

———. "'This Poor Widow . . .' (Mark 12:43): From Donation to Diatribe." Pages 183–94 in *A Most Reliable Witness: Essays in Honor of Ross Shepard Kraemer.* Edited by Susan Ashbrook Harvey, Nathaniel DesRosiers, Shira L. Lander, Jacqueline Z. Pastis, and Daniel Ullucci. Brown Judaic Studies 358. Providence, RI: Brown University, 2015.

———, ed. *"Women Like This": New Perspectives on Jewish Women in the Greco-Roman World.* Atlanta: Scholars Press, 1991.

———. "Women's Humor and Other Creative Juices." Pages 120–26 in Brenner, *Are We Amused?*

Levine, Amy-Jill, and Marianne Blickenstaff, eds. *A Feminist Companion to Matthew.* Sheffield: Sheffield Academic, 2001.

Levine, Amy-Jill, and Ben Witherington III. *The Gospel of Luke.* New Cambridge Bible Commentary. Cambridge: Cambridge University Press, 2018.

Lightman, Marjorie, and William Zeisel. "Univira: An Example of Continuity and Change in Roman Society." *Church History* 46, no. 1 (1977): 19–32.

Lincoln, Andrew T. "The Promise and the Failure: Mark 16:7, 8." *Journal of Biblical Literature* 108, no. 2 (1989): 283–300.

Lindemann, Andreas. "Die Osterbotsghaft des Markus. Zur Theologischen Interpretation von Mark 16.1–8." *New Testament Studies* 26, no. 3 (1980): 298–317.

Lockwood, Peter F. "The Woman at the Well: Does the Traditional Reading Still Hold Water?" *Lutheran Theological Journal* 36 (2002): 12–24.

Longenecker, Richard N. "Taking Up the Cross Daily: Discipleship in Luke-Acts." Pages 50–76 in *Patterns of Discipleship in the New Testament.* Edited by Richard N. Longenecker. Grand Rapids: Eerdmans, 1996.

Love, Stuart L. "The Household: A Major Social Component for Gender Analysis in the Gospel of Matthew." *Biblical Theology Bulletin* 23 (1993): 21–31.

Luttick, Janine. "Little Girl, Get Up and Stand on Your Own Two Feet!" Pages 631–42 in *Reading the Gospel of Mark in the 21st Century: Method and Meaning.* Edited by Geert van Oyen. Bibliotheca Ephemeridum Theologicarum Lovaniensium 301. Leuven: Peeters, 2019.

Lyons-Pardue, Kara J. "A Syrophoenician Becomes a Canaanite: Jesus Exegetes the Canaanite Woman in Matthew." *Journal of Theological Interpretation* 13 (2019): 235–50.

Maccini, Robert G. "A Reassessment of the Woman at the Well in John 4 in Light of the Samaritan Context." *Journal for the Study of the New Testament* 53 (1994): 35–46.

Malbon, Elizabeth Struthers. "Fallible Followers: Women and Men in the Gospel of Mark." *Semeia* 28 (1983): 29–48.

———. "The Poor Widow in Mark and Her Poor Rich Readers." *Catholic Biblical Quarterly* 53, no. 4 (1991): 589–604.

Marcus, Joel. *The Way of the Lord: Christological Exegesis of the Old Testament in the Gospel of Mark.* Edinburgh: T&T Clark, 1992.

McGinn, Sheila E. "Why Now the Women? Social-Historical Insights on Gender Roles in Matthew 26–28." *Proceedings: Eastern Great Lakes and Midwest Biblical Societies* 17 (1997): 107–14.

Meier, John P. *A Marginal Jew: Rethinking the Historical Jesus.* Vol. 3, *Companions and Competitors.* Anchor Bible Reference Library. New York: Doubleday, 2001.

Meiselman, Moshe. *Jewish Women in Jewish Law.* Library of Jewish Law and Ethics 6. New York: Ktav/Yeshiva University, 1978.

Menéndez-Antunã, Luis. "Male-Bonding, Female Vanishing: Representing Gendered Authority in Luke 23:26–24:53." *Early Christianity* 4 (2013): 490–506.

Meye, Robert P. *Jesus and the Twelve: Discipleship and Revelation in Mark's Gospel.* Grand Rapids: Eerdmans, 1968.

Meyers, Carol. *Rediscovering Eve: Ancient Israelite Women in Context.* Oxford: Oxford University Press, 2013.

Michaels, J. Ramsey. "John 12:1–11." *Interpretation* 43 (1989): 287–91.

Miller, Amanda C. "Cut from the Same Cloth: A Study of Female Patrons in Luke-Acts and the Roman Empire." *Review and Expositor* 114 (2017): 203–10.

Miller, Susan. *Women in Mark's Gospel.* Journal for the Study of the New Testament Supplement Series 259. Edinburgh: T&T Clark, 2004.

Mitchell, Joan L. *Beyond Fear and Silence: A Feminist-Literary Reading of Mark.* New York: Continuum, 2001.

Moloney, Francis J. "Can Everyone Be Wrong? A Reading of John 11.1–12.8." *New Testament Studies* 49 (2003): 505–27.

Moss, Candida R. "The Man with the Flow of Power: Porous Bodies in Mark 5:25–34." *Journal of Biblical Literature* 129 (2010): 507–19.

Moss, Candida R., and Joel S. Baden. *Reconceiving Infertility: Biblical Perspectives on Procreation and Childlessness.* Princeton: Princeton University Press, 2015.

Mukansengimana-Nyirimana, Rose, and Jonathan A. Draper. "The Peacemaking Role of the Samaritan Woman in John 4:1–42: A Mirror and Challenge to Rwandan Women." *Neotestamentica* 46 (2012): 299–318.

Mulgan, Richard. "Aristotle and the Political Role of Women." *History of Political Thought* 15, no. 2 (1994): 179–202.

Munro, Winsome. "The Pharisee and the Samaritan in John: Polar or Parallel?" *Catholic Biblical Quarterly* 57 (1995): 710–28.

———. "Women Disciples in Mark?" *Catholic Biblical Quarterly* 44, no. 2 (1982): 225–41.

Murphy-O'Connor, Jerome. "Prisca and Aquila: Travelling Tentmakers and Church Builders." *Bible Review* 8 (1992): 40–51, 62.

Navarro Puerto, Mercedes. "Female Disciples in Mark? The 'Problematizing' of a Concept." Pages 145–72 in *Gospels: Narrative and History.* Edited by Mercedes Navarro Puerto and Marinella Perroni. Vol. 2.1 of *The Bible and Women: An Encyclopedia of Exegesis and Cultural History.* Atlanta: SBL Press, 2015.

Neyrey, Jerome. "What's Wrong with This Picture? John 4, Cultural Stereotypes of Women, and Public and Private Space." *Biblical Theology Bulletin* 24 (1994): 77–91.

Niccum, Curt. "A Note on Acts 1:14." *Novum Testamentum* 36 (1994): 196–99.

O'Brien, Kelli S. "Written That You May Believe: John 20 and Narrative Rhetoric." *Catholic Biblical Quarterly* 67 (2005): 284–302.

O'Collins, Gerald. "The Fearful Silence of the Three Women (Mark 16:8c)." *Gregorianum* 69, no. 3 (1988): 489–503.

O'Collins, Gerald, and Daniel Kendall. "Mary Magdalene as Major Witness to Jesus' Resurrection." *Theological Studies* 48 (1987): 631–46.

O'Day, Gail R. "Surprised by Faith: Jesus and the Canaanite Woman." Pages 114–25 in Levine and Blickenstaff, *Feminist Companion to Matthew*.

Olivares, Carlos. "The Term *oligopistos* (Little Faith) in Matthew's Gospel: Narrative and Thematic Connections." *Colloquium* 47 (2015): 274–91.

Osiek, Carolyn. "The Women at the Tomb: What Are They Doing There?" Pages 205–20 in Levine and Blickenstaff, *Feminist Companion to Matthew*.

Osiek, Carolyn, and Margaret Y. MacDonald. *A Woman's Place: House Churches in Earliest Christianity*. Minneapolis: Fortress, 2006.

Ottermann, Monika. "'How Could He Ever Do That to Her?!' Or, How the Woman Who Anointed Jesus Became a Victim of Luke's Redactional and Theological Principles." Pages 103–16 in *Reading Other-wise: Socially Engaged Biblical Scholars Reading with Their Local Communities*. Edited by Gerald O. West. Atlanta: Society of Biblical Literature, 2007.

Oudshoorn, Jacobine G. *The Relationship between Roman and Local Law in the Babatha and Salome Komaise Archives: General Analysis and Three Case Studies on Law of Succession, Guardianship and Marriage*. Leiden: Brill, 2007.

Park, Wongi. "Her Memorial: An Alternative Reading of Matthew 26:13." *Journal of Biblical Literature* 136 (2017): 131–44.

Parsons, Mikeal C. *Acts*. Paideia Commentaries on the New Testament. Grand Rapids: Baker Academic, 2008.

———. *The Departure of Jesus in Luke-Acts: The Ascension Narratives in Context*. Journal for the Study of the New Testament Supplement Series 21. Sheffield: JSOT Press, 1987.

Parvey, Constance. "The Theology and Leadership of Women in the New Testament." Pages 117–49 in *Religion and Sexism*. Edited by Rosemary R. Ruether. New York: Simon & Schuster, 1974.

Perkinson, Jim. "A Canaanitic Word in the Logos of Christ; or the Difference the Syro-Phoenician Woman Makes to Jesus." *Semeia* 75 (1996): 61–85.

Pervo, Richard I. *Profit with Delight: The Literary Genre of the Acts of the Apostles*. Philadelphia: Fortress, 1987.

———. "Unnamed Women Who Provide for the Jesus Movement." Pages 441–42 in *Women in Scripture: A Dictionary of Named and Unnamed Women in the Hebrew Bible, the Apocryphal/Deuterocanonical Books, and the New Testament.* Edited by Carol Meyers, Toni Craven, and Ross S. Kraemer. Grand Rapids: Eerdmans, 2001.

Pesch, Rudolf. *Das Markusevangelium II*. Herders theologischer Kommentar zum Neuen Testament. Freiburg: Herder, 1977.

Phillips, Victoria. "The Failure of the Women Who Followed Jesus in the Gospel of Mark." Pages 222–35 in Levine, *Feminist Companion to Mark*.

———. "Full Disclosure: Towards a Complete Characterization of the Women Who Followed Jesus in the Gospel according to Mark." Pages 13–31 in *Transformative Encounters: Jesus and Women Reviewed.* Edited by Ingrid Rosa Kitzberger. Biblical Interpretation Series 43. Leiden: Brill, 2000.

Phipps, William E. *Assertive Biblical Women*. Contributions in Women's Studies 128. Westport, CT: Greenwood, 1992.

Pomeroy, Sarah B. *Goddesses, Whores, Wives, and Slaves: Women in Classical Antiquity*. 2nd ed. New York: Schocken, 1995.

Powell, Denise. "Elizabeth's 'Seclusion': A Veiled Reference to Her Bold Belief?" *Bulletin for Biblical Research* 29 (2019): 488–98.

Rand, J. A. du. "The Characterization of Jesus as Depicted in the Narrative of the Fourth Gospel." *Neotestamentica* 19 (1985): 18–36.

Reeder, Caryn A. *The Samaritan Woman's Story: Reconsidering John 4 after #ChurchToo*. Downers Grove, IL: IVP Academic, 2022.

Reid, Barbara E. *Choosing the Better Part? Women in the Gospel of Luke*. Collegeville, MN: Liturgical Press, 1996.

———. "'Do You See This Woman?' Luke 7:36–50 as a Paradigm for Feminist Hermeneutics." *Biblical Research* 40 (1995): 37–49.

———. "The Gospel of Luke: Friend or Foe of Women Proclaimers of the Word?" *Catholic Biblical Quarterly* 78 (2016): 1–23.

———. "Luke: The Gospel for Women?" *Currents in Theology and Mission* 21 (1994): 405–14.

Reid, Barbara E., and Shelly Matthews. *Luke 1–9*. Edited by Amy-Jill

Levine. Wisdom Commentary 43A. Collegeville, MN: Liturgical Press, 2021.

Reimer, Ivoni Richter. *Women in the Acts of the Apostles: A Feminist Liberation Perspective*. Translated by L. Maloney. Minneapolis: Fortress, 1995.

Reinhartz, Adele. "From Narrative to History: The Resurrection of Mary and Martha." Pages 161–84 in Levine, *"Women Like This."*

Remaud, Michel. "Les femmes dans la généalogie de Jésus selon Mattieu." *Nouvelle revue théologique* 143 (2021): 3–14.

Rhoads, David. "Jesus and the Syrophoenician Woman in Mark: A Narrative-Critical Study." *Journal of the American Academy of Religion* 62, no. 2 (1994): 343–75.

Runesson, Anders. "Saving the Lost Sheep of the House of Israel: Purity, Forgiveness, and Synagogues in the Gospel of Matthew." *Melilah* 11 (2014): 8–24.

Sabin, Marie. "Women Transformed: The Ending of Mark Is the Beginning of Wisdom." *CrossCurrents* 48, no. 2 (1998): 149–68.

Saller, Richard P. *Patriarchy, Property and Death in the Roman Family*. Cambridge Studies in Population, Economy and Society in Past Time. Cambridge: Cambridge University Press, 1994.

Schaberg, Jane. "Luke." Pages 275–92 in *The Women's Bible Commentary*. Edited by Carol A. Newsom and Sharon H. Ringe. Louisville: Westminster John Knox, 1992.

Scheffler, Eben. "Caring for the Needy in the Acts of the Apostles." *Neotestamentica* 50 (2016): 131–65.

Schierling, Marla J. "Women as Leaders in the Marcan Communities." *Listening* 15 (1980): 250–56.

Schmahl, Günther. *Die Zwölf im Markusevangelium*. Trier: Paulinus-Verlag, 1974.

Schneiders, Sandra M. "Touching the Risen Jesus: Mary Magdalene and Thomas the Twin in John 20." Pages 153–76 in Koester and Bieringer, *Resurrection of Jesus*.

———. "Women in the Fourth Gospel and the Role of Women in the Contemporary Church." Pages 123–43 in Stibbe, *Gospel of John*.

Schottroff, Luise. *Lydia's Impatient Sisters: A Feminist Social History of Early Christianity*. Translated by Barbara and Martin Rumscheidt. Louisville: Westminster John Knox, 1995.

Schrock, Jennifer Halteman. "'I Am among You as One Who Serves': Jesus and Food in Luke's Gospel." *Daughters of Sarah* 19 (1993): 20–23.

Schüssler Fiorenza, Elisabeth. "A Feminist Critical Interpretation for Liberation: Martha and Mary: Lk. 10:38–42." *Religion and Intellectual Life* (1986): 21–36.

———. *In Memory of Her: A Feminist Theological Reconstruction of Christian Origins*. New York: Crossroad, 1989.

Scott, J. Martin C. "Matthew 15.21–28: A Test-Case for Jesus' Manners." *Journal for the Study of the New Testament* 62 (1996): 21–44.

Sechrest, Love L. "Enemies, Romans, Pigs, and Dogs: Loving the Other in the Gospel of Matthew." *Ex Auditu* 31 (2015): 71–105.

Seim, Turid Karlsen. *The Double Message: Patterns of Gender in Luke-Acts*. Nashville: Abingdon, 1994.

———. "Roles of Women in the Gospel of John." Pages 56–73 in *Aspects of the Johannine Literature*. Edited by Lars Hartman and Birger Olsson. Uppsala: Almqvist & Wiksell, 1987.

Selvidge, Marla J. "Alternate Lifestyles and Distinctive Careers: Luke's Portrait of People in Transition." *Sewanee Theological Review* 36 (1992): 91–102.

Shin, In-Cheol. "Matthew's Designation of the Role of Women as Indirectly Adherent Disciples." *Neotestamentica* 41 (2007): 399–415.

Sievers, Joseph, and Amy-Jill Levine, eds. *The Pharisees*. Grand Rapids: Eerdmans, 2021.

Sim, David C. "The Women Followers of Jesus: The Implications of Luke 8:1–3." *Heythrop Journal* 30 (1989): 51–62.

Simon, Louis. "Le sou de la veuve: Marc 12/41–44." *Etudes théologiques et religieuses* 44 (1969): 115–26.

Spencer, F. Scott. *Journeying through Acts: A Literary-Cultural Reading*. Peabody, MA: Hendrickson, 2004.

———. "Out of Mind, Out of Voice: Slave-Girls and Prophetic Daughters in Luke-Acts." *Biblical Interpretation* 7 (1999): 133–55.

———. *Salty Wives, Spirited Mothers, and Savvy Widows: Capable Women of Purpose and Persistence in Luke's Gospel*. Grand Rapids: Eerdmans, 2012.

———. "Those Riotous—yet Righteous—Foremothers of Jesus: Exploring Matthew's Comic Genealogy." Pages 7–30 in Brenner, *Are We Amused?*

Spencer, Patrick E. "'Mad' Rhoda in Acts 12:12–17: Disciple Exemplar." *Catholic Biblical Quarterly* 79 (2017): 282–98.

Spina, Frank Anthony. *The Faith of the Outsider: Exclusion and Inclusion in the Biblical Story*. Grand Rapids: Eerdmans, 2005.

Stibbe, Mark, ed. *The Gospel of John as Literature: An Anthology of Twentieth-Century Perspectives*. New Testament Tools and Studies 17. Leiden: Brill, 1993.

Strecker, Georg. *Der Weg der Gerechtigkeit: Untersuchung zur Theologie des Matthäus*. Göttingen: Vandenhoeck & Ruprecht, 1962.

Strelan, Rick. "Tabitha: The Gazelle of Joppa (Acts 9:36–41)." *Biblical Theology Bulletin* 39 (2009): 77–86.

———. "To Sit Is to Mourn: The Women at the Tomb (Matthew 27:61)." *Colloquium* 31 (1999): 31–45.

Tannehill, Robert C. "The Disciples in Mark: The Function of a Narrative Role." *Journal of Religion* 57, no. 4 (1977): 386–405.

Thiele, Walter. "Eine Bemerkung zu Act 1,14." *Zeitschrift für die neutestamentliche Wissenschaft und die Kunde der älteren Kirche* 53 (1962): 110–11.

Thurston, Bonnie. "Who Was Anna? Luke 2:36–38." *Perspectives in Religious Studies* 28 (2001): 47–55.

Vaage, Leif E. "An Other Home: Discipleship in Mark as Domestic Asceticism." *Catholic Biblical Quarterly* 71, no. 4 (2009): 741–61.

Van Iersel, Bas M. F. "Failed Followers in Mark: Mark 13:12 as a Key for the Identification of Intended Readers." *Catholic Biblical Quarterly* 58, no. 2 (1996): 258.

Van Til, Kent A. "Three Anointings and One Offering: The Sinful Woman in Luke 7.36–50." *Journal of Pentecostal Theology* 15 (2006): 73–82.

Via, E. Jane. "Women, the Discipleship of Service, and the Early Christian Ritual Meal in the Gospel of Luke." *St. Luke's Journal of Theology* 29 (1985): 37–60.

Wainwright, Elaine M. *Towards a Feminist Reading of the Gospel according to Matthew*. Beihefte zur Zeitschrift für die neutestamentliche Wissenschaft 60. Berlin: de Gruyter, 1991.

Wallace, Daniel B. *Greek Grammar beyond the Basics*. Grand Rapids: Zondervan, 1996.

Wassen, Cecilia. *Women in the Damascus Document*. Academia Biblica 21. Atlanta: Society of Biblical Literature, 2005.

Wasserman, Tommy. "Bringing Sisters Back Together: Another Look at Luke 10:41–42." *Journal of Biblical Literature* 137 (2018): 439–61.

Watts, Rikk E. *Isaiah's New Exodus in Mark*. Rev. ed. Grand Rapids: Baker, 2001.

———. "Women in the Gospels and Acts." *Crux* 35 (1999): 22–33.

Weaver, Dorothy Jean. "'Wherever This Good News Is Proclaimed':

Women and God in the Gospel of Matthew." *Interpretation* 64 (2010): 390–401.

Webb, Natalie. "Overcoming Fear with Mary of Nazareth: Women's Experience alongside Luke 1:26–56." *Review and Expositor* 115 (2018): 96–103.

Weeden, Theodore J. *Mark: Traditions in Conflict.* Minneapolis: Fortress, 1971.

Wegner, Judith Romney. *Chattel or Person? The Status of Women in the Mishnah.* New York: Oxford University Press, 1988.

Weiser, Alfons. "Die Rolle der Frau in der urchristlichen Bewegung." Pages 158–81 in *Die Frau im Urchristentum.* Edited by Gerhard Dautzenberg, Helmut Merklein, and Karlheinz Müller. Quaestiones Disputatae 95. Freiburg: Herder, 1983.

Weren, Wim J. C. "The Five Women in Matthew's Genealogy." *Catholic Biblical Quarterly* 59 (1997): 288–305.

Wilkins, M. J. "Disciples and Discipleship." Pages 202–12 in *Dictionary of Jesus and the Gospels.* Edited by Joel B. Green, Jeannine K. Brown, and Nicholas Perrin. 2nd ed. Downers Grove, IL: IVP Academic, 2013.

Williams, Ritva H. "The Mother of Jesus at Cana: A Social-Science Interpretation of John 2.1–12." *Catholic Biblical Quarterly* 59 (1997): 679–92.

Wilson, Brittany E. *Unmanly Men: Refigurations of Masculinity in Luke-Acts.* Oxford: Oxford University Press, 2015.

Witherington, Ben, III. "On the Road with Mary Magdalene, Joanna, Susanna, and Other Disciples—Luke 8:1–3." *Zeitschrift für die neutestamentliche Wissenschaft und die Kunde der älteren Kirche* 70 (1979): 243–48.

———. *Women in the Ministry of Jesus.* Society for New Testament Studies Monograph Series 51. Cambridge: Cambridge University Press, 1984.

Woodington, J. David. "Charity and Deliverance from Death in the Accounts of Tabitha and Cornelius." *Catholic Biblical Quarterly* 79 (2017): 634–50.

Yarbro Collins, Adela. *Mark.* Hermeneia. Minneapolis: Fortress, 2007.

Index of Authors

Index of Subjects

Index of Scripture and Other Ancient Sources